AFRIKA-STUDIEN Nr. 49

Publication series "Afrika-Studien" edited by Ifo-Institut für Wirtschaftsforschung e. V., München, in connexion with

Prof. Dr. PETER VON BLANCKENBURG, Berlin
Prof. Dr. HEINRICH KRAUT, Dortmund
Prof. Dr. OTTO NEULOH, Saarbrücken
Prof. Dr. Dr. h. c. RUDOLF STUCKEN, Erlangen
Prof. Dr. HANS WILBRANDT, Göttingen
Prof. Dr. EMIL WOERMANN, Göttingen

*Editors in Chief:*

Dr. phil. WILHELM MARQUARDT, München
Afrika-Studienstelle im Ifo-Institut
Prof. Dr. HANS RUTHENBERG, Stuttgart-Hohenheim,
Institut für Ausländische Landwirtschaft

IFO-INSTITUT FÜR WIRTSCHAFTSFORSCHUNG MÜNCHEN
AFRIKA-STUDIENSTELLE

# Status and Use of African Lingua Francas

By

BERND HEINE

WELTFORUM VERLAG · MÜNCHEN

SPONSORED BY THE FRITZ THYSSEN-STIFTUNG, KÖLN

All rights, especially that of translation into foreign languages, reserved.
It is also forbidden to reproduce this book, either whole or in part, by photomechanical means (photostat, microfilm and/or microcard) or by other procedure without written permission from Weltforum-Verlag
© by Weltforum-Verlag GmbH, München 1970
Library of Congress Catalog Card Number 71—101979
ISBN 3 8039 0033 6
Print: Druckerei G. J. Manz AG, Dillingen/Donau
Printed in Germany

*Handwritten at top:*
Ifo-Institute für Wirtschaftsforschung München
Afrika-Studienstelle

\* STATUS AND USE OF AFRICAN LINGUA FRANCAS
by Bernd Heine

Weltforum Verlag, München.

## Review of Published and Forthcoming Studies within the African Research Programme

The entire research programme being conducted up to January 1970 by the African Studies Centre of the Ifo Institute – partly by the Centre itself, partly in conjunction with other institutes and researchers – covers the studies listed below (see also introductory remarks in vols. 1 and 2 of "Afrika-Studien").

For readers' information on changes, supplements, and forthcoming publications, each volume of "Afrika-Studien" will contain a review of the programme as a whole.

Vols. 1–18 have been issued by Springer Publishing House, Berlin–Heidelberg–New York, subsequent volumes by Weltforum Publishing House, Munich, in co-operation with publishing houses in the United Kingdom and the United States. The studies published as mimeographs (African Research Reports) can be obtained through the African Studies Centre of the Ifo Institute for Economic Research (early editions only); the more recent editions (from 1968 onwards) are available through the Weltforum Publishing House, Munich.

A chronological list of published and forthcoming studies is attached at the end of this book.

### General Economic Studies

a) Tropical Africa

N. AHMAD / E. BECHER, Development Banks and Companies in Tropical Africa (printed as volume 1), in German

R. GÜSTEN / H. HELMSCHROTT, National Accounting Systems in Tropical Africa (printed as volume 3), in German

N. AHMAD / E. BECHER / E. HARDER, Economic Planning and Development Policy in Tropical Africa (mimeograph), in German

H.-G. GEIS, The Monetary and Banking Systems of the Countries of West Africa (printed as volume 20), in German

Africa-Vademecum (Basic Data on the Economic Structure and Development of Africa), prepared by F. BETZ (series Information and Documentation, vol. 1), in German, with additional headings in English and French

\* title

H. Harlander / D. Mezger, Development Banks and Institutions in Africa (Series Information and Documentation, volume 2), in German

H. Amann, Operational Concepts of the Infrastructure in the Economic Development Process (mimeograph), in German

K. Erdmann, Development Aid to Africa – with Special Reference to the Countries of East Africa (mimeograph), in German

### b) East Africa

L. Schnittger, Taxation and Economic Development in East Africa (printed as volume 8), in German

R. Güsten, Problems of Economic Growth and Planning: The Sudan Example (printed as volume 9), in English

P. v. Marlin, The Impact of External Economic Relations on the Economic Development of East Africa (mimeograph), in English

R. Vente, Planning Processes: The East African Case (printed as volume 52), in English

F. Goll, Israeli Aid to Developing Countries with Special Reference to East Africa (mimeograph), in German

W. Fischer, Problems of Land-Locked Countries: Uganda (printed as volume 41), in German

H. Hieber, Economic Statistics in Developing Countries: The Example of Uganda (printed as volume 40), in German

G. Hübner, Importance, Volume, Forms and Development Possibilities of Private Saving in East Africa (mimeograph), in German

M. Yaffey, Balance of Payments Problems in a Developing Country: Tanzania (printed as volume 47), in English

E.-J. Pauw, Money and Banking in East Africa (Kenya, Tanzania, Uganda) (printed as volume 35), in German

D. Bald, Administration and Economic Exploitation of German East Africa before 1914 (being printed as volume 54), in German

M. Bohnet / H. Reichelt, Applied Research in East Africa and Its Influence on Economic Development (in preparation), in English

P. v. Marlin and Contributors, Financial Aspects of Development in East Africa (being printed as volume 53), in English

## Agricultural Studies

### a) Tropical Africa

H. Klemm / P. v. Marlin, The EEC Market Regulations for Agricultural Products and Their Implications for Developing Countries (mimeograph), in German

H. Pössinger, Agricultural Development in Angola and Moçambique (printed as volume 31), in German

J. O. Müller, The Attitude of Various Tribes of the Republic of Togo, Especially the Ewe on the Plateau de Dayes, towards the Problem of Commissioned Cattle Herding by the Fulbe (Peulh) of West Africa (printed as volume 14 in German, mimeographed in French)

E.-S. El-Shagi, Reorganization of Land Use in Egypt (printed as volume 36), in German

H. Thorwart, Methods and Problems of Farm Management Surveys in Africa South of the Sahara (in preparation)

B. Mohr, Rice Cultivation in West Africa – A Presentation of the Economic and Geographical Differences of Cultivation Methods (printed as volume 44)

R. Bartha, Fodder Plants in the Sahel Zone of Africa (in German, English and French), (printed as volume 48)

b) **East Africa**

*1. Basic Studies*

H. Ruthenberg, Agricultural Development in Tanganyika (printed as volume 2), in English

H. Ruthenberg, African Agricultural Production Development Policy in Kenya 1952–1965 (printed as volume 10), in English

H. Dequin, Agricultural Development in Malawi (mimeograph), in English

H. Kraut/H.-D. Cremer (ed.), Investigations into Health and Nutrition in East Africa (printed as volume 42), in English

H. Blume, Autonomous Institutions in East African Agricultural Production (completed), in English

*2. Studies Concerning Grassland Use and Animal Husbandry in East Africa*

H. Leippert, Botanical Investigations in the Masai Country/Tanzania (an Example from the Semi-Arid Areas of East Africa), (mimeograph), in German

H. Klemm, The Organization of Milk Markets in East Africa (mimeograph), in German

K. Meyn, Beef Production in East Africa with Special Reference to Semi-Arid Areas (completed), in English

H. Späth, Development Possibilities of the Pig and Poultry Industry in East Africa (in preparation)

Walter/Dennig, Comparative Investigations into the Efficiency of Utilizable Ruminants in Kenya (in preparation)

*3. Studies in the Organization of Smallholder Farming in East Africa*

D. v. ROTENHAN, Land Use and Animal Husbandry in Sukumaland/Tanzania (printed as volume 11), in German

H. PÖSSINGER, Investigations into the Productivity and Profitability of Smallholder Sisal in East Africa (printed as volume 13), in German

S. GROENEVELD, Problems of Agricultural Development in the Coastal Region of East Africa (printed as volume 19), in German

V. JANSSEN, Agrarian Patterns in Ethiopia and their Implications for Economic Growth (in preparation), in German

H. RUTHENBERG (ed.), Smallholder Farming and Smallholder Development in Tanzania – Ten Case Studies (printed as volume 24), in English

M. ATTEMS, Smallholders in the Tropical Highlands of East Africa. The Usambara Mts. in the Transition Period from Subsistence to Market Production (printed as volume 25), in German

F. SCHERER, Vegetable Cultivation in Tropical Highlands: The Kigezi Example (Uganda) (mimeograph), in English

v. HAUGWITZ/THORWART, Farm Management Systems in Kenya (in preparation)

W. SCHEFFLER, Smallholder Production under Close Supervision: Tobacco Growing in Tanzania. A Socio-Economic Study (printed as volume 27), in German

H. RABE, Crop Cultivation on the Island of Madagascar with Special Reference to Rice Growing (mimeograph)

E. BAUM, Traditional Farming and Land Development in the Kilombero Valley/Tanzania (mimeograph), in German

R. GOLKOWSKY, Irrigation in Kenya's Agriculture with Special Reference to the Mwea-Tebere Project (printed as volume 39), in German

*4. Other Studies Concerning Agricultural Development*

M. PAULUS, The Role of Co-operatives in the Economic Development of East Africa, and Especially of Tanganyika and Uganda (printed as volume 15), in German

N. NEWIGER, Co-operative Farming in Kenya and Tanzania (mimeograph), in English

J. VASTHOFF, Small Farm Credit and Development – Some Experiences in East Africa with Special Reference to Kenya (printed as volume 33), in English

F. DIETERLEN / P. KUNKEL, Zoological Studies in the Kivu Region (Congo-Kinshasa) (mimeograph), in German

W. ERZ, Game Protection and Game Utilization in Rhodesia and in South Africa (mimeograph), in German

M. BARDELEBEN, Co-operatives in the Sudan: Their Characteristics, Functions and Suitability in the Socio-Economic Development Process (in preparation)

## Studies in Commerce, Trade and Transport

H. HELMSCHROTT, Structure and Growth of the East African Textile and Garments Industry (printed as volume 45), in German

H. KAINZBAUER, Trade in Tanzania (printed as volume 18), in German

K. SCHÄDLER, Crafts and Small-Scale Industries in Tanzania (printed as volume 34), in English

K. SCHÄDLER, Manufacturing and Processing Industries in Tanzania (mimeograph), in English

H. REICHELT, The Chemical and Allied Industries in Kenya (mimeograph), in English

R. GÜSTEN, Studies in the Staple Food Economy of Western Nigeria (printed as volume 30), in English

G. W. HEINZE, The Role of the Transport Sector in Development Policy – with Special Reference to African Countries – (printed as volume 21), in German

H. AMANN, Energy Supply and Economic Development in East Africa (printed as volume 37)

R. HOFMEIER, Problems of the Transport Economy in Tanzania with Special Reference to Road Transport (in preparation), in English

P. ZAJADACZ and Contributors, Studies in Production and Trade in East Africa (being printed as volume 51), in English

T. MÖLLER, Mining and Regional Development in East Africa (in preparation)

H. MILBERS, The Requirements for the Means of Transport in East Africa with a View to the Economic Expansion of these Countries (in preparation)

## Sociological and Demographic Studies

A. MOLNOS, Attitudes towards Family Planning in East Africa (printed as volume 26), in English

O. RAUM, The Human Factor in the Development of the Kilombero Valley (mimeograph), in English

O. NEULOH a. o., The African as Industrial Worker in East Africa (printed as volume 43)

H. W. JÜRGENS, Contributions to Internal Migration and Population Development in Liberia (printed as volume 4), in German

I. ROTHERMUND, The Political and Economic Role of the Asian Minority in East Africa (printed as volume 6), in German

J. Jensen, Continuity and Change in the Division of Labour among the Baganda (Uganda) (printed as volume 17), in German

W. Clement, Applied Economics of Education – The Example of Senegal – (printed as volume 23), in German

H. W. Jürgens, Examination of the Physical Development of Tanzanian Youth (mimeograph), in English

H. W. Jürgens, Investigations into Internal Migration in Tanzania (printed as volume 29), in German

A. v. Gagern, The African Settlers and How They Organize Their Life in the Urambo-Scheme (Tanzania) (printed as volume 38), in German

Gerken / Schubert / Brandt, The Influence of Urbanization upon the Development of Rural Areas – with Special Reference to Jinja (Uganda) and Its Surroundings (in preparation)

E. C. Klein, Social Change in Kiteezi (Buganda), a Village within the Sphere of Influence of the Township of Kampala (Uganda) (printed as volume 46), in German

U. Weyl, Population Trends and Migration in Malawi with Special Reference to the Central Region of Lake Malawi (in preparation)

M. Meck, Population Trends in Kenya and Their Implications for Social Services in Rural and Urban Areas (in preparation)

Staewen/Schönberg, Cultural Change and Anxiety Reaction among the Yoruba of Nigeria (printed as volume 50), in German with English Summary

J. Muriuki, The Mau-Mau Movement: Its Socio-Economic and Political Causes and Implications upon British Colonial Policy in Kenya and Africa (in preparation), in English

H. Desselberger, Education's Contribution to Economic Development of a Tropical Agrarian Country – the Example of Tanzania (in preparation)

## Legal Studies

H. Fliedner, Land Tenure Reform in Kenya (printed as volume 7), in German

H. Krauss, Land Legislation in the Cameroons 1884–1964 (printed as volume 12), in German

G. Spreen, The Present State of Legislation in East Africa (in preparation)

K. v. Sperber, The Implications of Tanzania's Administrative System for Her Economic Development (completed), in English

F. v. Benda-Beckmann, Development of Law in Malawi (completed), in German

## Studies in Economic Geography

W. Marquardt, The Interrelationship between Man, Nature and Economy: the Example of Madagascar (in preparation)

H.-O. Neuhoff, Gabun: History, Structure and Problems of the Export Trade of a Developing Country (printed as volume 16), in German

H. D. Ludwig, Ukara: A Special Case of Land Use in the Tropics (printed as volume 22), in German

R. Jätzold/E. Baum, The Kilombero Valley/Tanzania: Characteristic Features of the Economic Geography of a Semihumid East African Flood Plain and Its Margins (printed as volume 28), in English

A. J. Halbach, The Economy of South West Africa (a Study in Economic Geography) (mimeograph), in German

J. A. Hellen, Rural Economic Development in Zambia 1890–1964 (printed as volume 32), in English

K. Engelhard, The Economico-Geographical Pattern of East Africa (in preparation)

J. Schultz, Iraqw Highland/Tanzania: Resource Analysis of an East African Highland and its Margins (in preparation)

K. Gerresheim, Evaluation of Aerial Photography in East Africa (an Inventory) (mimeograph), in German

## Bibliographies and Others

D. Mezger / E. Littich, Recent English Economic Research in East Africa. A Selected Bibliography (mimeograph), in German

A. Molnos, Annotated Bibliography of Social Research in East Africa 1954–1963 (printed as volume 5), in German

B. Heine, Status and Use of African Lingua Francas (printed as volume 49), in English

M. Bohnet, Science and Development Policy: The Problem of Applying Research Results (mimeograph), in German

## Foreword

The work here presented is based on an investigation published in German, which was brought out in 1968 under the title "Afrikanische Verkehrssprachen" by the Institute Infratest, Munich, and the radio broadcasting service Voice of Germany (Deutsche Welle). In the meantime various more recent publications have been evaluated, and results of my own sociolinguistic investigations have been revised, these having been carried out in Kenya from August to December 1968 within the framework of the German Research Association (Deutsche Forschungsgemeinschaft), which financed the project 'Mapping of Africa' ('Kartenwerk Afrika').
At this stage I would like to convey my deeply felt thanks to my esteemed teacher, Professor KÖHLER, for his stimulation and help, which contributed in a considerable measure to the creation of this work. Last not least, my thanks go to Mr. Hans Freiherr VON REDWITZ for translation into English as well as to the FRITZ-THYSSEN FOUNDATION in Cologne, who generously contributed the funds for translation and printing.
In order to facilitate reading, the following indication should be observed: in addition to the sub-divisions according to the table of contents the paragraphs of the whole text are arranged in numerical order. These paragraphs are referred to in the Index of Authors and in the General Index at the end of this book. The numerical order makes possible a more precise sub-division than would be achieved if these Indices were merely referring to pages; the research work is thus facilitated and the reader can more easily find those parts of the text he is interested in.

Cologne, July 1969

Bernd HEINE

# Contents

A. Introduction . . . . . . . . . . . . . . . . . . . . . . . . . . . . . . 15
B. Definitions and Characteristics . . . . . . . . . . . . . . . . . . . 19
    I. Range of Functions of Lingua Francas . . . . . . . . . . . . 19
    II. "A" Type and "B" Type Languages . . . . . . . . . . . . . 23
    III. Basis Form and Lingua Franca Form . . . . . . . . . . . . . 25
    IV. Distribution of Lingua Francas . . . . . . . . . . . . . . . . 29
    V. Lingua Francas and Diachrony . . . . . . . . . . . . . . . . . 30
    VI. Spread of Lingua Francas . . . . . . . . . . . . . . . . . . . 34
    VII. Borders of Spread . . . . . . . . . . . . . . . . . . . . . . . 37
    VIII. National State, European Languages and African Lingua Francas . 40
    IX. Lingua Franca and Dialect Continuum . . . . . . . . . . . . 45
C. African Lingua Francas: A Survey . . . . . . . . . . . . . . . . . 47
    I. Southern Africa . . . . . . . . . . . . . . . . . . . . . . . . . 47
        a) FANAGALO . . . . . . . . . . . . . . . . . . . . . . . . 47
        b) TSWANA . . . . . . . . . . . . . . . . . . . . . . . . . 52
        c) LOZI . . . . . . . . . . . . . . . . . . . . . . . . . . . . 52
        d) UMBUNDU . . . . . . . . . . . . . . . . . . . . . . . . 54
        e) LWENA . . . . . . . . . . . . . . . . . . . . . . . . . . 56
        f) Town BEMBA . . . . . . . . . . . . . . . . . . . . . . 56
        g) NYANJA . . . . . . . . . . . . . . . . . . . . . . . . . . 60
    II. Congo Basin . . . . . . . . . . . . . . . . . . . . . . . . . . . 64
        a) LUBA lingua franca . . . . . . . . . . . . . . . . . . . 64
        b) KITUBA . . . . . . . . . . . . . . . . . . . . . . . . . . 67
        c) LINGALA . . . . . . . . . . . . . . . . . . . . . . . . . 72
    III. Eastern Africa . . . . . . . . . . . . . . . . . . . . . . . . . . 80
        a) SWAHILI . . . . . . . . . . . . . . . . . . . . . . . . . 80
        b) GANDA . . . . . . . . . . . . . . . . . . . . . . . . . . 105
        c) AMHARIC . . . . . . . . . . . . . . . . . . . . . . . . . 107
    IV. Central Sudan and North Africa . . . . . . . . . . . . . . . 110
        a) ZANDE . . . . . . . . . . . . . . . . . . . . . . . . . . 110
        b) SARA . . . . . . . . . . . . . . . . . . . . . . . . . . . 111
        c) KANURI . . . . . . . . . . . . . . . . . . . . . . . . . 112
        d) MABA . . . . . . . . . . . . . . . . . . . . . . . . . . . 114
        e) ARABIC . . . . . . . . . . . . . . . . . . . . . . . . . . 115
    V. Western Central Africa . . . . . . . . . . . . . . . . . . . . . 119
        a) BULU . . . . . . . . . . . . . . . . . . . . . . . . . . . 119
        b) YAUNDE . . . . . . . . . . . . . . . . . . . . . . . . . 122
        c) Pidgin A 70 . . . . . . . . . . . . . . . . . . . . . . . . 124

|        |                          |     |
| ------ | ------------------------ | --- |
|        | d) DUALA                 | 125 |
|        | e) BALI                  | 126 |
|        | f) Adamawa-FUL           | 127 |
|        | g) SANGO                 | 131 |
| VI.    | West African Coast       | 138 |
|        | a) YORUBA                | 138 |
|        | b) EWE                   | 139 |
|        | c) TWI                   | 141 |
|        | d) GA                    | 144 |
|        | e) MENDE and TEMNE       | 145 |
|        | f) SUSU                  | 146 |
|        | g) WOLOF                 | 147 |
| VII.   | Western Sudan            | 151 |
|        | a) HAUSA                 | 151 |
|        | b) SONG'AI               | 159 |
|        | c) MOSI                  | 161 |
|        | d) MANDINGO              | 163 |
|        | e) MALINKE               | 165 |
|        | f) DYULA                 | 166 |
|        | g) BAMBARA               | 168 |
|        | h) KANGBE                | 170 |

Bibliography . . . . . . . . . . . . . . . . . . . . . . . . . . 172
Index of Authors . . . . . . . . . . . . . . . . . . . . . . . . 191
General Index . . . . . . . . . . . . . . . . . . . . . . . . . . 193

## Maps

1. African Lingua Francas in Southern Africa . . . . . . . . . . . . 47
2. African Lingua Francas in the Congo Basin . . . . . . . . . . . . 64
3. African Lingua Francas in Eastern Africa . . . . . . . . . . . . 81
4. African Lingua Francas in Central Sudan . . . . . . . . . . . . 110
5. African Lingua Francas in Western Africa . . . . . . . . . . . . 120

## A. INTRODUCTION

A lingua franca is understood to be a common language which is habitually used as a medium of communication between groups of people whose mother tongues are different (cf. UNESCO 1953, 46; SAMARIN 1962, 54/6; GREENBERG 1965, 52). The question whether the language involved is one spoken as mother tongue by one of the groups in communication with one another or whether this language is employed by all groups as a second language only, remains unconsidered in this definition.

A class of languages is thereby defined, which in literature has become known under a multiplicity of termini. Since, however, the criteria of definition forming the basis of such termini are not uniform, more or less large variations result each time in their scope of application. As a rule, these criteria can be classified in three groups.

1. *Scope of the language's function.* This criterion forms the basis for such designations as "trade language" (Fr. *langue de traite* or *langue commerciale,* Ger. *Handelssprache*) or the designation of "vehicular language" (Fr. *langue véhiculaire,* Ger. *Verkehrssprache*) applied here.

2. *Function of the language as a medium of communication.* Under this heading fall all those designations stressing the importance of lingua franca as a medium of communication, such as "contact language" (Fr. *langue de relations*[1] or *langue "passe-partout"* [BURSSENS 1954, 29], Ger. *Kontaktsprache*).

3. *Linguistic characteristics of the language.* Lingua francas not only distinguish themselves by their scope of application and their function among communication media, but not rarely possess special linguistic structures. For this reason, designations are occasionally applied to them, such as "pidgin language" or "Creole"[2].

As a rule, artificial languages such as *Volapük, Esperanto,* etc., are counted among the lingua francas — an application which does not always seem

---

[1] "The contact languages are those used for the purpose of contact amongst each other by the populations separated by language barriers." ("Les langues de relation sont celles utilisées pour leurs rapports entre elles par des populations que sépare une barrière linguistique" [JACQUOT 1960, 30].)

[2] "Pidgin" and "Creole" are primarily taken as a concept of linguistics. In this connection, "Creole" — as opposed to "pidgin" — is to be understood exclusively as a terminus of diachronic linguistics (see par. 14).

justified (cf. SAMARIN 1962, 56). These languages, called "writing desk languages" by Ernst SCHULTZE, have in some cases not extended much beyond the restricted circle of their originator. As they do not possess any ascertainable value in Africa, they will not be further touched upon in the following.

Those languages which in Africa are not to be counted amongst the lingua francas, are described as v e r n a c u l a r languages. Accordingly, such languages are to be understood as languages which are habitually spoken only as first language and not as second or third. For such languages, the designation "tribal languages" (Fr. *langues tribales,* Ger. *Stammessprachen*) is often used. In consideration of the fact that the boundaries of the use of such languages do not always tally with those of the tribe, this designation is only used in cases in which this seems to be justified; it can therefore not be understood as synonymous to "vernacular languages".

In the above-named definition of "lingua franca" the concept of "mother tongue" is used, which suffers from its terminological inexactitude and for this reason has repeatedly become the subject of critical remarks (cf. CHRISTOPHERSEN 1948, 2 ff.). It is being understood in the present investigation as having the same meaning as "first language" (contrary to "second language", etc.) and describes a language which is initially learnt by an individual or by a group of people (WEINREICH 1953, 88). In this sense, individuals who ab initio have simultaneously learnt two languages, have two mother tongues (op. cit. 77). This usage thus is based on a diachronic criterion. The mother tongue, however, is not necessarily the language best mastered. It may happen — and this can in fact be demonstrated by various examples — that an individual through intensive use of a second language achieves a proficiency in it which exceeds that of the mother tongue[3]. It therefore proves itself necessary to introduce at least one further differentiation. Thus, the language which is best mastered is designated as p r i m a r y and all others are as s e c o n d a r y languages[4]. The primary language is not always identical with the mother tongue and, analogously, the concepts of "second language" and "secondary language" can, in the individual case, designate different communication media.

---

[3] An example of this is given by Uriel Weinreich in the immigrants to the United States, who have acquired a greater facility in English than in their mother tongue (WEINREICH 1953, 76). Similar observations can also be made in Africa. In Kecheibi in eastern Ghana I was able to ascertain that some inhabitants, although having learnt ANIMERE, the language of their parents, as mother tongue, they had later acquired a better knowledge of ADELE, the predominant language of the locality.

[4] This use of the termini does not tally with that of W. H. WHITELEY and M. HOUIS, whose criterion in the differentiation between primary language (Fr. *langue primaire,* Ger. *primäre Sprache*) and secondary language (Fr. *langue secondaire,* Ger. *sekundäre Sprache*) is not represented by the degree of mastery but by current usage of the language (WHITELEY/HOUIS 1962, 154/160).

In the treatment of the subject matter, the type and scope of the theme under discussion render it necessary to impose some restrictions which have not been taken into consideration in the title of the book. The lingua francas of Indo-European origin, which are spoken in sub-Saharan Africa, will not be included in the study. Among these belong more particularly English, French, Afrikaans and Portuguese, as well as the variants deriving their origins from these languages, such as *Pidgin-English, Français-Tirailleur, Crioulo,* etc. These languages differentiate themselves not only in their linguistic status, but frequently also in their sociolinguistic prerequisites from the African lingua francas; it is therefore not surprising that their treatment has hitherto stimulated lesser interest amongst the scholars of African languages than amongst the representatives of other fields of study — in particular the scholars of Romance philology, such as Hugo SCHUCHARDT and Marius F. VALKHOFF[5].

It is unknown how many lingua francas are spoken in Africa. This on the one hand is caused by the fact that not sufficient research has been conducted on the African languages up to the present. Some languages still exist which are unknown or known by name only. On the other hand, linguists as well as ethnologists have so far given little attention to the sociolinguistic aspects of lingua francas. Thus, as a rule, neither in papers dealing with the science of language nor in ethnological works, closer descriptions can be found of the spread and status of lingua francas. The languages dealt with in the present study may therefore represent only one part of the total number of African lingua francas.

In the following study, the reader will miss the names of languages such as IBO, SOMALI or GALLA, being amongst the "most important" African languages. The reason that these languages are excluded from further consideration is found in the fact that as lingua franca they fulfil only an unimportant function or none at all; nor could I learn of the existence of such a function with any degree of certainty. The question whether a language must be classified as a lingua franca or as vernacular language, cannot always be unequivocally answered on the basis of the contradictory statements not infrequently to be found in literature.

Lingua francas can be dealt with from very differing aspects. In principle, the present study restricts itself to one of those aspects which in the following will be defined as "sociolinguistics". The results of other fields of study — more particularly of philology — will be adduced in as far as they appear to be of importance in respect of this subject. Those two fields are subsumed under the designation of "sociolinguistics", which Trevor HILL on the one hand calls "sociological linguistics" and "institutional linguistics", in which

---

5 More recently, a greater importance is attached to the study of Indo-European forms of lingua francas in Africa, even by the scholars of African philology, not least through the influence of J. BERRY.

case under "sociological linguistics" he understands the occupation with the general principles of the relation between language and language user or language and community, and under "institutional linguistics" the study of special cases of language and communities as social institutions (HILL 1958, 455; cf. ELLIS 1965). The second part of this study dealing with various examples of African lingua francas would therefore fall within the scope of institutional linguistics, whereas in the first part, occupying itself with the comparison of lingua francas, the aspects of sociological linguistics are most of all taken into consideration.

In this connection, the study comprises in particular the following questions:

a) *Development into a lingua franca*. Here the factors having influenced the origin and development of a particular lingua franca under study should be ascertained.

b) *Present-day spread*. In this connection a difference will be drawn between the area in which a lingua franca is spoken as first language, and the area in which it is spoken as second or third language. The first is dealt with only in as far as it is of importance in respect to the status of the lingua franca. Otherwise, reference is made to the statements to be found in the series *Handbook of African Languages* published by the *International African Institute* as well as in other pertinent works. Moreover, the number of users of the lingua franca, as far as can be ascertained, is stated.

c) *The sociolinguistic status*. Subject of the study will in particular be the question under which circumstances and by whom a lingua franca is being used, and which functions it possesses.

The insufficient material hitherto published on African lingua francas does not in respect of any of these languages admit of the satisfactory treatment of any of the three mentioned points. In many cases the study can be based only on rudimentary data so that not only the description but also the comparison of the lingua francas of necessity remains fragmentary.

In the treatment of the various lingua francas, a short note on their linguistic status is added each time. Hitherto, the classification of languages in Africa has largely been undertaken with methods which cannot stand up to serious scientific criticism. Thus, the application of the comparative method has been restricted to few fields, such as the *Bantu* languages. Additionally, the question of the linguistic status of lingua francas, amongst them more particularly the p i d g i n s , is answered differently by individual scientists. The remarks on the status of African lingua francas can therefore be of a preliminary character only.

Many of the African lingua francas can be divided into a number of dialects which frequently differ very much from one another, conditioned in one case by geographical and in the other case by social factors. In the following, boundaries of dialects will not be dealt with unless they are of importance in respect of the sociolinguistic status of the relevant lingua franca.

# B. DEFINITIONS AND CHARACTERISTICS

## I. Range of Functions of Lingua Francas

1 As can already be presumed by designations like "trade language" these languages represent means of communication which, in comparison with other languages, are frequently specialised to some extent. The origin of lingua francas in many cases is connected to a specific situation of interethnic or international contact, by which not only the linguistic form but also the sociolinguistic status of the lingua franca is influenced. More particularly, it is trade, administration and communications which form the basis of such contact situations, and accordingly it is these very fields which are of importance for the function of lingua francas. To a lingua franca a specific function cannot infrequently be attributed, which particularly is characteristic with respect to the extent of its application.

2 These facts have already been pointed out in former papers on lingua francas, and frequently the range of functions of the languages was made the basis of their classification. Ernst SCHULTZE, for instance, sub-divided those lingua francas designated by him as "substitute languages"[1] into the following four types:

I. Settlement-gibberish (medley of languages spoken in the settlements),
II. Trading-gibberish (medley of languages made use of in trading),
III. The artificial international auxiliary languages (desk languages), and
IV. The slave and servant languages (SCHULTZE 1933).

This typology is primarily based on the origin of the languages, i.e. a diachronic criterion. Apart from the artificial international auxiliary languages, all type-designations refer to a special functional extent, which

---

[1] "I would like to define as substitute languages those languages which are used as means of communication by people speaking different languages, of whom neither speaks the other's tongue, thus obliging them to make a linguistic detour in order to converse with each other." ("Als Ersatzsprachen möchte ich diejenigen bezeichnen, die zur Verständigung zwischen verschiedensprachigen Menschen benutzt werden, von denen keiner die Sprache des anderen kennt, so daß sie eines sprachlichen Umweges bedürfen, um sich miteinander zu unterhalten" [SCHULTZE 1933, 380].) Accordingly, the "substitute" languages are to be dealt with as a sub-division of lingua francas.

has led to the formation of each of the languages. Thus, the settlement-gibberish finds its origin "in the need of linguistic communication between peoples of different tongues, who on account of living in the same settlement have become neighbours or have inter-mixed their dwelling places" (loc. cit. 381); the trading-gibberish "owes its origin to the trading contacts between peoples of different tongues" (loc. cit. 384). Finally, the slave and servant languages, to which Schultze amongst others counts SWAHILI "are formed in such areas where people of different languages come into contact, who ... face each other not as equals, but live socially on distinctly different levels. It is therefore always a question of a relation betwen d o m i n a t i o n and s u b o r d i n a t i o n, in most cases of a relation between masters and servants, if not masters and slaves" (loc. cit. 389).

Essentially, this typology was adopted by John E. REINECKE, who nevertheless on some points finds criticism for the work of SCHULTZE (REINECKE 1938). The sociolinguistic function also takes up a position of precedence in his classification. The types therein designated as (a) *trade jargons*, (b) *plantation creole dialects* and (c) *settlers' creole dialects* are comparable to SCHULTZE's types II, IV and I, respectively, whereas III remains unconsidered by REINECKE.

3   Also the African lingua francas frequently allow a specialization to be recognized in their range of application. HAUSA and DYULA, for instance, are thus deemed to be predominantly languages of t r a d e, and the designation "Dyula" in some parts of the western Sudan is synonymous with 'travelling traders'. Other lingua francas such as BAMBARA, LINGALA, NYANJA and in part also YAUNDE (see NEKES 1911, 2), are or were often designated as s o l d i e r languages since they served as means of communication amongst the generally ethnically heterogeneous troops of the former colonial powers or of the modern African states. Other lingua francas have spread along the great traffic routes and to a special degree merit the designation l i n g u a   f r a n c a. Especially the big African rivers, such as the Congo, Ubangi and Niger, offer favourable intercommunication and have contributed to the development of so called r i v e r languages, i.e. lingua francas having developed along river-courses. In this connection, especially LINGALA, SANGO and in part also SONG'AI can be mentioned.

4   It is not unjustified to speak in some cases of lingua francas as s c h o o l or a d m i n i s t r a t i v e languages because they are preponderantly used in these fields. As an example may be pointed out the comments by E. O. J. WESTPHAL on the position of TSWANA-TAWANA in Ngamiland, the northwestern province of Botswana, formerly Bechuanaland (WESTPHAL 1962). Examples of s c h o o l languages are numerous and can be found in almost all parts of anglophone Africa. Languages used exclusively or predominantly during work can be designated as w o r k i n g languages

(RICHARDSON 1962, 189). A typical example of this is represented by FANAGALO, as was demonstrated by Irvine RICHARDSON on the basis of the situation in the copperbelt of Zambia. There it serves more particularly as a means of communication between Africans and Europeans while at work. On the use of FANAGALO within the Republic of South Africa, the chief area of spread of this language, no reliable data is available to me, but it seems to be a similar case to that in Zambia. This can be gathered from the name *Silunguboi,* one of the designations used in South Africa for FANAGALO. *Silunguboi* approximately means "the language used by Europeans in contact with their African servants".

In this connection it would be of great importance to elaborate a typology of the African lingua francas in accordance with the scope of their functions. Considering the present stage of research such a project, however, would be premature. Our knowledge of these languages is still too fragmentary to justify a systematization.

5 Whereas, accordingly, there exist domains offering propitious prerequisites for the use of lingua francas, other domains can be found into which access by lingua francas is difficult. To these more particularly belong the family and the kinship group.

During his investigations in Bangui, the capital of the Central African Republic, André JACQUOT, for instance, ascertained that SANGO as lingua franca is spread throughout the town. Apart from one young woman, who had only been in Bangui a short time, all 1,412 persons interviewed stated that they had a command of SANGO. But only 2.5% of them were using the lingua franca as the sole means of communication within the family (JACQUOT 1961, 163).

A good example of this is also represented by the data supplied by Maria LEBLANC on the use of SWAHILI in Katanga (LEBLANC 1955). SWAHILI is the predominant lingua franca in this industrial area and in an increasing measure is replacing the vernacular languages. LEBLANC was able to ascertain that the use of the lingua franca is essentially more restricted within the family than between members of different families (loc. cit. 793). But even within the family considerable differences result in part in the use of SWAHILI. Whereas brothers and sisters converse amongst one another in SWAHILI in far more than 50% of the cases involved, 23% of the parents communicate with their children in this language, married couples making use of SWAHILI only in 3% of the cases (loc. cit. 794–7).

The observation that communication between married couples is specially resistant to the use of lingua francas is confirmed by investigations on other African lingua francas[2]. L. B. DE BOECK, for instance, made out during his

---

2 This, however, does not apply to such cases in which the marital spouses have grown up with different mother tongues.

studies in Kinshasa, the capital of the Congo, that the African coming from the country into the town first of all uses the lingua franca LINGALA in his contact with strangers but not with the members of his tribe or family. This undergoes a change later when his children learn LINGALA as sole or p r i m a r y language, and when in contact with other members of his tribe the use of LINGALA gains a stronger foothold. Thus, he frequently uses his mother tongue only in communication with his wife (BOECK 1953, 3/4).

6   Even when lingua francas often occur in connection with a certain range of functions, their use is only very rarely restricted to this one field. The above-mentioned termini such as s o l d i e r language or r i v e r language relate only to a single — even though important — aspect, but give little indication as to the total range of application of a lingua franca. The fact that lingua francas as a rule have several functions, is frequently reflected by the designations under which they have become known. KITUBA, for instance, is designated, inter alia, as *Kikongo commercial,* i.e. 'KIKONGO trading language', *Kileta,* i.e. 'language of the state, of the government', and as *Kisodi,* i.e. 'language of soldiers'. Thereby, already three ranges of functions of a lingua franca are nominated, which J. BERRY has classified as *pidgin of restricted function* (BERRY 1962, 225). SANGO also has received different names, permitting certain conclusions in respect of its range of application: *Sango commercial* 'SANGO trading language', *sango tí tulugú* 'SANGO of soldiers', or *sango tí salawísi,* which means the 'SANGO of those leaving the village in order to work for money' and points to the importance of this language for modern labour migrations. Thanks to the assiduous efforts of William J. SAMARIN and André JACQUOT we know that the functions of this lingua franca have by no means been exhausted thereby. Within this range of functions FANAGALO, which above was adduced as a w o r k i n g language, embodies further differentiations. Thus, inter alia, it has become known under the designations *Mine-Kafir* and *Kitchen-Kafir,* which already point to two different ranges of functions of this language, i. e. on the one hand, within the South African mines, and, on the other hand, within the households of families of European origin.

7   It does not occur infrequently that with the differentation of various ranges of functions within a lingua franca, there is also connected with it a linguistic differentiation. SWAHILI, for instance, has various p i d g i n dialects, each one of which is an expression of a different function. Thus, inter alia, a *ki-Setla* is differentiated, approximating a form of the w o r k i n g language, which preponderantly is used by Europeans in contact with their African personnel, as well as a *ki-Hindi,* representing the SWAHILI dialect of a major part of the Indian population in East Africa, or a *ki-Shamba,* predominantly the contact language of the plantation workers in large

areas inland. Moreover, a *ki-Vita* (lit.: 'war language') is mentioned, a possibly extinct SWAHILI dialect having the function of a s o l d i e r language (cf. BRYAN 1959, 128).

## II. "A" Type and "B" Type Languages

8   The difficulties encountered during the attempt to set up a typology of African lingua francas, has already been pointed out. Some of these languages are known by name only, and others, on which material is available, have only been investigated in part. A comparison of lingua francas therefore rests on a very inconsistent point of departure. On the basis of diachronic points of view a difference, however, can be noted, which is also of importance in respect of the synchronic observation of African lingua francas. Depending on whether the origin and development of a lingua franca has occurred independently or in dependence on the Afro-European contact-situation, the difference between languages of an "A" type or "B" type can be determined.

9   The development of languages of an "A" type seems in the majority of cases to have been the result of warlike events in pre-colonial times. As languages of the conquering powers they were carried into the territory of the subjected peoples and there spread as lingua francas. This can be demonstrated in particular with regard to the various languages of the western Sudan. Thus MANDINGO as language of the *Mali* empire, SONG'AI as language of the empire of the same name, KANURI as language of the *Kanem-Bornu* empire or TWI as language of the *Ashanti* empire presumably owe a large or even decisive part of their importance to their genetic position within these state formations. But also in other parts of Africa lingua francas can be found whose development is closely connected with the history of conquering peoples. Thus ZANDE spread in the Mbomu-Uele territory as a result of the invasion of the bellicose *Avongara*, and the development of LOZI into the lingua franca of the Upper-Zambezi was the result of the empire-building by the *Kololo* conquerors.

The pre-colonial trade was the cause of another important factor which in turn favoured the development of important lingua francas mainly in the western Sudan. Here can primarily be named HAUSA[1] and DYULA, a dialect of MANDINGO. Furthermore, religion seems to have played its part in the spread of "A" type languages. Thus, for instance, E. RAPP reports

---

1 HAUSA, however, also owes its importance as lingua franca to the expansion of the *Ful* empires *Sokoto* and *Gwandu*, amongst whom it served as the predominant language (cf. GREENBERG 1965, 53).

that TWI found entrance not only by the expansion of the *Ashanti* empire, but also as a language of r e l i g i o n amongst the neighbouring tribes (RAPP 1955, 229). In this connection the question is of great importance as to the relation existing between the spread of Islam to that of some "A" type languages — more particularly ARABIC. Thus it can be presumed that the advance of this world religion has influenced the development of some African lingua francas to no small degree.

10 The spread of the "B" type languages occurred to a major extent thanks to the improvement and extension of the communication network following the arrival of the Europeans. The interior of the African continent was opened up by the railway, but even to a larger extent by the motor car, and tribes hitherto living in seclusion came into contact with other tribes. Thereby new centres were formed from which the language spread. It is a characteristic fact of many "B" type languages that they spread along the newly-created ways of communication, be it along the great motorways, the railway lines or navigable rivers. Further important stimuli were received by the "B" type languages through trade with products of European culture.

The modern labour migrations also exerted their influence on the development of lingua francas. Areas intensively cultivated or industrialized became the points of attraction for labourers of differing origin, and thus offered fertile ground for the origin of lingua francas. Not infrequently the language of the indigenous population was learned by the inflowing people as second language, thus, for instance, WOLOF by the FUL-speaking *Tukuleur* in Dakar or GANDA by the immigrant labourers in the kingdom of Buganda (see GREENBERG 1965, 55).

11 The languages of the "B" type not infrequently derive an important portion of their origin and development from the educational and administrative systems introduced by the colonial powers. The schools established by the governments and Christian missions led to the development of a special type of lingua franca, which may be named a s c h o o l language (see par. 4). BULU in the southern Cameroons, for instance, became the language of school education thanks to the American Presbyterian Mission, and it seems not in the very least due to this fact that it was taken over by the neighbouring tribes as lingua franca (NIDA 1955, 157). Various African lingua francas could be furthered in their importance as languages of administration. TSWANA-TAWANA has already been mentioned in this connection. A further example is offered by KITUBA in the area of the Lower Congo, which for this reason has often been called *Kileta* "the language of the state, of the government"\*. The number of factors defining the development of "B" type languages is undoubtedly thereby not yet exhausted. Thus, for instance, the two modern mass media, newspapers and radio broadcasting, cannot be underestimated in their importance.

---

\* ... 'die Sprache des Staates, der Regierung' (HULSTAERT 1950, 47).

12  The differentiation between languages of "A" type and "B" type, however, may not be deemed a classification of the African lingua francas. Even with a sufficient knowledge of the historical events, on the one hand, it cannot always be unequivocally decided whether the development of a lingua franca must be looked upon as connected with the Afro-European contact-situation. A good example of this is supplied by the history of the two r i v e r languages LINGALA and SANGO. Already in the time before the arrival of the Europeans both seem to have occupied a position of importance — however a regionally limited and modest one — as lingua francas along the Congo and Ubangi rivers. In respect of both languages the development into a supra-regional lingua franca set in during the nineties of the last century and is the result of the contacts between Africans and Europeans in the beginning of the colonial times. In taking the former epoch of the development of the two lingua francas as a basis of the classification, they would have to be grouped amongst the "A" type and, in the other case, however, amongst the "B" type. Some other lingua francas, contrariwise, such as SWAHILI, HAUSA or MANDINGO, demonstrate that one language can combine the characteristics of both types.

13  It is therefore not possible to classify each language under one single type. It is rather more important to investigate in how far a language under study belongs to the "A" type and/or to the "B" type. Thus KANURI, for instance, preponderantly possesses the characteristics of the "A" type, whereas other languages, such as FANAGALO or Town-BEMBA, are exclusively languages of the "B" type. Some languages, moreover the important lingua francas such as SWAHILI, HAUSA and MANDINGO blend the characteristics of both types in more or less equal proportions. The older period in development of these lingua francas falls into the pre-colonial age and was independent of any European influence. Its more recent development, however, was to a large extent determined by the Afro-European encounter.

## III. Basis Form and Lingua Franca Form

14  In their sociolinguistic and linguistic characteristics, lingua francas can utterly differ. In the sociolinguistic field, a differentiation according to the function of the lingua franca can be made between t r a d i n g languages, s o l d i e r languages, etc., in the linguistic field perhaps between languages with a p i d g i n structure and c r e o l e languages[1]. A lingua franca as

---

1 i.e. pidgin languages, which have become the mother tongue to a group of people, and thereby have undergone a process which shall here be designated as c r e o l i z a t i o n.

a rule has its origin in a n a t u r a l language[2], which is learned by people speaking other languages as their mother tongues, and is habitually used by them as their second language. This development causes a particular language to split principally into two forms which in the following shall de designated b a s i s  f o r m and l i n g u a  f r a n c a  f o r m. Such a split can as a rule be proved not only in the linguistic but also in the extra-linguistic field. The basis form is that form of the language which is still being used as mother tongue, whereas the lingua franca form is spoken as second language, i.e. not as mother tongue. The lingua franca form can be differentiated from the basis form by the fact of its having to undergo a process which often is defined as *"simplification"*, and which will in the following be called p i d g i n i z a t i o n. The result of this process is, for instance, that the lingua franca form in comparison with the basis form shows less differentiation in grammar, vocabulary and phonology. To this must be added that the lingua franca form is being influenced by the linguistic habits of those people using it. The difference between basis form and lingua franca form is as a rule recognized without difficulty by the speakers of the basis form, whereas this is not always the case in respect of those speaking the lingua franca form.

15 The degree of this difference diverges from one lingua franca to another. It can be so large that both are separated by a language border, i.e. that they form different languages. In other cases the basis form and lingua franca form act like two dialects of the same language, and in other cases again they are so similar to each other, that it does not seem to be justified to speak of different forms of dialects. More particularly remarkable are the divergencies within the linguistic structure. By the above-mentioned process, the lingua franca form undergoes a change of structure, which in the extreme leads to a development of a p i d g i n, i.e. to a linguistic form with "minimum" differences. The other extreme constitutes that lingua franca form, the structural change of which is so slight that it hardly differs from the basis form. It remains to be investigated whether the structural change under special circumstances can amount to nil, which would mean that basis form and lingua franca form would be identical.

16 Differences between the various lingua francas are also revealed in the relations between basis form and lingua franca form. In the case of many lingua francas it can be observed that the basis form exerts a certain influence upon the lingua franca form. This influence can be explained, inter alia, by the fact that the basis form represents a norm to the speakers of the lingua franca form, which they are attempting to imitate. The larger the influence of the basis form, the less the difference between the two forms tends to be.

---

2 The concept "natural language" defines all languages adopted as a first language by a group of people through the process of enculturation (cf. SAMARIN 1962, 56).

In the case of a small influence of the basis form, however, an increasing tendency towards p i d g i n i z a t i o n frequently asserts itself in the case of the lingua franca form. In this respect, however, the question is problematic as to how in an individual case[3] the degree of such influence can be measured by linguistic means.

17 The relations between basis form and lingua franca form are influenced by various extra-linguistic factors. One of these factors is the relation of the number of speakers with regard to the two language forms. If one takes the amount of speakers of the basis form as constant and applies to it an index value of 1.00, this value can be contrasted with the corresponding proportionate number of lingua franca speakers, which then will lie between the extremes of infinity and zero. In the case of the number of speakers of the lingua franca form being just as large of that of the basis form, it will also receive the index value 1.00; if, on the other hand, the number of speakers of the lingua franca form is only half as large, it will be given the value of 0.50. An index value of zero would mean that there is no lingua franca form — and consequently no lingua franca — present; an index value of infinity, on the other hand, would have to be applied to a language having no basis form and therefore not being spoken as mother tongue. The smaller the value of the lingua franca form, the larger the influence of the basis form tends to be. Contrarily, the influence of the basis form in respect of a high index value of the lingua franca form (more particularly in the case of 1.00 and more) inclines to become smaller. In respect of the lingua franca form of some African lingua francas the following index values of the number of speakers accordingly result:

| | |
|---|---|
| MOSI (pursuant to DELAFOSSE 1912) | 0.13 |
| TWI[4] | 0.34 |
| ARABIC in the Sudan (pursuant to MURRAY 1963) | 0.39 |
| WOLOF[4] | 0.43 |
| NYANJA (pursuant to ATKINS 1950) | 0.56 |
| SONG'AI[4] | 0.60 |

Whereas, accordingly, MOSI makes up only a relatively small number of speakers of the lingua franca form, in NYANJA and SONG'AI the figure amounts to already more than half of the speakers of the basis form; other African lingua francas — such as, for instance, SANGO in the Central African Republic — achieve index values which sometimes may amount to

---

[3] An approach in this connection is offered, for example, by the research into loan-words. It must thus be expected that the influence is the larger the more loan-words are adopted by the lingua franca form from the basis form. The identification of the loan-words, however, is rendered more difficult by the fact that both forms frequently differ but slightly and possess a large number of semantically and formally conforming words.

[4] These figures, here taken as a basis, represent estimates.

more than 100.00. The number of speakers of the African lingua francas is unfortunately still too little known in order to calculate exact values in respect of a larger number of them.

18 In conformity with the relation between basis form and lingua franca form, the African lingua francas can be classified into various classes. The lack of knowledge of these languages, however, does not permit the undertaking of a detailed classification; in the following review, therefore, a differentiation is only made between three main types:

1. The influence of the basis form on the lingua franca form is strong, and both forms differ but slightly. An example for this is supplied by EWE in Togoland and East Ghana. It is used by various tribes, such as the *Avatime, Nyangbo-Tafi, Logba, Ahlo* and *Likpe*, as lingua franca. Only a few thousand people belong to these tribes, whereas the basis form is spoken by altogether more than a million people. Moreover, the basis form has gained a certain importance as written language within the area of spread of the lingua franca form. Both forms are so much alike that the differences are frequently noticed only by the speakers of the basis form.

2. An influence of the basis form on the lingua franca form can be observed: both forms, however, are separated by a dialect or language border and have clearly differentiated structures. This, inter alia, applies to BEMBA in Zambia, the basis form of which is called BEMBA *(Cibemba)* and the lingua franca form of which is defined as *Town* BEMBA. BEMBA exercises a certain control over the linguistic form of Town BEMBA; the latter, however, has already developed its own linguistic structure, which reveals a tendency towards p i d g i n i z a t i o n (RICHARDSON 1961; RICHARDSON 1962).

3. The basis form exerts no influence upon the lingua franca form; between them runs a dialect or language border, and their structures are very different. An example of this presumably is SANGO. The lingua franca form of SANGO is apparently independent of the basis form, a dialect being spoken by a limited number of people around the village of Mobaye on the Ubangi River[5]. The structures of the two forms more particularly differ in the basis form being a natural language and the lingua franca form a pidgin.

19 The types (1) and (3) represent extreme forms of lingua francas. Unless belonging to these two types, all of them can be classified along a scale between (1) and (3), such as is the case for (2), for example[6].

---

5 Since SANGO is a dialect of NGBANDI, which is spoken in large parts of the area of spread of the lingua franca, it remains to be investigated whether NGBANDI, in a larger sense, does not constitute the basis form of the lingua franca SANGO.

6 The contrast between the types (1) and (3) approximately corresponds to the differentiation between *'langues communes'* and *'langues "passe-partout"'*,

20 The question arises as to which position the creole languages occupy in this classification. Tendencies towards development from the p i d g i n to the c r e o l e have been observed in various African lingua francas, thus, for instance, in SANGO, KITUBA and LINGALA. However, not many details have become known of the sociolinguistic position or the linguistic structure of the creole languages[7]. It may, however, be looked upon as certain that the African creole languages can be counted amongst the natural languages, and just like these they can also become the basis form of lingua francas.

## IV. Distribution of Lingua Francas

21 The spread of African lingua francas differs considerably according to age, sex and vocation of the speakers and fluctuates from one language to the other. Generally speaking, lingua francas are widespread particularly amongst the population at a vocational age; in comparison, the use amongst the older people and children declines. Some lingua francas are predominantly the languages of the working youth. This, for instance, applies to LINGALA, Town BEMBA and SANGO. These languages are learned mostly by the migrant labourers who have left their rural homes in order to earn money in the towns. When they return to their families later on they frequently give up the use of the lingua franca.

22 Men and women often have a different attitude towards a lingua franca. Amongst the *Dagomba* living in the north of Ghana, the men mostly speak

---

pursuant to A. BURSSENS, and between '*languages principales*' and '*langues véhiculaires*', pursuant to A. JACQUOT (BURSSENS 1954, 27–9; JACQUOT 1960*, 30). Thus JACQUOT remarks: "The first (i.e. *langues véhiculaires,* author's note) are in general extremely simplified in comparison with the languages from which they are derived and their area is rather large; they do not really belong to one certain population. The second are languages which in fact belong to a certain defined ethnic group, but are spoken in a more or less widespread area because of particular economic and social reasons." ("Les premières [i.e. *langues véhiculaires,* author's note] sont généralement très simplifiées par rapport aux langues dont elles dérivent et leur aire est assez étendue; elles n'appartiennent pas en propre à une population déterminée. Les secondes sont des langues appartenant effectivement à des ethnies déterminées, mais employées dans un rayon plus ou moins étendu, en dehors de leur aire normale, en raison de conditions économiques ou sociales particulières" [JACQUOT 1960a, 30].)

7 Eugene A. NIDA notes on the c r e o l i z a t i o n of KITUBA: "In such centres as Leopoldville, Leverville, and Kikwit, there are thousands of people who no longer speak any tribal language ... Kituba is now acquiring vocabulary at an amazing rate and is elaborating its morphological and syntactic structure by the addition of more noun classes and greater complexity in the verb expressions" (NIDA 1955, 156). Otherwise there are few notes on creole languages in Africa. See, however, SAMARIN 1966.

HAUSA as lingua franca, whereas the women — and especially the market women — are making use more of TWI (RAPP 1955, 229). The knowledge of lingua francas is as a rule more widely established amongst the men than the women. This surely applies to the languages LINGALA, Pidgin A 70, FANAGALO and SWAHILI. In the case of Town BEMBA, however, Irvine RICHARDSON ascertained that its use is as widespread amongst men as amongst women (RICHARDSON 1961, 26). Whereas, pursuant to William J. SAMARIN, the knowledge of SANGO is greater amongst the men than in the female population (SAMARIN 1955, 263), André JACQUOT observed amongst the women a superiority in the knowledge of that language (JACQUOT 1960, 174). We unfortunately have no comprehensive statistical data on the African lingua francas, so that these remarks can be taken as possessing only provisional character. Undoubtedly the African men demonstrate on the average a greater mobility in comparison with the women: they travel much, have more inter-ethnic contacts, and accordingly they are supplied with better opportunities to learn a lingua franca. Moreover, the proportion of the male population in school attendance is still essentially larger than that of the female population and the importance of school attendance in the spread of lingua francas cannot be underestimated. On the other hand, the African woman has good opportunities in the market-place of making herself familiar with foreign languages, the market being a meeting-place for people of different origins. A special investigation would be required to ascertain the surpassing importance to be attributed to it in the origin and spread of lingua francas.

23 The spread of a lingua franca in relation to the vocations of the speakers depends on its respective sociolinguistic position. Whereas, in the use of Town BEMBA domestic servants and prostitutes in particular are more evident, in the case of lingua francas, the significance of which rests on its being furthered by the government, administration officials, teachers and clergymen form important groups. The African lingua francas are spoken as a rule mostly by traders. Another important vocational group is formed by the lorry drivers, who fulfil an important function in African inland traffic. That, for example, Pidgin A 70 is often called *bulu bediliva,* i.e. the 'BULU of the lorry drivers', points to the importance of this vocational group in the use of the lingua franca.

## V. Lingua Francas and Diachrony

24 A lingua franca finds its origin under specific historical prerequisites, it develops and can in turn decay as soon as these conditions change. A description of the African lingua francas at the present time for this reason only

represents an infinitesimal portion of their development. Two lingua francas, which synchronically observed hardly differ, can be the result of opposing developments and could also go very different ways in the future. For instance, in the copperbelt of Zambia, more particularly FANAGALO and Town BEMBA have become widespread as African lingua francas. The development of both languages, however, differs considerably. FANAGALO was the predominant lingua franca in the early days of its development history. Later on another lingua franca, Town BEMBA, evolved, and in increasing measure replaced FANAGALO, the functional domain of which became more and more narrowed down, until in the end it still had its use in only one single domain, namely that of work. The knowledge of this process renders prognoses possible in respect of the future development of the sociolinguistic situation in the Zambian copperbelt: it may be presumed that FANAGALO will continue to lose in importance, whereas Town BEMBA has surely not yet reached the zenith of its capacity. Thus Irvine RICHARDSON considers that in twenty years Town BEMBA next to English will have become the most important language in the entire territory of Zambia (RICHARDSON 1962, 196).

Also Eugene A. NIDA pointed out that the development of lingua francas can take very different courses. He traces the history of two African lingua francas and brings to light the factors which have influenced their development. Whereas KITUBA, a lingua franca form of KIKONGO, allows a growing tendency to be recognized, BULU in the southern Cameroons can be cited as an example of the decay of a lingua franca (NIDA 1955).

25  In the following it will be shown by way of example under which conditions lingua francas can originate and how, in turn, they can decay in a changed sociolinguistic situation[1].

In the eastern part of the Niger delta, in the former Rivers province of Nigeria, various small ethnic groups are living, who for linguistic and other reasons to be explained later can be classified into coastal and hinterland inhabitants. The coastal inhabitants are sub-divided into *Kalabari* (in the east) and *Nembe* (in the west). Both are speaking closely-related dialects of IJO (Ijaw), which pursuant to Joseph H. GREENBERG belongs to the *Kwa* branch of the *Niger-Congo* family. The inhabitants of the hinterland are sub-grouped into *Abua, Odual* and *Ogbia*, who speak closely-related languages[2]. The *Abua, Odual* and *Kalabari* are direct neighbours just like the *Ogbia* and *Nembe*.

During the 19th century, the coastal tribes controlled the palm oil trade with European firms. Since no palm oil is procured in the coastal area the population there acquired this product from their neighbours in the hinter-

---

1 The statements rely on investigations made by Hans WOLFF (WOLFF 1967).
2 WOLFF supplies no data on the genetic position of the languages ABUA, ODUAL and OGBIA.

land and delivered it to the Europeans. By this role as middlemen the coastal tribes gained esteem and influence in comparison with the inland inhabitants — presumably this was to a great extent caused by their contact with the Europeans. The inland tribes proceeded to learn the languages of the coastal inhabitants as lingua franca, the men in particular excelling in this connection. Thus a large number of *Abua* and *Odual* people spoke KALABARI, and a still larger number of *Ogbia* mastered NEMBE.

The coastal languages gained such importance that in the interior they were used occasionally even during village gatherings. More particularly, they were promoted by the European missionaries, who as a rule settled at the coast, taught at first the local population, used their language in the churches and ultimately elevated them to written languages. Thus KALABARI and NEMBE became the languages of the mission, and in their roles as clergymen as well as teachers, the members of the coastal tribes contributed still more to the spread of their languages in the interior.

During the last 30 to 40 years the political and economic situation, and with it also the sociolinguistic one, changed in this area. The palm oil trade, the basis of economic relations between coastal and inland tribes, ceased to exist. Simultaneously, in the case of the inland inhabitants, a growing consciousness of ethnic individuality became evident. Vent was given to the opinion that they were exploited and suppressed by the trading states on the coast, and that this situation would have to be changed. Since the independence of Nigeria in 1960, more particularly the inland tribes developed a brisk political activity, the target being recognition as individual ethnic groups, achieving, as a consequence, political self-administration independent from the coastal tribes.

The effects of this change on the sociolinguistic situation can be summarized as follows: KALABARI and NEMBE are hardly learned as lingua francas any longer, their role having been taken over by important languages of the interior, most of all by IBO and English. During village gatherings, in church and during lessons of the lower primary school forms, it is not the coastal language which is being used, but their own mother tongue.

26 In the case of a lingua franca having gained a foothold in the area of spread of another language, different possibilities arise in respect of its further development. It may be possible on the one hand, that the preconditions causing their spread change to such an extent that it loses its function as a lingua franca and becomes a vernacular language again, as seems to be the case with KALABARI and NEMBE. This, for instance, according to the statements made by Nida, applies to BULU. It may, however, not infrequently be observed that the lingua franca to a growing extent adopts the role of the vernacular languages which are spoken in their sphere of influence. Such a process often leads to the dying out of the vernacular languages.

27 In both above-mentioned possibilities the lingua franca as an inter-linguistic means of communication forms a provisional solution, leading to a stage of development in which the lingua franca itself becomes a vernacular language — be it that those who avail themselves of it as second language are not using it any more, or because it is adopted as mother tongue by such people and thereby relinquishes its characteristics as lingua franca. Moreover, there exists a third possibility, according to which the existence of a lingua franca does not indicate a provisional stage, but represents the ultimate conclusion of a development. This development as a rule takes the following course: One language is adopted by the speakers of another language as lingua franca. The range of functions of the two languages acts in a complementary way. In the case of a lingua franca it often comprises such fields as trade, communications, administration, etc. This use becomes more strongly established and there arises a situation of s t a b l e b i l i n g u a l i s m. Joseph H. GREENBERG reports that such a situation existed, for example, in Timbuktu: "The Tuareg and the Arabs have been bilingual for centuries, employing Songhai and their own language without loss of ethnic identity or serious impairment of group membership" (GREEN-BERG 1965, 56).

In respect of not a few African lingua francas such a development can be proved. The number of speakers at first takes a tremendous upsurge, and the knowledge of the language spreads like wildfire. After some time the spread reaches its point of satiation and begins to stagnate. Following onto this a certain equilibrium arises and the further development of the lingua franca takes its course without significant fluctuations. Simultaneously, however, a group of people not infrequently forms, to which the lingua franca becomes a mother tongue. Such groups are found in particular in the urban centres and are predominantly comprised of the descendants of people who have migrated from rural districts, and who had not learnt as their first language the language of their parents, but the lingua franca. This, for instance, seems to apply to the two Congo languages LINGALA and KITUBA (see particularly HULSTAERT 1946, 128/9).

Graphically the development can be shown as follows:

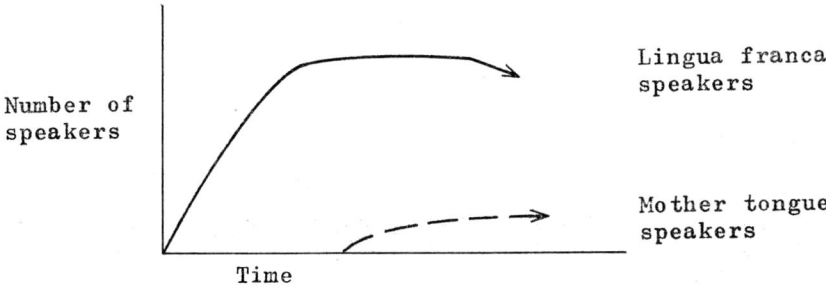

In this connection, a differentiation between two types of lingua francas is of importance. Starting from the difference between *bilinguisme généralisé* and *bilinguisme orienté*, attention to which was drawn by Maurice Houis (Houis 1962, 111/2), Gabriel Manessy differentiated between "assimilating languages" *(langues assimilatrices)* and "trading languages" *(langues de commerce)*. As examples of the first he cited FUL, ZANDE, WOLOF and SANGO, as instances of the latter the languages SWAHILI, HAUSA and MANDINGO. The "assimilating languages" are tending to oust the vernacular languages, but are limited in respect of the possibility of spreading. On the "trading languages", however, Manessy notes:

"These trading languages (the word "trading" implying the widest sense), in contrast to the assimilating languages, are really international, in as far as they are wholly indifferent to ethnics, social structure and mode of life. They are, on the other hand, liable to expand indefinitely, as long as subsist the needs which they can satisfy, and as long as they do not collide with other languages of the same category ... Such a language does not in the least take the place of the mother tongue, since it is only spoken in certain situations, i.e. on the market or in administration offices, in situations in which only people charged with 'exterior relations' of the group in question are employed." ("Ces langues de commerce [en donnant au mot 'commerce' son sens le plus large], contrairement aux langues assimilatrices, sont réellement internationales, en ce qu'elles sont indifférentes aux distinctions d'ethnie, d'organisation sociale et de genre de vie. Elles demeurent, d'autre part, susceptible d'expansion indéfinie tant que subsistent les besoins qu'elles permettent de satisfaire, et tant qu'elles n'entrent pas en concurrence avec une autre langue de même categorie ... Une telle langue ne se substitue aucunement à la langue maternelle, puisqu'elle n'est employée que dans des situations bien déterminées, au marché ou bien dans les bureaux de l'administration, situations où ne sont engagés que les gens chargés des 'relations extérieures' du groupe en question" [Manessy 1964, 78].)

## VI. Spread of Lingua Francas

28  The fact of a language developing into a lingua franca is not infrequently accounted for by its possessing a "simple" structure and being "easy to learn", through these characteristics achieving an advantage over other languages as lingua franca. Maurice Houis, however, notes: "... it does not seem, in a bilingual situation, that the structure of the language intervenes at all with the acceptance of this language." * It is useful in this connection to distinguish between languages, the structure of which can be designated as p i d g i n , and other languages not possessing such a structure. Per definitionem, pidgin languages have a "simple" structure, i.e. in comparison

---

\* "... il ne nous semble pas que, dans une situation bilingue, la structure de la langue intervienne en quoi que ce soit dans l'acception de cette langue" (Houis 1962, 108).

with natural languages they are less differentiated in phonology, morphology, syntax and vocabulary. A language, however, becomes pidginized only by the fact of having served for some time as a lingua franca. The "simple" structure therefore cannot be adduced in this case as an explanation of the development into a lingua franca. Moreover, the question as to whether a language is easy or difficult to learn must remain open when viewed in the light of the present stage of research.

29 More importance is attached to the question whether the spread of a lingua franca is promoted by the fact that it takes place in an area in which languages related to it are spoken. Thus, inter alia, Johannes LUKAS and Emmi KÄHLER-MEYER have asserted, that the spread of SWAHILI was furthered by the coincidence of its predominantly being spoken in the territory of the related *Bantu* languages (see LUKAS 1942, 18; MEYER 1944, 259). Contrariwise, HOUIS offers for consideration that "... one could offer a number of African examples showing that bilingual people adopted as second language languages of quite a different structure in comparison with their first language."\*

A glance at the linguistic map of Africa shows that the spread of lingua francas often occurs in areas in which closely-related languages are spoken. Thus, SWAHILI has spread more particularly in the *Bantu* domain, whereas amongst languages belonging to other families such as MASAI or SOMALI, it could gain but small foothold. It was especially the linguistically homogenous *Bantu* area which proved in particular manner to be fertile soil for the genesis of lingua francas. A further example is represented by SANGO in the Central African Republic, which has preponderantly spread in the area of BANDA–GBAYA–NGBANDI.

The possibility of language relationship being able to influence the development of lingua francas, cannot be excluded. Language relationship, however, is a concept of diachronic linguistics, which may be considered irrelevant with regard to synchronic observation. The spread of FUL in Adamawa took place in an area in which a large number of languages related to it are spoken. This relationship, however, is so distant that it is hardly felt by the speakers, let alone its possible contribution to the spread of FUL. Hitherto, it has not been possible in anyone case to prove a causal connection between language relationship and the spread of an African lingua franca. These facts coincide with the conclusions reached by L. F. BROSNAHAN, pursuant to which "... nothing in the study of language, so far as I am aware, suggests that any internal features of the language concerned, features of phonology or grammar, or of vocabulary, are likely to be very influential in determining the outer history of that language. Important though these features are in

---

\* "... on pourrait avancer de nombreux exemples africains montrant que des bilingues ont adapté comme langue seconde des parlers très differents dans leurs structures de celles de leur langue première" (HOUIS 1962, 108).

some respects, the influence they can exert on the use of a language is certainly negligible in comparison with that exerted by the interplay of social, political and military forces" (BROSNAHAN 1963, 15).

Tribes speaking closely-related languages frequently also show affinities in extra-linguistic fields of culture[1]. The influence attributed to the language relationship in the spread of lingua francas is presumably not infrequently a result of such extra-linguistic affinities. Thus it is possible that the spread of SWAHILI in the *Bantu* areas rests on fewer linguistic bases but much rather is the result of extra-linguistic features between the *Bantu* tribes, which culturally distinguish themselves not inconsiderably from the *Masai* or *Somali*.

30 Another problem presenting itself during the sociolinguistic study of the African lingua francas is the question as to how and to what extent Islam has influenced the spread of these languages. In a comparison, for example, of the area of spread of the important lingua francas ARABIC, SWAHILI, HAUSA or MANDINGO with that of the Islamic religion, important agreement emerges which can hardly be the result of chance. It is indeed shown that the spread of these and other lingua francas, such as Adamawa-FUL or KANURI, was accompanied by the spread of Islam.

The face of Africa was considerably altered through the appearance of Islam. One of its effects caused the reduction of ethnic frictions and their replacement by other antagonisms, such as, for instance, the oppositions between Mohammedans and non-Mohammedans, or between Mohammedans and Christians. Moreover, trade and communications obtained fresh stimuli. These factors have undoubtedly supplied propitious preconditions for the development of lingua francas. Diedrich WESTERMANN observes: "Suaheli, Hausa and Mandingo owe their early spread in part to Islam, which as a world religion dissolved the narrowness of tribe and clan, broadened their vision and prepared paths for innate entrepreneurial spirits." * The question as to how this process has taken its course in the individual case still remains unexplained and is in need of detailed investigation.

---

1 It must, however, be emphasized that there are sufficient examples, pursuant to which ethnic groups with closely-related or even identical languages can have very different cultures.

* "Suaheli, Hausa und Mandingo verdanken ihre frühe Ausbreitung zum Teil dem Islam, der als Weltreligion die Stammes- und Sippenenge sprengte, den Blick weitete und angeborener Unternehmungslust die Wege ebnete" (WESTERMANN 1940, 404).

## VII. Borders of Spread

31  Beside the factors which can be favourable to the spread of a lingua franca there are others which, in turn, offer resistance to its spread.
One of these factors is the rivalry between lingua francas. Joseph H. GREENBERG remarks in this connection: "The only thing that is likely to arrest its spread is a rival lingua franca" (GREENBERG 1965, 52). If a lingua franca intrudes into the sphere of a neighbouring lingua franca it cannot infrequently be observed that its expansion begins to stagnate. As a result a tendency can be found towards formation of a border zone between the area of spread of the two lingua francas. This border zone is characterized by the fact that the population living within it is to a particularly large degree trilingual, i.e. that this population apart from its own mother tongue understands and speaks both lingua francas.

32  Various examples indicate, however, that the spread of a lingua franca is not in every case kept at bay by the existence of a rival lingua franca. It is possible that one of the two languages can prove itself dominant and advance to the same extent as the other loses ground. An example for this is the sociolinguistic situation on the coast of the Cameroons towards the end of the 19th century. Coinciding with the decay of the *Duala* trade, pidgin English, which at that time could look back upon a tradition of more than a hundred years, intruded into the sphere of influence of another lingua franca, that of DUALA, the area of spread of which gradually shrank.

33  On the other hand, the African linguistic map is not poor in areas where more than one lingua franca is being spoken, i.e. areas in which the borders of spread of lingua francas overlap. In some cases it becomes evident that these languages are not used within the same environments but possess complementary functional domains. Depending on ethnic origin, social position or sex of the speakers, these functional domains can be different. In southern Ghana, for instance, HAUSA is the lingua franca of the immigrants from the north (ROUCH 1956, 162), whereas with regard to the rest of the population TWI represents the predominant lingua franca. A complementary use of lingua francas conforming to the social positions of their speakers can be observed in various parts of Africa. Thus the elite of a country makes use of a lingua franca introduced by the former colonial power (in most cases English or French), whereas the lower strata use an African lingua franca. As an example of this may serve the remarks by W. J. SAMARIN on the situation in the Central African Republic. SANGO is the lingua franca of a predominant part of its population, but not the language of the *évolués,* so called:

"These are those Africans who have had sufficient education in French to be fluent in it. This fluency has made it possible for them to acquire positions that, because of superior remuneration, set them apart from the others. Among themselves the *évolués* use French, but its use seems to vary in proportion to the degree of social evolution" (SAMARIN 1955, 265).

A situation of a complementary use of lingua francas on a vocational basis seems to be present in the copperbelt of Zambia. Whereas FANAGALO fulfils the function of a working language, NYANJA more particularly is the language of the police and the army. Town BEMBA, finally, disposes of the largest functional domain and has become the language of modern life in town (RICHARDSON 1961).

34 As already mentioned repeatedly, the spread of lingua francas can further be impaired as soon as it reaches the territory of ethnic groups strong in numbers. To SWAHILI, thus, a resistance has chiefly been put up by the large East African tribes such as *Ganda, Kikuyu, Luo*, etc.; LINGALA could establish itself only slowly amongst the large group of *Bakongo* in Kinshasa, and HAUSA up to now was hardly able to gain a foothold in the territory of the *Yoruba, Ibo* or *Kanuri*. It is characteristic in respect of some of these tribes that although resisting the use of the African lingua francas, they adopted all the more readily the language — generally English or French — of the former colonial power. This applies, for instance, to the *Ganda* with regard to SWAHILI or to the *Yoruba* and *Ibo* in respect of HAUSA.

On the basis of their numerical strength as well as their political importance, large tribes not infrequently develop a marked ethnic consciousness which may go hand in hand with a depreciation of everything foreign. This characteristic has its effect also in the attitude towards the lingua franca by deprecating it as *"nobody's language"*[1] (SUTHERLIN 1962, 75). It must be added that on account of its characteristic as inter-ethnic means of communication the lingua franca is occasionally even looked upon as a danger for the unity and autonomy of the group. This, inter alia, can be demonstrated by the example of the Kingdom of Buganda. Since approximately 1920 the British administration in Uganda showed tendencies to elevate SWAHILI to one of the official languages of that country. This plan met with strong resistance amongst the population of the Kingdom of Buganda which found a passionate expression in 1929 in a declaration by the then *Kabaka* Daudi Chwa.

The fact that a large ethnic group can consider itself threatened in its existence and its position by the inroads of a lingua franca is also demonstrated by the sociolinguistic situation in Kinshasa, the former Leopoldville, at the beginning of the nineteen fifties. Amongst the numerous tribes represented in this town the *Bakongo*, making up three-quarters of the population, constituted by far the strongest group. Its language, however, KIKONGO, carried only very limited importance, all the more so as it

---

[1] i.e. a language which as a rule is not spoken as mother tongue but as second language.

was split up into various dialects. Contrariwise, LINGALA as a lingua franca had achieved such spread that L. B. DE BOECK, one of the foremost experts on this language, designated the then town of Leopoldville as "LINGALA town". It happened not infrequently that the *Bakongo* amongst themselves conversed not in their joint mother tongue, but in LINGALA (BOECK 1953). Under such circumstances passionate resistance developed amongst the *Bakongo* against LINGALA. An association of *Bakongo* was founded, with the object of promoting the importance of KIKONGO, of adapting the language to modern requirements and of strengthening the unity of the *Bakongo* population. In an manifesto published by this association it says, inter alia (see WING 1953):

"Our numerous children who go to the town schools are instructed in an heteroclite African language (i.e. LINGALA; author's note) and ignore the beauties and infinite riches of their own literature. Some of them, after a few years of school studies, are even ashamed to express themselves in Kikongo... The experience shows the observers that our children who are thus shaped in this heteroclite African language are losing more and more the delicacy, the prudence and the gentleness which is characteristic for the Mukongo population." *

35 But there seems to be another reason responsible for the fact that the spread of lingua francas often stagnates as soon as it intrudes into the territory of large tribes. In the case of a tribe distributed over a small area and with a small population the acquisition of an inter-ethnic means of communication in many cases is a scarcely avoidable necessity. Communication in the tribe's own language is possible only with relatives or with immediate neighbours; the nearest major market place is situated perhaps already in the territory of another tribe speaking another language. Contrariwise, communication in widely-distributed tribes is restricted to a larger extent to their own tribesmen. The necessity of having to use another means of communication apart from their own language is therefore small by comparison, and thus the knowledge of foreign languages is more particularly to be found among members of those groups of population who by reason of their vocation are forced to entertain inter-ethnic contacts, such as, for instance, traders[2].

---

\* "Nos nombreux enfants fréquentant les écoles de la ville sont instruits en une langue africaine hétéroclite (i.e. LINGALA, author's note) et ignorent la beauté et les richesses infinies de leur propre littérature. Certains d'entr'eux, après quelques années d'écolage éprouvent une certaine honte à s'exprimer en Kikongo... L'expérience montre aux observateurs que nos enfants ainsi formés en cette langue hétéroclite, perdant de plus en plus la délicatesse, la pudeur et la douceur caractéristique de peuple Mukongo" (see WING 1953).

2 Examples of languages with a smaller number of speakers, however, can also be given, who have assiduously resisted the adoption of lingua francas. Thus Emmi KÄHLER-MEYER reports of the *Vute* (Wute), who live in the Cameroons south of Tibati, having offered successful resistance against the intrusion of Adamawa-FUL (MEYER 1944, 268).

36  Cultural factors, finally, can also influence the spread of lingua francas disadvantageously. In the case of a lingua franca being carried into an area with an economic system, social structure, religion, etc. strongly deviating from the one of its carriers, its spread may meet with resistance there — possibly on account of its being regarded as "embodiment of a foreign culture". It must also be added that frequently a close relation can be observed to exist between the degree of cultural difference and the density of communication; that is to say that the more the ways of life of two groups differ the smaller become the contacts between them, or vice versa. The smaller now the intensity of such contact, the less importance can be attributed to the lingua franca. The *Masai*, for example, in East Africa, distinctly differ in their culture from most of the so-called *Bantu* tribes, up to most recent times they pursued relatively little contact with the outside world and the SWAHILI lingua franca could gain but a small foothold in the area they inhabit. In a similar manner, the cultural differences between the peoples of the inner Sudan and the coastal tribes living further to the south explains in part the fact that the important lingua francas HAUSA, SONG'AI and MANDINGO could not establish themselves in the areas near the coast of West Africa.

The number of factors is not yet exhausted by far; tribal rivalries, determined by their historical background, can thus render difficult the spread of a lingua franca — as Joseph H. GREENBERG has demonstrated by the example of HAUSA in the *Kanuri* territory [3] — just as much as a language policy carried on by government administrations and missions.

## VIII. National State, European Languages and African Lingua Francas

37  In order to be able to better appraise the spread of a lingua franca an exact knowledge of the sociolinguistic situation in which it is found is required. Since the national states today preferably constitute the set-up for the development of lingua francas, an important task arises in the investigation of the sociolinguistic situation in the various states. Approaches to a typology of the language situation in African states can be found in the paper *Problèmes linguistiques des Etats négro-africains à l'heure de l'In-*

---

3 "Hausa was the language of the Fulani-dominated Muslim empire of Sokoto, which fought for supremacy with the Kanuri empire of Bornu in the pre-European period. This traditional attitude of hostility still finds expression in an unwillingness to recognize the dominant position of Hausa and to accommodate to it" (GREENBERG 1965, 53).

*dépendence* by Pierre ALEXANDRE, in which he differentiates between three groups:

1. States relatively homogeneous in respect of language. The majority of the population in these states converse in mutually intelligible languages. Ruanda, Burundi and the (present) Somali Republic are examples of this group.

2. States linguistically heterogeneous, but speaking one or more predominant languages; thus for instance, Nigeria with HAUSA, YORUBA and IBO, Uganda with GANDA, Kenya, Tanzania and the Comores Islands with SWAHILI, the Sudan with ARABIC, Zambia with BEMBA, Rhodesia [Zimbabwe] with SHONA or Malawi with NYANJA.

ALEXANDRE furthermore counts among this group the Senegal with WOLOF and SERER, (the present state of) Upper Volta with MOSI, (the present state of) Mali with MALINKE-BAMBARA, as well as Gabon with FANG. The last named languages — contrary to the first-mentioned languages of this group — are not made use of in government administration and education.

3. States linguistically heterogeneous. In this case again a differentiation must be made between such states making use of African languages in government administration and education — such as Ghana, Sierra Leone and Congo-Kinshasa — and other states in which this is not the case, such as Congo-Brazzaville, Central African Republic, Chad, Togoland, Dahomey, the Cameroons, Niger, the Ivory Coast and Guinea (ALEXANDRE 1961, 184/5).

38 This classification surely has little practical value. The attribution to the groups (2) and (3) seems to be arbitrary in some cases and hardly measures up to reality. Nevertheless it contains some leads which may be of importance to future investigations. Undoubtedly, a three-type scheme will hardly suffice satisfactorily to group the multiplicity of language situations in Africa. It will therefore depend on adducing further classification criteria, such as has been attempted by Charles A. FERGUSON (FERGUSON 1962). He proposes the following parameters:

a) The use of a language as written language;
b) The degree of standardization of a language;
c) The number of *major languages* of a nation, this meaning languages understood by at least ten million people or spoken by one tenth of the total population of a nation;
d) The type of "dominance" of a language;
e) The use of *"languages of wider communication"* within a nation (loc. cit. 12).

39 Of an importance not to be underestimated is, for example, the last-mentioned parameter, which inquires into the use of the world languages, so called — in Africa more particularly French and English. These languages,

41

introduced by the former colonial powers and adopted by the independant African governments as languages of state, frequently determine the functional domain of the African lingua francas. It would be vain to deliberate on the importance of SWAHILI without the presence of English in Uganda today, or on the importance of other African lingua francas in territories formally administered by France without the presence of French. It is, however, certain that there existed serious competition between the European languages and some African lingua francas, which occasionally found expression in passionate press campaigns. Not infrequently this competitive struggle was decided in favour of the European languages. The question, however, which language is more deserving of promotion, belongs still to the important subjects of language policy in some African states. An exact knowledge of the field of application of the European languages is an indispensable prerequisite with regard to the understanding of the African lingua francas. Attempts such as, for instance, undertaken by E. G. Lewis prove useful here. He classifies some African countries pursuant to their use of English as official language as follows:

i) English constitutes the only official language (Ghana, Gambia, Sierra Leone, Kenya, Uganda);

ii) English is the official language, in conjunction with an African language (Tanzania, Botswana, Swaziland, Lesotho formerly Basutoland);

iii) English, together with several African languages, is the official language (Rhodesia, Malawi, Zambia);

iv) English and French are the only official languages (Mauritius).

These classifications are further sub-divided, in connection wherewith the criterion such as, inter alia, the manner of use of the official language in school education (for example as school language or as school subject) is being adduced (Lewis 1962, 86/7).

40 The question is of interest in this connection as to what influence the Europeans and their languages had on the linguistic form of the African lingua francas. It must primarily be pointed out that it is those languages in particular which have adopted loan-words from European languages, and it cannot infrequently be observed that the European loan-words to be met with in vernacular languages have found their way there not directly but via the medium of an African lingua franca. Thus, for instance, the Togo Remnants languages spoken in the Volta region of Ghana have received the loan-words of European origin via the lingua francas EWE and TWI. Similar observations were also made in other parts of Africa (cf. East 1937).

41 The European missionaries and administration officials often went to great lengths to standardize the use of African lingua francas, which as a rule were not uniform. An important means in the achievement of this was writing. Orthographies based on the Latin alphabet, were created, periodicals and

books were published, and the lingua francas were employed in school instruction as well as in government administration. This development did not remain without influence on their linguistic structure. The origin of the s c h o o l languages, so called, represents one of the results of this process.

42 If, on the one hand, the tendency towards p i d g i n i z a t i o n prevalent in the lingua franca was not infrequently counter-acted by these efforts on the part of the Europeans, it became evident, on the other hand, that the very contact situation between Europeans and Africans often led to the creation of pidgin forms. *Ki-SETLA* ('settler's language'), one of the pidgin forms of SWAHILI, derives its origin from the contact between white people and the Africans just like TSHITUBA (not to be confused with KITUBA), a pidgin dialect of TSHILUBA, as well as BANGALA, a dialect of LINGALA. Also in the formation of FANAGALO, a pidgin form derived from the *Nguni* languages, the Europeans seem to have taken a considerable part.

43 The influence exerted by the national state borders in Africa upon the development of lingua francas, had its advantages as well as disadvantages. SANGO, for example, is the predominant language of the Central African Republic. The borders of its area of spread more or less tally with the frontiers of this state, and SANGO has become a symbol of unity in respect of this young republic with its linguistically and ethnically heterogeneous population. In 1965, it was declared the national language of the Central African Republic (ALEXANDRE 1967, 22). Although this development aided the spread of SANGO within the country's borders, it hindered its spread outside of this republic. In neighbouring countries, SANGO is considered the language of a foreign state and presumably for this reason it is rejected as lingua franca there. Instead of this, the lingua franca of one's own country is employed, such as for example, LINGALA in Congo-Kinshasa.

44 Those lingua francas which have already spread beyond the borders of a state are also influenced in their development. The language policy pursued in the individual countries shows important differences — particularly with regard to the lingua francas. Whereas, for example, SWAHILI in Tanzania receives considerable support from the government, it is hardly taken into consideration in the language policy of Uganda, where, however, the sociolinguistic prerequisites are of a different nature (see WHITELEY 1962). The role of the lingua franca occupied by SWAHILI in Tanzania, was in Uganda transferred in part to English.

45 Still in another sense the national state borders prove themselves to be of importance. The orthographies used in writing African languages are as a rule very different depending on the nationality of the former colonial power. The languages HAUSA and YORUBA, the main area of spread of which lies in Nigeria, are furthermore spoken in the neighbouring territories

formerly under French administration. The publications appearing in these languages in Nigeria are, however, hardly read by the *Hausa* and *Yoruba* in the francophone areas, since the orthographies employed in Nigeria are unfamiliar there (ALEXANDRE 1962, 184).

46 Orthographies have influenced the sociolinguistic position of lingua francas in varying degrees of importance. They may contribute towards the fact that a unified, highly-esteemed written language evolves from a language dialectically split up and of low prestige.

How much, on the other hand, the absence of a uniform orthography can affect the position of a language, has been demonstrated by B. W. ANDRZEJEWSKI by the example of the SOMALI language. In comparison with other African states the Somali Republic finds itself in an enviable position in that almost the entire population of the country speaks SOMALI as their first language, and this republic counts amongst the linguistically most homogeneous states of the continent. Nevertheless, the sociolinguistic situation of Somalia is hardly less problematic than that of other African states. The reason for this is the non-existence of an officially sanctioned SOMALI orthography, although, thereby, no obstacles are put in the way of SOMALI being understood as vernacular language in all parts of the country. This is all the more so as there exists a kind of "Common SOMALI", i.e. a dialect performing the function of a lingua franca amongst the SOMALI dialects, which in part differ very much from one another. SOMALI, however, is not used in written form. ARABIC, Italian and English serve this purpose. The merchant conversing with his customer in SOMALI makes out his bills in one of these three languages, and also the policeman who interrogates the witnesses to a traffic accident in SOMALI, will not make his report in this language. Although the parliamentary debates are carried on in SOMALI, the parliamentary reports are written down in Italian, ARABIC and English. The situation is aggravated by the fact that each of these three languages is mastered only by part of the population. In the southern part of the country English is hardly spoken, whereas in the northern part this is the case with Italian. Although ARABIC is used in all parts of the country, the number of people able to use it is limited. Because of the disunity within the population of Somalia, there is little hope of a uniform SOMALI orthography establishing itself in the near future (ANDRZEJEWSKI 1962).

Rival orthographies can disadvantageously influence the use of a lingua franca. Thanks primarily to the language policy of the missionaries of the 19th century, TWI is sub-divided today into two groups of dialects with rivalling orthographies. The Europeans, who first settled on the coast, elevated the FANTE dialect of TWI to the position of a written language. Later on they recognized the importance of the inland dialects and created a further orthography on the basis of the AKUAPEM dialect. Attempts undertaken in more recent times to create a regularized written form in respect of all dialects, failed on account of the resistance of the population to whom the various orthographies had become a symbol of linguistic and sociological individuality.

47 The use of African lingua francas as written languages shows considerable differences. Charles A. FERGUSON has classified the languages of the world into the following three types [1]:

I. Languages not used in normal written communication;

II. Languages used in normal written communication. "Normal written communication" is in this connection to be understood as a) communication by letter, b) the publication of newspapers and periodicals, and c) books not translated from other languages;

III. Languages regularly used for the publication of results *"of original research in physical sciences"* (FERGUSON 1962).

All African lingua francas can be classified under one of the two types I or II, whereas III is not represented. Languages of the type I are, for example, FANAGALO, Town BEMBA and Pidgin A 70, amongst many others. To these belong almost all African lingua francas spoken in the territories formerly under French administration. The languages of the type II however, are less numerous. To it, more particularly, can be counted SWAHILI and HAUSA. On the other hand, this typology requires further differentiations in order to do justice to the great variety of African lingua francas.

## IX. Lingua Franca and Dialect Continuum

48 A lingua franca is not only a means of communication used between speakers of different languages. It can also fulfil an important function within a group of dialects, i.e. in a d i a l e c t   c o n t i n u u m. The more pronounced the linguistic and sociolinguistic differences between the individual dialects, the larger is the likelihood of a linguistic form emerging from them, having the function of a lingua franca. This form has been designated K o i n e [1] by Trevor HILL, who defines this concept in a very general way, i.e. as "... any tongue distinct from his own vernacular, that a person shares with the speakers of some other vernaculars" (HILL 1958, 443/4). It therefore tallies to a large extent with the terminus "lingua franca" applied here.

49 Frequently it is one of the dialects of the dialect continuum which takes on the role of a K o i n e, in which connection the selection of such a dialect

---

[1] A fourth type is also mentioned, which, however, can remain out of consideration at this point (FERGUSON 1962, 9 below).

[1] Cf. the use of the concept K o i n e by Charles A. FERGUSON (FERGUSON 1959, 616/7).

can rely on different bases. In one case it may depend on the numerical superiority of the speakers of a dialect, in another on the political preeminence of its speakers or on their vocational activity (for example, as traders). Important, inter alia, is also the influence of the Christian missionaries in Africa, who were able to create propitious conditions for the genesis of a K o i n e by elevating a certain dialect to a written language and introducing it within school instruction. The example of EWE in Togoland shows, however, that the last-mentioned factor need not be decisive. In contrast to eastern Ghana where the written language used is based on the ANG'LO dialect, in Togoland the MINA dialect promoted comparatively little by the mission finds itself on the way to becoming the K o i n e of the EWE dialects.

Examples of such "lingua francas on a dialect basis" can be found in all parts of Africa. B. W. ANDRZEJEWSKI reports, for instance, on the situation in Somalia:

"With the exception of the Rahanwiin dialect... all Somali dialects are mutually intelligible. Even among the speakers of the Rahanwiin dialect, many people are bidialectal and speak also a generally acceptable type of dialect which I would like to call *Common Somali*, unterstood in all Somali-speaking territories, from Jibouti to Isiolo and from the heart of the Ogaden to the coast of the Indian Ocean" (ANDRZEJEWSKI 1962, 177).

Also Yoruba in south-western Nigeria possesses a K o i n e , which is often called "Standard Yoruba" and which is based on the OYO dialect but is not identical with it. "Standard Yoruba" is employed in school instruction, in literature and in communication between people speaking different YORUBA dialects (BAMGBOSE 1966, 2).

# C. AFRICAN LINGUA FRANCAS: A SURVEY

## I. Southern Africa

### a) FANAGALO

50  FANAGALO is known under a number of different names, as follows: *Isikula,* a designation originating in ZULU and meaning 'coolie language' (COLE 1953, 2; DUNCAN 1954, 45) or 'Indian language' (TRAPP 1908, 508);

Map 1. *Southern Africa*

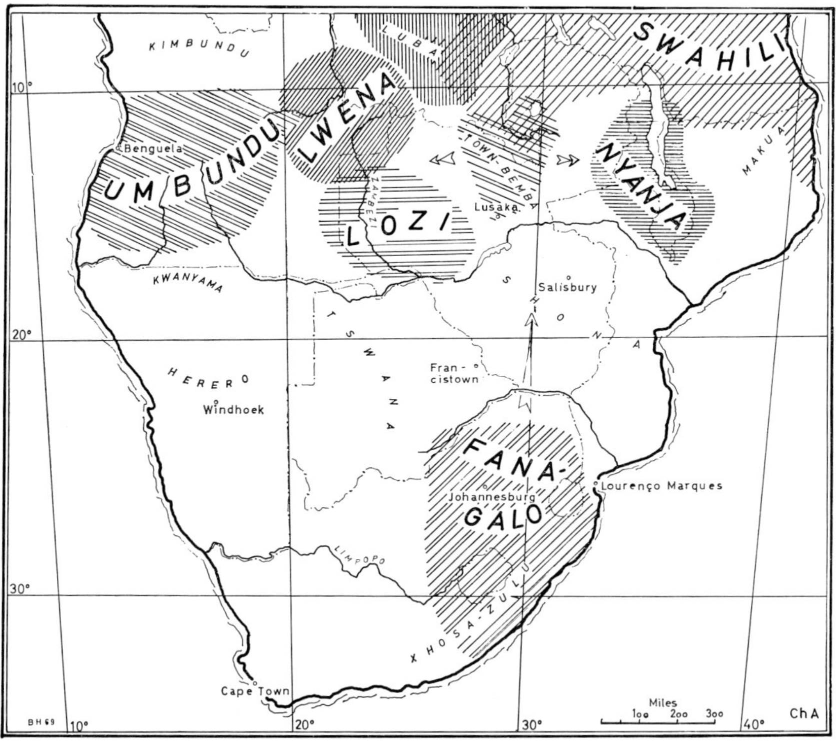

*Note:* The hatchings indicate the distribution of the different lingua francas.
*Source:* Author.

*Kitchen-Kafir,* presumably so called because the language has been used much in the kitchen between the white women and their African "boy" and still is used;

*Mine-Kafir,* so called on account of its importance in the South African mines;

*Silunguboi,* which is composed both of the ZULU *isilungu* 'European language' as well as *boy* and means 'the language used by Europeans in conversation with their servants';

*Isilololo, Cilololo* or the *lo-lo* language on account of the repeated occurrence of the particle *lo*, which i.a. has the function of the demonstrative pronoun and of the definite article;

*Cilapalapa* or the *lapa* language, so called on account of the frequent usage of the locative formative *lapa* in this language;

*Isipiki;*

*Cikabanga;*

*Pidgin Bantu;*

*Basic Bantu;*

*Basic Nguni* or *Basic Modified Nguni;*

*Basic Zulu;*

*Conversational Zulu* (see BOLD 1951, 6/7; COLE 1953; EPSTEIN 1959; BRYAN 1959, 154; RICHARDSON 1961).

It can be assumed that the list of names in respect of this language is not yet exhausted. The name FANAGALO *(Fanakalo, Fanekalo),* predominantly used in scientific literature, means: 'in this manner, thus' and is derived from the words *fana* 'to be similar', *ga* 'like, as', *lo* 'this' (COLE 1953, 6) occurring in that language. In their contact with Africans, one of the sentences most used by the Europeans ran like this: *enza fanagalo!* 'do it like this!'. The abbreviated form *fanagalo!* soon imprinted itself to such an extent on the people's mind that it became the name of the language.

51 Little agreement prevails on the linguistic status of FANAGALO. Pursuant to D. T. COLE, the vocabulary of the language derives 70% from the *Nguni* group belonging to the *Bantu* — and in particular from the ZULU language which is to be counted as part of this group, 24% from English and 6% from Afrikaans (COLE 1953, 1). Similarly, in the phonological, morphological, syntactical and semantic fields borrowings can be found. Although COLE ascertained that FANAGALO is not spontaneously understood by the *Bantu* population in South Africa but must be learnt in the same manner as by the white people, and although he called it a hybrid language, an examination of the basic vocabulary hardly admits of a doubt that in spite of its deviating structure it is a *Bantu* language, i.e. that next to the ZULU, XHOSA and other languages, it belongs to the *Nguni* group [1].

---

1 In this connection, compare Otto TRAPP's note on FANAGALO: "Zulu, simplified to the utmost, provides the basic construction; the words necessary in

*The development into a lingua franca*

52 The origin of FANAGALO can presumably be traced back to the middle of the 19th Century. We attribute the first knowledge of this language to Canon CALLAWAY, who in 1866 spoke of "miserable gibberish, composed of anglicised Kaffir, and kaffirised English and Dutch words, thrown together without any rule but the caprice and ignorance of the speaker" (DUNCAN 1954, 45). In 1908, Otto O. TRAPP remarked that the Indians who had immigrated into South Africa had participated in the formation of this language (TRAPP 1908, 508), and also COLE tends towards this view, all the more so as the designation *Isikula* (see par. 50) suggests such an interpretation (COLE 1953, 2/3). This, however, is doubted by Patrick DUNCAN, who points out that the Indians arrived in Natal only in 1860, i.e. at a time when FANAGALO presumably already existed (DUNCAN 1954, 45). Additionally, it must be observed that the language hardly exhibits any traces of a notable influence of Indian languages (COLE 1953, 3). On the other hand, it is a fact that the Indians took an important part in the dispersion of FANAGALO.

53 It can be assumed that Natal on the east coast of South Africa is the area of origin. During the period after the Chaka wars, a zone of contact established itself there between the Europeans and the *Bantu* population — in particular between the English-speaking settlers and the *Zulu*. The attempt of these two groups to make themselves understood most likely led to the birth of a new language, i.e. FANAGALO (COLE 1953, 2).

54 In subsequent times FANAGALO spread beyond the borders of Natal. The Europeans played a considerable part in its being brought to the South African gold and diamond mines, where a fresh nucleus leading to its spreading was built up. FANAGALO became the language of the mines (cf. *Mine-Kafir*, par. 50), more particularly so of the Witwatersrand mines, where among the multilingual population from various parts of South Africa, Angola, Rhodesia, Zambia, Malawi and Tanzania it became an indispensable medium of communication.

But not only within the *Bantu* population but also in the communication between white employer and African employee the language attained large importance. Many mining companies look upon the command of the lingua franca as a necessary prerequisite to the work underground and have introduced courses in FANAGALO for newly-employed labourers (COLE 1953, 3).

> modern culture are borrowed from English." ("Ein bis auf das äußerste vereinfachtes Zulu gibt die Grundkonstruktion, aus dem Englischen werden die in moderner Kultur nötigen Worte entlehnt" [TRAPP 1908, 508].) Carl Meinhof also entertained no doubts that FANAGALO is a *Bantu* language (MEINHOF 1939, 312).

55 FANAGALO spread beyond the frontier of South Africa into Rhodesia, where several dialects grew out of it. Mention should be made of the fact that it was introduced there by the "pioneers" of Cecil RHODES, who advanced northwards in 1890 and still in the same year laid the foundation stone for the later capital of Salisbury. As a rule they had a good command of FANAGALO and used that language as communication medium with the Africans in Rhodesia (HOPKIN-JENKINS 1947, Introduction). It furthermore spread into the industrial districts of Zambia and Katanga (COLE 1953, 3; EPSTEIN 1959, 236), where further centres of an ethnic and linguistic medley grew up.

56 Up to World War II, FANAGALO was the lingua franca recognized by everybody in the copperbelt of Zambia, the former Northern Rhodesia. After the war, however, its importance waned very fast. It became the w o r k i n g  l a n g u a g e, i.e. it was only used during working hours, and then only as a means of communication between Whites and Africans (RICHARDSON 1961, 28).

There were two reasons for the sudden decrease of influence of this lingua franca in the copperbelt. Firstly, this process took place during a period of growing self-assertion amongst the African population. FANAGALO was looked upon as a language created by the little-loved colonial masters. In this connection Irvine RICHARDSON remarks:

"The 'blacks' have to learn it from the 'whites' or from their servants – often a somewhat painful process. It is not surprising, therefore, that amongst Africans it is now regarded as a slave-driving jargon, while to many Europeans it is a means of 'keeping the Kafir in his place'. It denies Africans their tribal status while refusing to admit that they are fit to speak English or Afrikaans" (loc. cit. 29).

The second reason was that another inter-ethnic medium of communication offered itself, i.e. the "Town BEMBA", a younger lingua franca gaining popularity, which benefited from the resentments against FANAGALO and — supported by a large BEMBA-speaking body of workmen — developed itself into the predominant language in the copperbelt.

*Present spreading and status*

57 Thereby, the present area of spreading of the FANAGALO language has been sketched, on which, otherwise, few data are available. The lingua franca is spoken chiefly in the north and east of the Republic of South Africa, between Witwatersrand, Durban and East London, and furthermore in Rhodesia, in the copperbelt of Zambia and possibly also in Katanga. Outside of South Africa FANAGALO is, however, of no noteworthy importance — not in the least because in those areas in which it spread, either other lingua francas were already spoken or developed themselves later, thus, for instance, the "Town BEMBA" in the copperbelt, SWAHILI-NGWANA

in the south eastern Congo. Pursuant to M. A. BRYAN, FANAGALO is widespread among the men (BRYAN 1959, 154). Amongst the female population, however, it seems to be less known.

58 Contrary to other African lingua francas, which as a rule hold a certain prestige in comparison with the vernacular languages, FANAGALO is of low repute. It must be said, though, that it has found a large number of devotees, who have great expectations for the language. Characteristic of this is the opinion represented by Otto TRAPP in 1908:

"Isikula will grow, will become the family language of the lower working population, and for a long time will not be considered worthy of being written, but will refine itself during this period of repression, gain in richness of vocabulary, become strong and powerful and one day lead and reign supreme in our country (i.e. South Africa, author's note)." *

59 During the sixty years which have passed since then this prophesy has not come true. After World War II — particularly since 1947 — an extensive literature on the lingua franca in the form of grammar books and dictionaries, has come into existence. The comments of some of the supporters of the language which have been compiled and discussed by COLE show, however, that these supporters did not assess the importance of the language realistically. Mention is made of it as the "lingua franca of southern Africa", which "is being used daily by millions", and which "is spoken everywhere between the Cape and the Great Lakes, wherever Black meets White". It is said that Pygmies in the heart of the Congo answered in FANAGALO after all attempts to communicate with them in English, French, Afrikaans or in one of the *Bantu* languages had failed (COLE 1953, 2).

60 In comparison with the devotees, however, the opponents of FANAGALO are by far in the majority. CALLAWAY had already called the language a "miserable gibberish" (DUNCAN 1954, 45), and TRAPP remarked that FANAGALO was "rejected by everyone with disdain". Although COLE admits that the language fulfils an important function in the industrial areas of South Africa, he nevertheless passionately advocates that "in the interest of improved relations between the races" the use of this "bastard" language should be restricted (COLE 1953, 1/9).

61 Not only amongst the white but also amongst the black population of South Africa, FANAGALO does not seem to be appraised very highly. Although no detailed statements are available, the situation in South Africa should not essentially differ from the one in Zambia, where FANAGALO is almost exclusively used in the communication between Whites and Africans. From

---

\* "Isikula wird wachsen, wird Familiensprache der unteren Arbeiterbevölkerung werden, wird lange nicht des Schreibens würdig erachtet werden, wird sich aber in diesem Zurückgestoßensein feiner ausbilden, an Wortreichtum gewinnen, wird stark und kräftig werden und eines Tages die führende alleinherrschende Sprache in unserem Lande (d. i. Südafrika, Anm. Verf.) sein" (TRAPP 1908, 511).

there A. L. EPSTEIN reports that FANAGALO "... remains essentially the language of command and direction, and by more educated Africans at least is invariably associated with European racialist attitudes, and the denial of African claims to full equality on the human plane" (EPSTEIN 1959, 237; cf. par. 56).

Hence, the language is not looked upon as serving the purpose of overcoming racial barriers, but rather that of strengthening them. Whereas English is the language of the upper stratum of society, FANAGALO is deemed to be the l a n g u a g e  o f  t h e  l o w e r  c a s t e, namely that of the Africans. Thus, a European expects an African to address him in FANAGALO, and he would look upon it as impudent if this man used the English language [2].

## b) TSWANA

62  Next to English, TSWANA, a *Bantu* language, is the official tongue of the South African State of Botswana. There it also occupies a function — though restricted — as lingua franca. Data on the importance of this language in Ngamiland, the north western province of Botswana, have been compiled by E. O. J. WESTPHAL. Six *Bantu* languages and two *Khoisan* languages are spoken in this province. Measured by the number of people using it, YEI spoken by 23,000 people is the most important language. Of greatest importance, however, is TAWANA, the local dialect form of TSWANA, which is only spoken by 3,000 people as their mother tongue. By the British policy of *indirect rule*, the authority of the TSWANA-speaking population was strengthened in the then Protectorate of Bechuanaland, and the dominating position in Ngamiland was vested in the *Tawanians*.

TAWANA was declared the official language of Ngamiland. It is the only African language employed there in the administration as well as in the schools. Thereby, it gained a certain prestige. It is being learned by the members of the other tribes in Ngamiland and is used as second language. If only to represent their affairs appropriately before the State authorities, they require a knowledge of TAWANA — quite apart from the fact that *Tawanians* only rarely learn any other language which is spoken in Ngamiland (WESTPHAL 1962).

## c) LOZI

63  LOZI, which has become known also under other names, such as *Rozi, Rotse, Kololo, Sikololo* i.a., belongs to the group of *Bantu* languages. The question

---

[2] It may be presumed that this situation has changed after the independence of Zambia, but the attitude of the African population towards FANAGALO has hardly altered.

as to the position occupied by LOZI in this group has, however, not yet finally been settled (see below).

64 In 1823, approximately 30,000 Sotho people assembled round Sebitwane, who was but 20 years of age, and, being pressed by the *Griqua*-Hottentots as well as the *Zulu* ruler Chaka, left their homeland north of the Vaal River. This group, having received the name *Kololo*, at first moved to the west to Kuruman and then turned towards the north. During a long migration, which proved to be rich in bellicose events, they crossed the Zambezi west of the Victoria Falls and penetrated into the country of the *Lozi* tribes. In 1840, the *Lozi* were conquered, and Sebitwane established an empire among them, having removed the dynasty of the *Luyi* and having occupied all important offices with his *Kololo* henchmen (see WESTERMANN 1952, 436/7).

65 KOLOLO *(sikololo)*, the language of the conquerers and a dialect of SOTHO, was forcibly imposed as the State language and spread to the same extent as LUYI (Luyana), the language of the inferior subjects lost its influence. When the Scottish explorer David LIVINGSTONE in 1851 reached Sebitwane's residence Linyanti, KOLOLO had already gained a certain influence as lingua franca of the Upper Zambezi River and as language of the courts (STIRKE 1922, 13). In that year, Sebitwane died of pneumonia in the presence of LIVINGSTONE.

66 In 1864, the *Lozi* rose against the ruling caste of the *Kololo,* killed all men and elevated the ancient *Luyi* dynasty to the throne of the empire. The most important ruling figure of this clan was Lewanika (Luanika, Lobosi), who governed from 1878 to 1916. In 1890 he requested the help of the *British South Africa Company* and subordinated his empire to the British colonial power. In spite of this development, KOLOLO could not only maintain its status as lingua franca of the entire empire, but was even able to expand itself. Under the ruling *Luyi* clan KOLOLO, however, became subject to a quick change, chiefly caused by the influence of the Luyi language (STIRKE 1922, 13/4; 40/1). In consideration of this linguistic change, the designation of KOLOLO from this time on was frequently replaced by LOZI, a description which henceforth will be applied (cf. TURNER 1952, 12). The designation LOZI has established itself more particularly in recent literature[3]. By subduing the different tribes such as the *Ila* and *Tonga*, Lewanika enlarged his empire and thereby also the influence of LOZI. He called young people

---

3 Not only the status but also the designation of this language still seem to be little clarified. The name "Lozi" has not only been used in the aforesaid sense, but also as a synonym for the designation "Luyi" (Luyana) (cf. WESTERMANN 1952, 439). In connection with this, mention must be made of a differing concept of the status of LOZI, which, on the one hand, is associated by some people with LUYI, on the other hand by others with SOTHO, and by other people still is described as a "mixed language" (cf. BRYAN 1959, 151).

of noble families from the conquered territories to come to his court, who, upon their return to their home countries, spread the knowledge of LOZI (WESTERMANN 1952, 439). Thus LOZI penetrated into very remote regions. In the north it found its way into the territory of the *Lwena* (Luvale) and *Lunda*, in the east extended as far as the *Tonga* and in the south included the *Totela* country (cf. STIRKE 1922, 40). To the west, it reached as far as the *Mbunda*, in the Angola territory administrated today by the Portuguese (cf. JENSEN 1947, 1127).

67 In spite of the influence exerted by LUYI on LOZI, LOZI remained on the basis of its origin – closely related to SOTHO. Thus the French missionary COILLARD 1870—1879 was able to communicate with the LOZI-speaking population (WESTERMANN 1952, 439), and the mission, to whom were available books of instructions and grammars of SOTHO only, introduced SOTHO as language of the schools into the spreading area of LOZI. Later on, however, this procedure was abolished and LOZI was given its own alphabet and literature.

68 LOZI has retained its importance as lingua franca in Barotseland up to today. It is the predominant language of the south-western part of Zambia and was acknowledged as one of the four official languages of that country. In the city of Livingstone on the Zambezi, in which various lingua francas are spoken, it is the most widespread language (RICHARDSON 1961, 26).

G. FORTUNE summarizes the spreading of LOZI as follows:

"It is the first language of most people now in the central Barotse plain to the north and south of Mongu and on either side of the Zambezi to a considerable distance inland and is spoken to the virtual exclusion of almost anything else. This is the case also along the river all the way to Livingstone, though here the situation is complicated in certain places by other languages. Away from this central area Lozi is a lingua franca used in public life all over the Province in courts, in schools and administration in addition to English. It is generally understood by men even in remote areas, e.g. in the south-west along the Mashi river and in Mankoya district. Women who tend to travel less and have a more restricted social horizon do not show the same competence although even among them and especially among the younger people its use is widespread and growing" (FORTUNE 1968, 3).

## d) UMBUNDU

69 UMBUNDU is the language of the *Ovimbundu*, inhabiting the Benguela-Highlands of southern Angola. This language should not be confused with the KIMBUNDU, which is likewise a *Bantu* language and also spoken in Angola, north of UMBUNDU.

70 The history of UMBUNDU as a lingua franca is in part connected with trade in south-western Africa. Since the early 19th Century, the *Ovimbundu* people have become known as traders, and, along with the Arabs from

Zanzibar, were reputed to be the biggest traders in *Bantu*-speaking Africa (CHILDS 1949, 191). They brought European goods into the interior and sold ivory and later on chiefly rubber to the Europeans who lived in the coastal area. Thereby, their language spread into the interior of the country and also gained a foothold at the coast.

71 This process of spreading UMBUNDU — called "Umbunduisation" by G. M. CHILDS (CHILDS 1949, 179) — is still continuing today, although the *Ovimbundu* people largely lost their predominant status as traders already at the beginning of the 20th Century (McCULLOCH 1952, 9). Various tribes relinquished their own languages and adopted UMBUNDU as mother tongue. Amongst them can be counted i.a. the *Cenge* (Cengi), *Sanga*, *Namba* and *Kasongi* living in the northern part of the Benguela-Highlands (CHILDS 1949, 179).

72 In 1904, the construction of the Benguela railway was started, and planned to connect the coast with the hinterland. It led straight through the centre of the *Ovimbundu* territory and in 1929 reached the frontier of the then Belgian Congo. With this event, the period of trading caravans, in which the Ovimbundu participated to a large extent, came to an end. The UMBUNDU language, however, found fresh possibilities to spread along the railway line. It became the predominant lingua franca amongst the *Nganda* and *Hanya* tribes living close to the railway. Chiefly, however, it was spread in the towns along the coast, in which a large number of members of different tribes had settled. It is presumed that already during the period from 16th to 19th Centuries sizeable groups of *Ovimbundu* emigrated to the coast and settled in the vicinity of Catumbela and Benguela. In more recent years the UMBUNDU language gained such an importance on account of the fresh arrival of emigrants that the other African languages are hardly used any more there. Thus, G. M. CHILDS notes that in Lobito and Catumbela, apart from UMBUNDU hardly any other *Bantu* language is spoken (CHILDS 1949, 180). In the south it penetrated as far as the surrounding of Mossamedes, and in the north as far as Novo Redondo (op. cit. 179/80).

73 The present-day spreading area of UMBUNDU as lingua franca comprises almost the entire southern part of Angola, in which case, however, it is much less spoken in the east than in the west. The approximate northern border of its spreading seems to be formed by Quibala and Mussende, whereas the largest density of the UMBUNDU-speaking population can be found in the districts of Benguela and Bihe (VIE).

The number of *Ovimbundu* is stated to be 1,331,087, pursuant to the census of 1940[4], whereas according to an estimate made by Th. TUCKER in 1955,

---

4 According to CHILDS this number must be decreased by 150,000, since also non-*Ovimbundu* had erroneously been included in the census. On the other hand, in this total of 1,331,087 not all the *Ovimbundu* are accounted for who live out-

A. C. EDWARDS works it out to amount to 1.5 Million (EDWARDS 1962, 21). If each person using UMBUNDU as lingua franca were added to this figure, the overall number of UMBUNDU users would amount to approximately 1.8 to 2 Million.

## e) LWENA

74 LWENA *(Luena, Lovale, Luvale)* is included by M. A. BRYAN in the *Chokwe-Lunda* group of *Bantu* languages (BRYAN 1959, 67). It is spoken as lingua franca in eastern Angola, south-western Congo and in the north-western part of Zambia. In particular it is used as a second language by the *Lunda, Luchazi* and *Chokwe* (WHITE 1951, 67). According to C. M. N. WHITE, more than one million people are said to speak or understand LWENA (WHITE 1949, Introduction). It spread especially in the industrial and densely populated areas (WHITE 1944, 3) and was carried by the labour migrations even to the Zambian copperbelt, where, however, it could not gain a foothold and on account of the competition of rival lingua francas — more particularly "Town BEMBA" – could not achieve any notable importance. It is being used today in Zambia as a language of education in the primary schools and beyond that even as a subject of instruction.

## f) Town BEMBA

75 The designation "Town BEMBA" (abbreviated TB) was introduced by Irvine RICHARDSON, the foremost expert on this language. By its users themselves it is mostly called *cikopabeeluti*[5], i.e. 'the language of the copperbelt'. Occasionally, however, this designation also applies to other languages spoken in the copperbelt (RICHARDSON 1961, 25).

76 "Town BEMBA" belongs to the *Bemba* group of *Bantu* languages. Since a user of the vernacular BEMBA language — from which "Town BEMBA" has derived — does at first hardly understand the lingua franca and requires about five to six months to master it appropriately, it does not seem unjustified to look upon BEMBA and Town BEMBA as two different languages of the same group (cf. RICHARDSON 1961, 30).

*Development into a lingua franca*

77 On the soil of Zambia, the former Northern Rhodesia, to the south of Katanga, a very productive copper industry originated, which became the

---

side Angola, and altogether should certainly amount to more than 150,000 (CHILDS 1949, 9).

5 As RICHARDSON observes, there are various ways of spelling this name. Thus, for instance, A. L. EPSTEIN uses the spelling *Cicopperbelti* (EPSTEIN 1959, 250).

centre of attraction for people of many different nations and races. European mining experts, who had gained experience in South Africa, artisans, engineers, geologists, i.a., met here with a multilingual body of labourers. Added to this must be a somewhat smaller group of Asiatics, who tried their luck preponderantly in trade.

Between Whites and Africans, there quickly arose a social barrier, which found its expression in such matters as separate living areas. This barrier was chiefly based on differences in culture, education — the majority of Africans consisted of unskilled labourers — and last but not least on the colour of the skin. Added must be a frequent feeling of alleged "racial superiority" on the part of the White population.

78 This social situation also found its expression in the field of language. Whereas the Whites amongst themselves generally spoke English, they used FANAGALO when in contact with their subordinates. This language may be presumed to have originated in Natal in the middle of the 19th Century and spread to the gold and diamond mines of South Africa. Thence it was carried by the immigrated specialists and labourers into the Northern Rhodesian copperbelt and was used as a medium of communication between Whites and Africans.

79 Also amongst the African population FANAGALO experienced a further spreading and finally became the predominant lingua franca in the copperbelt (RICHARDSON 1961, 28). Indeed, the situation there demanded a lingua franca. The man who had left his tribal area in order to earn his living as an industrial labourer, usually understood only his mother tongue. He was therefore hardly capable of making himself understood by his colleagues or his white superiors. Here FANAGALO offered itself, which, on account of its simple grammatical structure and its limited vocabulary, was allegedly easy to learn. It became the language of the industrial population — a role which it already fulfilled in South Africa.

80 With the appearance of FANAGALO, however, two circumstances were connected which in the end proved to be of little promotional value for the spreading of this language. On the one hand it was considered in the copperbelt a "foreign" language on account of its South African origin. On the other hand it was a "command" language which deepened the social distance between White and Black, and by some Africans was often identified with racialistic attitudes (cf. EPSTEIN 1959, 237; RICHARDSON 1961, 29).

81 Contemporaneous with this situation was the development of "Town BEMBA". Its origin is said to go back to the time before World War I — approximately 1910. In those days, a sizeable body of *Bemba* men was hired for work in the mines (RICHARDSON 1961, 28). The proportion of BEMBA labourers in the copperbelt grew steadily. Today more than 60% of the labourers speak BEMBA or a closely related language as mother

tongue (loc. cit. 30). But not only the number but also the social importance of the BEMBA-speaking population rose. It soon boasted of making up a notable proportion of employees, teachers, trade union leaders and politicians.

82  Gradually BEMBA spread amongst the labour force in the copperbelt speaking different mother tongues. From the social intercourse of those people with the *Bemba*-speaking people, there developed a new language form, namely the "Town BEMBA", which was based on the vernacular language BEMBA, but steadily developed away from it. The BEMBA people living in the towns performed an important function in this development. They guarded against any excessive infiltration into this newly-formed language with words from the other languages represented in the copperbelt, and exerted a decisive influence on the acceptance of innovations in the language (RICHARDSON 1961, 31).

83  For a long time, however, the importance of "Town BEMBA" was limited — it was overshadowed by the predominant lingua franca FANAGALO. A decisive change occurred in the forties. The influence of FANAGALO suddenly decreased until in the end it was limited to one single domain, i.e. that of work. In the contact between Europeans and Africans, which as a rule was restricted to work, the FANAGALO language could maintain its position — not the least reason being because the Whites considered it their privilege to speak English and in their contact with the Africans used FANAGALO[6].

The decline of FANAGALO in the copperbelt since World War II is most likely based in part on the awakening self-assertion of the African population, which began to resist any European tutelage. FANAGALO was looked upon as the language of the Whites and its usage was avoided as far as possible (cf. par. 80).

84  The greater the decline of FANAGALO's importance, the wider the spreading of "Town BEMBA", until it finally became the predominant language of the copperbelt; a role which it has maintained up to today. It found its way into all spheres of activity — in the beer halls, at celebration dances and on the football field. Beyond this, it also appeared in printed form in the periodical *Nshila*; but up to now it has remained of limited importance as a written language.

*Spreading and arrangement*

85  Today "Town BEMBA" is to be found everywhere in the copperbelt, particularly in the towns of Ndola, Kitwe-Nkana, Chingola, Mufulira,

---

6  To be addressed in English by an African often amounted to a white man to be the "acme of Kaffir insolence" (EPSTEIN 1959, 237).

Luanshya, Bancroft, Kabulushi and Chibuluma. Apart from these localities it is found — though less wide-spread — in Broken Hill, Lusaka, Fort Roseberry, Livingstone, Zomba, and partly even in Salisbury (RICHARDSON 1962, 190). It is furthermore spoken — predominantly by former mine labourers — in the east of Zambia and in Malawi. There, however, NYANJA, which as language spoken in the army and by police has experienced a wider spreading, is the predominant lingua franca.

86 Amongst the Europeans, "Town BEMBA" up to today has not much been in vogue. In comparison with BEMBA of the rural districts it is designated as "slang", "broken BEMBA", "English with BEMBA grammar", or "mixed gibberish". This also applies to the missionaries, who had declared against the use of "Town BEMBA", but had on the other hand significantly promoted the tribal language of BEMBA as language of education in the schools[7] (RICHARDSON 1961, 27).

87 In the case of the African population, however, "Town BEMBA" has become a p r e s t i g e language, by the learning of which entry is obtained into the free, modern life of the town. The ability to speak "Town BEMBA" fluently is one of the prerequisites of social success. In this connection, RICHARDSON notes:

"It is the speech of those who have emerged from the bush to wrest from the white man's town the wealth which will promote them to demi-gods in the eyes of their rustic cousins... For the successful then, TB (i.e. Town BEMBA, cf. par. 75; author's note) is the sign of wealth, *savoir-vivre* and urbanity as they conceive it. For the unsuccessful and the newly-arrived ones..., it is a cloak under which to hide their deficiencies" (RICHARDSON 1961, 31).

Amongst the most zealous learners of "Town BEMBA" belong the prostitutes, who by the knowledge of this language hope for an increased prestige and advantages in their profession (loc. cit. 26).

88 The recognition of "Town BEMBA" found among the Africans in the copperbelt can possibly be explained by its being an African language in a particular sense, which is mastered well only by very few Europeans. Also in its origin and development the Europeans took no direct part. On the other hand, the other lingua francas represented in the copperbelt, i.e. FANAGALO, English and NYANJA owe their importance in a large measure to the European expansion in Central Africa[8].

---

7 On account of the zealous preference on the part of the missionaries for the rural BEMBA, this language has also been called "the BEMBA of the white Fathers" (RICHARDSON 1961, 27).

8 Concerning FANAGALO, see above. NYANJA, the predominant language in Malawi, reached Zambia more particularly as a medium of communication in the army and the police – both looked upon as little-loved auxiliaries of the Whites. Moreover, a sizeable group of strongly "Europeanized" *Nyanja* people – the *Nyanja* had come into early contact with European culture – can be found in the copperbelt.

89 "Town BEMBA" is used in all situations of town life — during work as well as during leisure time. There are, however, also restrictions on its application. Thus, it could not obtain a foothold in religious life; the reason for this has already been alluded to (par. 86). Also during political meetings the vernacular BEMBA is preferred to "Town BEMBA". Moreover, there exist certain social contexts in which "Town BEMBA" is not employed. Thus, for instance, a *Bemba* in an elevated position in social intercourse with equal-ranking members of the same tribe avails himself of vernacular BEMBA; with lower-ranking members and with people of different ethnical origin, however, he will communicate in "Town BEMBA" (RICHARDSON 1961, 26).

90 The servants, who form the third strongest occupational group in the towns of the copperbelt, as well as the prostitutes (see par. 87), particularly excell in speaking "Town BEMBA". Amongst women "Town BEMBA" is spread in the same way as amongst men. On the other hand, differences can be found in the spreading of this language depending on the tribal membership of the user. Thus, for instance, "Town BEMBA" is mastered to a far lesser extent by the *Lwena* (Luvale) than by most of the other tribes (RICHARDSON 1961, 26).

91 The application of this language also varies according to the age of the user. "Town BEMBA" is primarily the language of the working population and beyond that preponderantly the language of y o u t h. It is an expression of today's widely-spread disregard of tradition, law and order. Older men, who give up work in the copperbelt and return to their rural home country in order to spend their old age there, relinquish the use of "Town BEMBA" in favour of their mother tongue (RICHARDSON 1961, 27/8; 32).

92 The development leading to the spreading of "Town BEMBA" has not come to its end. It was selected as a basis for publications and has thereby improved its position as a written language. It furthermore gained in prestige and enlarged its area of spreading. Irvine RICHARDSON presumes that if the present tendency continues, "Town BEMBA" will in twenty years have become the most important language in Zambia next to English (RICHARDSON 1962, 195/6).

## g) NYANJA

93 NYANJA, the predominant language in the Central African State of Malawi, belongs to the *Bantu* group of languages.

*Development into a lingua franca*

94 The development of NYANJA into a lingua franca can presumably be connected with the arrival of Europeans in Central Africa. In 1856 David LIVINGSTONE had already discovered Lake Nyasa, and 19 years later the

Christian Mission named after him began its work there. At the beginning of the 20th Century the missionaries were joined by a considerable number of European settlers, who planted tea and tobacco on the southern plateaux of the British Protectorate named Nyasaland in 1907. Contrary to many of their neighbours, the *Nyanja* thereby came early into contact with the Europeans. They hired themselves out as house servants or as farm labourers. An important lead over other Central African tribes was gained by them through the fact that in their territory schools were established at an early date and that possibilities of learning technical trades were created. Thereby originated amongst the *Nyanja* a new class of workers, composed of office clerks, overseers, artisans and specialists. On account of a lack of skilled workers existing in the neighbouring territories, the *Nyanja* soon spread themselves into these areas (SCOTT/HETHERWICK 1951, V). Their travels led them more particularly into Southern and Northern Rhodesia, the Zambia of today.

95 With this expansion of the *Nyanja* population, their language was also carried beyond its original borders. In the south it penetrated across the Zambezi River, in the west as far as the mining area of the copperbelt, and is said to have found a modest foothold in Livingstone (RICHARDSON 1961, 26). In particular, NYANJA achieved a certain importance as lingua franca in the urban areas. Sizeable groups of NYANJA users settled here and on the basis of their better education in comparison with the other African peoples formed an elite class, which acted as an intermediary between Europeans and Africans. The Europeans, too, promoted NYANJA to an extent which should not be underrated. It became the official language of the police and the army — a function which decisively favoured its spreading; on the other hand, it also impeded it to a certain extent, as will be shown later. By the policemen and soldiers NYANJA was carried as far as the remote areas of the present-day states of Zambia and Malawi (see THOMSON 1955, 6). This support also exerted its influence on other fields of administration and upon instruction in schools. NYANJA became the official language of the then territory of Nyasaland (now Malawi) and was elevated to one of the four African literary languages in Northern Rhodesia, the present-day Zambia (PRICE 1940, 125; ATKINS 1950, 35). It seems that some groups in Malawi have relinquished their mother tongue in favour of NYANJA, for instance, the *Mbo* (Ambo) and the *Ngoni* — the latter originating from South Africa — who live in the central province of Malawi and the eastern province of Zambia (ATKINS 1950, 35).

96 In the copperbelt of Zambia NYANJA for some time served as lingua franca next to FANAGALO, "Town BEMBA" and English. In particular, it was widely used among office clerks, interpreters and technicians (RICHARDSON 1961, 28). Not the least important reason why it could gain no foothold there, but succumbed to the competition of "Town BEMBA", can be traced

back to its function as language of the police and army — both institutions being considered media for exerting pressure on the part of the Europeans, and for this reason being deprecated (RICHARDSON 1961, 30).

*Present-day spread and dialects*

97 As a lingua franca, NYANJA is spoken today almost in the entire territory of Malawi, in eastern Zambia, in the territories of Mozambique bordering on Malawi, and presumably also in various parts of Rhodesia (SCOTT/ HETHERWICK 1951, V). The language is divided into a number of dialects, of which, however, only the following are of greater importance (see PRICE 1940, 126/7; ATKINS 1950, 38; BRYAN 1959, 139/40):
MANG'ANJA in the south-east, CEWA in the west, LAKE NYANJA (named simply "Nyanja" by H. H. JOHNSON) in the north-east.
Not the least reason for the contrasts between these dialects lies in their being invigorated by the different language policies of the various Christian missions. After the Livingstonia Mission having at first taken into consideration the northern NYANJA dialects, the likewise Scottish Blantyre Mission settled on the Shire plateau south of Lake Nyasa in 1876 and elevated the MANG'ANJA dialect to the position of a standard language (PRICE 1940, 128/9). For a long time, the area of the CEWA dialect was in the hands of the bellicose *Ngoni* and was only later developed by the mission. The missionaries of the Dutch Reformed Church finally settled there and helped the CEWA dialect to achieve an importance, which especially after World War I challenged the leading position of MANG'ANJA. The Universities Mission to Central Africa, in turn, promoted the LAKE NYANJA and published a number of works, basing them on the lesser known dialect. The attempt to overcome the cleavage between these dialects finally led to the publication of a Bible translation in 1922, in which a language form, the "Union Nyanja", deriving from the rivalling dialects, was created. This form, however, could not gain a foothold because the contrast between the groups of dialects had already deepened far too much. The MANG'ANJA users looked upon the work as the "CEWA Bible", and the users of CEWA, on their part, complained that MANG'ANJA was represented in it much beyond its merits (PRICE 1940, 132).

*Demographic statements*

98 Thanks to an investigation by Guy ATKINS we possess more detailed statements on the number of the users of NYANJA (ATKINS 1950). ATKINS not only ascertained the number of those who use NYANJA as mother tongue, but also those who speak it as lingua franca in Malawi and the eastern

province of Zambia. It can, however, be assumed that the number of users of the lingua franca in the following table is based on estimates and that this table therefore possesses only a restricted value as evidence.

*Number of users of NYANJA*

| Territory | Mother tongue | Lingua franca | Total |
|---|---|---|---|
| Malawi | 1,183,292 | 670,826 | 1,854,118 |
|   Southern province | 304,259 | 588,421 | 892,680 |
|   Central province | 834,887 | 51,082 | 885,969 |
|   Northern province | 24,278 | 21,868 | 46,146 |
|   Likoma and east of Lake Nyasa | 19,868 | 9,455 | 29,323 |
| Zambia (eastern province) | 115,157 | 59,670 | 174,827 |
| Total | 1,298,449 | 730,496 | 2,028,945 |

99 As NYANJA is also being spoken outside the territories listed here, the total number of NYANJA users should approximately comprise 2.1 to 2.2 million. The spreading of this language, however, differs very much in the various territories. According to the statements by ATKINS, the following percentage figures can be given on the proportion in each category made up of NYANJA users within the total population:

*Percentage proportion of NYANJA users within the total population*

| Territory | |
|---|---|
| Malawi | *81.1%* |
|   Southern province | *83.9%* |
|   Central province | *99.5%* |
|   Northern province | *15.2%* |
|   Likoma and east of Lake Nyasa | *100 %* |
| Zambia (eastern province) | *72.9%* |

I.a., this table shows the eminent importance of NYANJA for the state of Malawi. It should be mentioned, however, that in the northern part of the country, the language is little known.

100 In respect of the various dialects, the following figures relating to users result:

*Number of NYANJA users*

| Dialect | Mother tongue | Lingua franca | Total |
|---|---|---|---|
| MANG'ANJA | 304,259 | 588,412 | 892,671 |
| CEWA | 974,312 | 132,620 | 1,106,932 |
| Lake NYANJA | 19,868 | 9,455 | 29,323 |
| Total | 1,298,439 | 730,487 | 2,028,926 |

Accordingly, all three dialects are used also as lingua franca. Although CEWA disposes of the largest number of users, it is of small importance as a lingua franca in comparison with MANG'ANJA. Compared with these two dialects, Lake NYANJA possesses only a small number of users, both as mother tongue and as lingua franca (see ATKINS 1950, 36–8).

## II. Congo Basin

### a) LUBA lingua franca

101 The LUBA lingua franca belongs to a multiplicity of languages and dialects which are collectively designated as the "LUBA group". This group, in turn, forms part of the *Bantu* languages. The study of this language is thereby rendered difficult because almost every author on the subject calls it by a

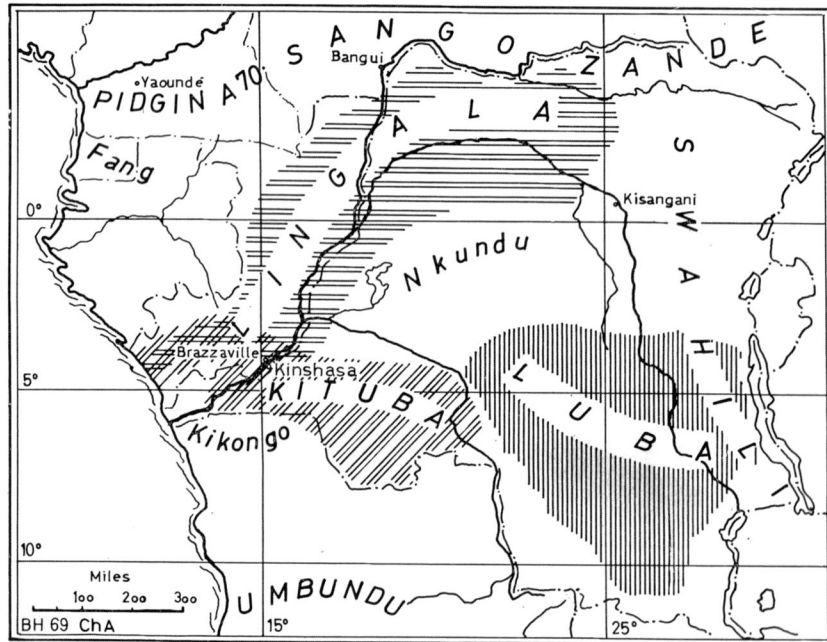

Map 2. *Congo Basin*

*Note:* The hatchings indicate the distribution of the different lingua francas.
*Source:* Author.

different name¹. Often, additionally, there is no terminological distinction made between the lingua franca and the corresponding vernacular form — called TSHILUBA in the following text.

102 The spreading of the LUBA lingua franca can presumably be traced back to the period after the arrival of the Europeans in Central Africa. Leo STAPPERS, on the other hand, notes that outside the areas inhabited by the LUBA population TSHILUBA was used already before the arrival of the Whites (STAPPERS 1952, 51). After the Arabs, under whose inroads the LUBA population suffered very much, had been driven out by Europeans, the south-eastern Congo was to an increasing extent developed by Belgium as a colonial power. Railways were constructed, roads built, and mines were opened up in the provinces of Kasai and Katanga. Whereas most of the tribes regarded these undertakings with suspicion, the *Luba* people readily put a large number of labourers at the disposal of the Europeans. The reason for this lay, on the one hand, in the overpopulation of the *Luba* territory and, on the other hand, in the good relations which had developed between various *Luba* chiefs and Europeans (BIEBUYCK 1961, 23). A mass migration of the Luba population began. Everywhere in the Kasai province where a new mine, a railway line or a river harbour came into existence, *Luba* tribesmen settled down, let their families follow later on, and founded *Luba* enclaves. Through hard work and adeptness they soon succeeded in finding a place for themselves among the groups of skilled workers. Thus they provided an important number of mechanics, car drivers and office staff.

103 In this situation of contact between the various *Luba* groups and the tribes in whose territory they had settled themselves, the LUBA lingua franca developed. According to G. VAN DER KERKEN, apart from TSHILUBA the languages of the *Song'e*² and *Kuba* are said to have participated in the growth of the LUBA lingua franca (KERKEN 1944, 239).

104 Not the least part played in the spreading of the language was that by the missionaries, who, by means of instruction in schools, helped it to attain considerable importance among the *Mbagani* and *Kuba* (HULSTAERT 1950, 35). *Luba* settlements sprang up around the newly built mission stations. They travelled with the white missionaries and thus among the local

---

1 Thus, for instance, A. VERBREKEN calls the lingua franca by the designation *Tshituba* and the vernacular form *Tshiluba* (VERBREKEN 1928, 5). G. VAN DER KERKEN, on the other hand, gives the lingua franca the name of *Kiluba-Kituba* and the vernacular language that of *Kiluba* (KERKEN 1944, 239/248) and G. HULSTAERT calls the vernacular form *Tsiluba* and the lingua franca *Tshiluba de traite* or *Kituba* (HULSTAERT 1950, 34–6/47; BURSSENS 1954, 30). A confusion of terminology occurred in particular through the lingua franca form of KIKONGO also having become known under the designation of *Kituba* (cf. NIDA 1955, 155); see KITUBA.

2 According to G. HULSTAERT SONG'E belongs to the LUBA group of languages (HULSTAERT 1950, 34).

tribes were the first to learn the benefits of a school education. Thereby they soon took up a large proportion of posts in the administration and became teachers and employees in trading companies. In short, while the *Luba* made up an absolute majority particularly in the clergy, and even though efforts were made to reduce the preponderance of the *Luba* in favour of other tribes, this scarcely altered the situation (STAPPERS 1952, 53/4). The *Luba* people became the ruling class in Kasai, and their language won considerable prestige.

105 In this way the LUBA lingua franca became the predominant lingua franca in the upper Kasai and in the Congo Basin (MORRISON 1906, iii). The present-day area of spreading of this language is not known with any degree of exactness as to its extent. G. VAN DER KERKEN notes that it limits itself particularly to the districts Kasai and Sankuru (KERKEN 1944, 255). According to O. LIESENBORGHS it is used beyond the *Luba* territory by the *Tetela, Kuba, Binji* (Bindi), *Bashilele, Cokwe* and the *Pende*, who speak a KIKONGO dialect (LIESENBORGHS 1942, 94/5). Apart from these, Amaat BURSSENS names the following *Bantu*-speaking tribes, throughout whose area the LUBA lingua franca is spread: Bena Tshofa, Bena Mpang'u, Bakwa Mbalayi, Bakwa Mbiye, Bakwa Mputu, Bena Kanyoka, Song'e (see above), Kete, Biombo, Sala Mpasu, Lualua and Tubeya (BURSSENS 1939, 267).

The area of influence of the LUBA lingua franca therefore reaches in the west to Kasai River, in other words, to the border of Angola; in the north-west presumably beyond Kasai to the area east of Kikwit; approximately along the 3rd s. latitude to Lualaba River in the east; and as far as Katanga in the south. The lingua franca is furthermore to be found in the large towns outside this area. Thus it is spoken, for example, in Kinshasa, the capital of the Congo, though there it does not have the function of a lingua franca, but is used only by the LUBA-speaking population (BOECK 1953, 4).

*Dialects*

106 According to Leo STAPPERS LUBA must be divided into western, central, eastern and southern dialect groups. The southern group disposes of the largest number of speakers, though the western group is the most important. This forms the basis of the LUBA lingua franca (STAPPERS 1952, 56). It is applied in school instruction and in the church and is acknowledged by the *Luba* as the predominant dialect form. The municipal centres of Luluaburg, Bakwanga, Tshikapa, Lusambo, Luebo, Tshimbulu, Muena Ditu and Luputa belong to its spreading area. The inhabitants of the rural districts learn this dialect form as soon as they come to town.

107 For contact between Europeans and Africans a particular lingua franca form came into existence, which is often given the name *Tshituba* (cf. par. 101, footnote). Its use seems to be restricted to those situations in which the native

population comes into contact with Whites, as, for example, in administrative affairs and legal proceedings (cf. STAPPERS 1952, 61). As can be presumed from STAPPERS' observations, a p i d g i n form of TSHILUBA seems to be in question here[3].

## b) KITUBA

108 Like other lingua francas, KITUBA has become known under a multiplicity of names, i.e.:

*Kikongo commercial;*
*Kikongo véhiculaire;*
*Kikongo simplifié;*
*Kikóngo ya Letá,* 'state Kikongo';
*Kileta,* the 'language of state and government';
*Kikongo keleve;*
*Ikeleve;*
*Kingala;*
*Kizabave;*
*Fiote;*
*Kisodi,* the 'language of the soldiers';
*Munukutuba (Monokutuba);*
*Kituba*[4];
*Kibulamatadi (Bula-Matari)* (LAMAN 1928, 379; CUVELIER 1944, 283/4; KERKEN 1944, 239; JONGHE 1933, 518; HULSTAERT 1950, 47; NIDA 1955, 155; SWIFT 1963, iii; REDDEN 1963, 18; FEHDERAU 1966, 7–10).
By the American Mennonite missionaries, who gained great merit in respect of the development of this language, it was called *Kikwango,* the 'Kwango' language (NIDA 1955, 156). Some of the above-mentioned names are not only designations for the entire language, but beyond that have gained special importance. Thus the western dialect spoken along the lower Congo River is often called *Kikongo ya Letá,* and the eastern dialect used in the Kwango-Kwilu region is designated Kituba or Kikongo (SWIFT 1963, X; REDDEN 1963, 18). The name *Munukutuba,* however, is above all applied to KITUBA as used in the Congo-Brazzaville territory (SWIFT 1963, X).

---

3 "This seems to be a succession of nouns and adjectives with a few expletives serving as conjunction or preposition." ("Het schijnt een aaneenrijging van noemvormen en naamwoorden te zijn met een paar partikels die dienst doen als voegwoord en voorzetsel" [STAPPERS 1952, 62].)

4 This designation has in particular spread more widely through the more recent works of American authors and for this reason will be used in this present paper. It may be pointed out that occasionally also other languages spoken in the Congo Basin were given this designation, thus, for instance, the LUBA lingua franca (HULSTAERT 1950, 47) and KUBA (KERKEN 1944, 248).

KITUBA forms a dialect of KIKONGO, which in turn belongs to the group of *Bantu* languages.

*Development into a lingua franca*

109 Pursuant to L. B. SWIFT and E. W. A. ZOLA, it may be presumed that KITUBA had already originated before the arrival of the Europeans in the interior of the Congo, more exactly, in contact between KIKONGO-speaking groups and tribes of the upper Congo. It derived from a pidginized form of KIKONGO. According to H. W. FEHDERAU its origin and early development occurred in the period between 1500 and 1875 (FEHDERAU 1966, 103). It was connected with the arrival of the Portuguese in the estuary area of the Congo River, by whom the trade in ivory and other goods was greatly enhanced in the interior. Nevertheless it does not seem likely that the Portuguese exerted direct influence either on the origin or the development of KITUBA. Of central importance for the development of KITUBA was the trading post of Manianga, situated on the caravan route between the Atlantic coast and Stanley Pool (op. cit. 100).

The basic reason for the importance gained by KITUBA in the lower Congo area were the interethnic contacts caused by the expanding trade. Although by the decline of this inland trade the situation leading to the spread of KITUBA underwent a change, the lingua franca did not lose prominence. A new phase of its development commenced with the formation of the Congo Free State in 1885 which caused an invigoration of trade as well as an increasing development of the interior. The lower region of the Congo became the meeting place for people of different tribal origins, who found employment in the administration, in trade or in railway construction. For them, KITUBA became the mutual medium of communication. On its expansion in the eastern region (see below) FEHDERAU remarks:

"European commerce expanded from the Lower Congo into the Kwango-Kwilu areas. The Kasai Company was already on the Kasai River in the 1890's. Lever Brothers began on the Kwilu River in 1912. These companies brought agents and native workers with them who knew Pidgin Kikongo. Local people who did business with them or entered into their employment adopted it as the means of communication" (FEHDERAU 1966, 110).

KITUBA was used by the white government officials, traders and settlers almost exclusively in their contact with the African population (NIDA 1955, 155). In the growing trading centres it soon became the sole medium of communication, and it was selected by the authorities as organ for official notices. It spread wherever members of different tribes came together on the plantations and in the factories (op. cit. 156).

110 As with other lingua francas used in the Congo Basin, the distribution extended in particular along the large rivers, in the case of KITUBA along

the Kwango and Kasai Rivers. In the Kwango district it was zealously taken up by the missionaries and turned into the basis of school instruction as well as religious teaching. Amongst the numerous smaller tribal groups of this area, the lingua franca gained special importance. In the areas, however, where vernacular forms of KIKONGO were spoken, the missionaries preferred this form of language and not the lingua franca.

KITUBA also extended along the Congo River between Matadi and Kinshasa and even penetrated far into the Congo-Brazzaville territory. In some of the multilingual areas the spread of KITUBA has till today not yet ceased (SWIFT 1963, XI). The language is employed for government publications and radio broadcasts.

111 The structure of KITUBA has altered by its becoming the mother tongue of many people. In the urban centres of Boma, Matadi, Pointe-Noire, Brazzaville, Kitwit or Feshi several thousands of members of various tribes have relinquished their language in favour of KITUBA and thus the pidgin language has turned into a c r e o l e language (NIDA 1955, 156; FEHDERAU 1966, 110).

*Spread and number of users*

112 Today, KITUBA is spoken in the entire lower Congo area — in particular along the southern tributaries of the Congo River. In its area of distribution 40–50 languages and dialects are spoken, all of which just like KITUBA belong to the Bantu group of the Niger Congo family. H. W. FEHDERAU, one of the foremost experts on KITUBA, distinguishes between three regions of distribution of the language (FEHDERAU 1966, 4 ff.):

1. The northern KITUBA region. It comprises the southern part of the Congo-Brazzaville territory. More particularly in the towns of Brazzaville, Dolisie and Pointe-Noire KITUBA boasts of a greater distribution. In one particular aspect, however, the position of the lingua franca differs from that of the other two areas. The State of Congo-Brazzaville was formerly under French administration, and the consequences of the French policy, solely directed towards the spread of the French language in disfavour of the African languages, can still be observed today. Thus it happens that *Munukutuba* — as KITUBA is called in this region (see above) — is the language used by the African population, whereas in communication between Africans and Europeans French represents the predominant medium (op. cit. 10/11).

113 2. The western KITUBA region. It embraces the western part of Congo-Kinshasa, which to the east is bounded by the Kwango River. Here, the lingua franca is especially widely spoken in the towns of Boma, Matadi and Thysville. There are, however, two factors restricting the importance of KITUBA in this region. On the one hand there are the Christian missions,

which prefer the use of the vernacular language KIKONGO. Thus FEHDERAU remarks:

"However, missions in the western region have been particularly disdainful of Kituba, some even refusing to acknowledge the extent of its usage. Even in the large centers where many of the younger generation use Kituba as a primary language, missions have continued to use the tribal Kikongo dialects in their work" (op. cit. 10).

On the other hand the importance of KITUBA is limited by LINGALA, a rival lingua franca, which as predominant language of Kinshasa is gaining influence in the areas neighbouring the capital. Thus, it is alleged, LINGALA is spreading between Kinshasa and Thysville to the impairment of KITUBA (op. cit. 5).

114   3. The eastern KITUBA region. It lies to the east of the Kwango River in the Kwango-Kwilu district and includes such towns as Kikwit, Bandundu (Banningville) and Feshi. It appears that KITUBA has gained greatest importance in this region. This is in the least caused by the fact that KITUBA is the only lingua franca here in major distribution and that this area is characterized by a special linguistic heterogeneity. In the eastern region, KITUBA is widespread not only in the towns but also in the rural areas. Although to a lesser degree, this applies also to the northern region, but not to the west, where KITUBA is predominantly used in the towns and trading centres.

The situation of KITUBA, however, is different in the neighbouring capital cities of Brazzaville and Kinshasa. Kinshasa, although situated in the western KITUBA region, is undoubtedly governed by LINGALA as lingua franca. "Those who use Kituba in Leopoldville (i.e. Kinshasa), know the language from previous contacts in Kituba regions beyond the capital" (FEHDERAU 1966, 5). On Brazzaville, however, FEHDERAU notes:

"It is true that Africans from the northeastern regions of the Congo who have left their home villages to settle in Brazzaville will tend to continue to use Lingala. But those from the western area as far as the Atlantic port city of Pointe Noire use Kituba. Radio Congo (Brazzaville) broadcasts many more Kituba broadcasts than Radio Leopoldville, which concentrates on Lingala and French" (op. cit. 6).

DE BOECK, in contrast, maintains that in Kinshasa KITUBA is used by the *Bakongo* in contact with the Europeans or the other African inhabitants, KITUBA being not only more widespread but also possessing the higher prestige (BOECK 1953, 4).

115   Pursuant to SWIFT and ZOLA, KITUBA is spoken by altogether 1.5 million people (SWIFT 1963, X). According to Eugene A. NIDA, however, the numbers of users in Congo-Kinshasa amounts to two million and in Congo-Brazzaville to one million, i.e. three million in all (NIDA 1955, 156).

116   KITUBA has a number of dialects, which, although differing according to locality, are mutually intelligible (NIDA 1955, 156). More particularly, it

is divided into a western and an eastern dialect area. The western area is characterized, inter alia, by a larger number of borrowings from KIKONGO, whereas the eastern area is influenced above all by languages of the Kwango and Kwilu districts [5].

*The sociolinguistic situation*

117 In company with other pidgin languages in Africa, KITUBA also as a result of its "corrupted form" enjoys but small esteem amongst the missionaries, and they avoid its use as far as possible (NIDA 1955, 155). So they have refused to assist in the furtherance of KITUBA in the Bas-Congo district — apart from some towns with an ethnically heterogeneous population (CUVERLIER 1944, 284; HULSTAERT 1950, 47). In the Kwango district, however where a uniform (linguistically homogeneous) population is lacking, they were forced to employ KITUBA.

Differences of attitude towards KITUBA can in particular be found between the western and eastern areas of distribution. Whereas in the east "Kituba enjoys a much more elevated position... in the minds of the people" and "has a more independent status as a means of communication in its own right" (FEHDERAU 1966, 11), it is not so highly appraised in the west. FEHDERAU remarks in this connection:

"Those who speak Kikongo as their primary language usually look down on Kituba as something less than a language. This seems evident to them since it is not the characteristic language of a particular group of people. In commercial centers, however, Kituba enjoys the prestige of a big-city language. Urban dwellers, in turn, often regard Kikongo as a rustic, bush language of the 'uncivilized' "(op. cit. 10).

As it is supposed to be easy to learn and was therefore preferred by the Europeans, it was often identified with the colonial masters, a fact which hardly contributed towards creating esteem for KITUBA (SWIFT 1963, X).

118 That the KITUBA is liked above all by the youth is demonstrated by the fact that although KIKONGO is dutifully used in the classroom, the pupils out of school prefer to speak KITUBA, the language in which they understand one another better (NIDA 1955, 157). KITUBA is primarily the language of the administration. It is employed by government officials and in government communication. The available literature supplies no information on the extent of its usage being enhanced thereby.

---

5 In his paper "Descriptive Grammar of the Kituba Language, A Dialectical Survey" FEHDERAU has described the dialect position of KITUBA (FEHDERAU 1962; FEHDERAU 1964; see SWIFT 1963, X).

## c) LINGALA

119   LINGALA — also called the "language of the river" — has become known under various designations such as *Bangala, Mangala* or *Ngala*[6]. As a rule it is named *Mangala* by the African population in the Congo (REDDEN 1963, X). According to M. A. BRYAN it belongs to the *Ngala* group of *Bantu* languages. In this group must be counted amongst others the languages MABAALE and BOGANGI which are spoken on the banks of the Congo River round Nouvelle Anvers and further down to the south (BRYAN 1959, 37–42).

*The development into a lingua franca*

120   The European travellers, moving upstream on the Congo River in the second half of the 19th Century, reported of a brisk trade in slaves, ivory and red powder amongst the tribes along the river. Those tribes, which as a rule spoke closely-related languages amongst one another, had already availed themselves of a lingua franca before the arrival of the Whites (COURBOIN 1908, VII; TANGHE 1930, 345; JONGHE 1933, 514).

121   It can, however, no longer be ascertained in how far this lingua franca can be identified with the LINGALA spoken today. TANGHE reports, that around 1890 the KIBANGI language, which is derived from BOBANGI[7] and which like LINGALA belongs to the *Ngala* group, was the predominant language

---

6   There is little agreement on the designation of this language. In this connection, J. A. BARNEY notes: "There are so many divergent views regarding this commercial language that one hesitates to make any statements for fear of adding confusion to what has always been confused" (BARNEY 1934, 220). In 1903, Walter H. STAPLETON called the language *Bangala* (STAPLETON 1910, c). J. TANGHE, however, terms the lingua franca as *Lingala; Ngala* for the group of dialects, to which, amongst other, LINGALA belongs; and *Bangala* for the users of the *Ngala* dialect (TANGHE 1930, 341). He further notes, that *Bangala* is a creation of the Europeans, who deduced this term from *Mangala* – a designation of several *Ngala* villages. Additionally, he admits, however, that *Lingala* and *Bangala* are used synonymously (loc. cit. 343/4). Suzanne COMHAIRE-SYLVAIN, like TANGHE, calls the lingua franca *Lingala*, which according to her, derives its origin from the language *Mangala* which was used in the country of Bangala (COMHAIRE 1949, 239). Emmi MEYER, in turn, calls the language neither *Lingala* nor *Bangala*, but *Ngala* (MEYER 1944, 260). In 1943, Malcolm GUTHRIE arrived at a different conclusion. He differentiated between the following language forms: (1) *Bangala,* which spread to the north beyond the *Bantu* border and was used primarily in contact between Europeans and Africans; (2) *Lingala*, a younger language, which however, experienced no noteworthy spread; (3) *Mangala*, the language form identical with the lingua franca *Lingala*, thus named by TANGHE and COMHAIRE-SYLVAIN, amongst others. GUTHRIE chose this name on the designation applied by the users themselves (GUTHRIE 1943, 118).

7   G. HULSTAERT calls this language "Bobangi de traite" (HULSTAERT 1950, 45).

of the lower Congo. It is said that the KIBANGI language has absorbed a number of borrowings, amongst others from the SWAHILI. It spread as far as Kinshasa, where for some years it occupied a position of considerable importance (TANGHE 1930, 345).

122 According to GUTHRIE, LINGALA is a younger language orginating in the nineties of the last century (GUTHRIE 1943, 119). It is assumed to have derived from BOLOKI[8], which is spoken to the north-east and south-west of Nouvelle Anvers[9]. At first, LINGALA was used by members of different tribes along the Congo River and thereby achieved a limited supra-regional importance. With the arrival of European soldiers, colonial officials and traders, a new phase in the development of this language set in. In their search for a medium of communication with the Africans, the Europeans in the western Congo region happened upon LINGALA, which already fulfilled a function as lingua franca. The prerequisites for the spreading of a European language not yet being in existence at that time, the Whites zealously took up LINGALA and used it in their contact with the native population.

123 According to GUTHRIE, the efforts of the Whites to learn LINGALA led to the development of a new language, namely, *Bangala*. This language, which he derogatorily calls "a typical trade jargon that can scarcely be called a language" (GUTHRIE 1943, 118), is characterized especially by an impoverishment in grammatical form and vocabulary. *Bangala* gained no substantial importance among the African population in the Congo (GUTHRIE 1939, X); it was spread, however, by the soldiers in the Uele area and in the north-east of the Congo as lingua franca among the population not speaking *Bantu* languages (GUTHRIE 1943, 118; WING 1953, 177).

124 But it was not only the fact that the Europeans learnt and supported LINGALA which promoted the language to greater importance. In the development of the country the Belgian colonial power primarily made use of the communication possibilities, offered to them by the Congo River system. New stations and trading posts continued to spring up along the river, and via the tributaries the interior of the colony was conquered.

In this process of colonization, LINGALA took an important part. The labour force required for that purpose by the Belgians was primarily recruited from the tribes of the lower Congo. Amongst these tribes the *Ngala* (Bangala) particularly excelled, who at first had put up fierce

---

8 According to J. KNAPPERT and G. HULSTAERT, LINGALA has its origin not in BOLOKI, but in BOBANGI (KNAPPERT 1958, 193; HULSTAERT 1950, 44/5).

9 GUTHRIE notes that BOLOKI has already died out (GUTHRIE 1943, 120; see, however, BRYAN 1959, 39). According to VAN BULCK, "Boloki" signifies a nickname for the approximately 1,250 "People of the water", living on both sides of the Congo River and being divided into different clans such as *Bolombo, Bobeka* (Mobeka), and *Malundja* (VAN BULCK 1948, 614).

resistance against Stanley, but who later became the first allies of the Whites (EVERBROECK 1958, 5). By them, LINGALA was carried wherever the Europeans gained a foothold. Thus, LINGALA became the language of the crews of the river steamers, of the soldiers and the labourers at the stations and the trading posts (COURBOIN 1908, VII), and from them in turn the native population learnt it.

125 Within the armed forces, LINGALA gained a special importance — not for the least reason because a large part of the soldiers came from the area around Nouvelle Anvers and spoke as their mother tongue one of the *Ngala* dialects. It is alleged that in 1903 some thousands of soldiers spoke LINGALA as their mother tongue (STAPLETON 1910, g). As a s o l d i e r ' s l a n g u a g e LINGALA succeeded in penetrating in the east into the sphere of influence of another lingua franca, i.e. that of SWAHILI.

126 Already at the beginning of the 20th Century, LINGALA seems to have become the mother tongue of a considerable number of people outside of the army (STAPLETON 1910, g). Since the arrival of the Europeans the contacts between the various ethnic groups had considerably enlarged on account of the stamping out of tribal warfare and the improved means of communication. As a result intermarriage between members of the different tribes frequently occurred. The spouses were generally forced to communicate with each other in LINGALA, which became their children's mother tongue (COURBOIN 1908, VIII).

127 The spread of LINGALA was furthermore substantially promoted by the colonial policy of the Belgians. In this language the administrative officials saw a possibility of overcoming the language chaos in the Congo, and thus there was no lack of proposals to designate LINGALA as the official language of the Belgian Congo. A knowledge of this language was made a condition for entry into the army — every recruit had to have a command of at least 600 words of the language (Congo's 1943, 184).

In 1918, the colonial government finally attempted to elevate LINGALA to the position of official language of the Belgian Congo (JONGHE 1933, 521). This step, however, was condemned to failure, as it took no account of the linguistic situation of the country; undoubtedly, the importance of LINGALA was thus overestimated. It was not clearly enough perceived, that in the east and the south of the country there were other lingua francas, which not only in the number of users but also in the extent of their use were of second importance to LINGALA (see LUBA lingua franca, SWAHILI).

*Present-day spread*

128 There are no reliable data available on either the extent of use or the number of users of LINGALA. It is spoken today on both banks of the Congo River

between Kinshasa and Basoko, and even beyond that up to about 100 miles west of Stanleyville, the present-day Kisangani; it is, however, not known how far it has spread away from the river into the interior of the country. According to Amaat BURSSENS it is spoken in the whole area between Lualaba in the east and Kasai River in the south (BURSSENS 1954, 29). In the north the area where LINGALA is spoken stretches as far as the Ubangi-Uele territory, but its importance there is restricted because of the existence of another lingua franca by the name of SANGO. In the north-east LINGALA is said to have spread as far as the Nile (JONGHE 1933, 521).

129 In the Lower Congo LINGALA has advanced along the railway lines and in particular has obtained a foothold in the towns. It thereby penetrated into the sphere of influence of another lingua franca, namely, KITUBA *(Kikongo commercial)*. From Kinshasa it spread across the river also to Brazzaville and — again by following the railway line — up to Pointe-Noire, as well as along the Alima River (HULSTAERT 1950, 45). The area of its use today comprises a major portion of the Congo-Brazzaville and in part even reaches to the Gabon frontier. In that country it is spoken in the area between Quesso and Brazzaville and further to the east (JACQUOT 1960*, 30). According to Janet ROBERTS LINGALA is spoken by a total of 1,200,000 people (ROBERTS 1962, 116) — a figure which undoubtedly is underestimated.

*The sociolinguistic situation*

130 Although the use of LINGALA was furthered to a considerable measure by the missionaries it rarely enjoyed a high esteem amongst them, since as a pidgin language it was looked upon by them as 'inferior' in comparison to the vernacular languages. Characteristic of this attitude is the following remark by J. WHITEHEAD:

"It is not an indigenous language, it is a hotchpotch of ignoramuses. As means of conveying thought, it is of less value than the lowest savage dialect" (LAMAN 1928, 379).

131 This opinion, however, as a rule is not shared by the African population. LINGALA to the inland inhabitants symbolizes modern, free life with its allurements and possibilities of liberating themselves from the fetters of the tribal existence. By learning this language, the user hopes to come into possession of money as well as other elements of culture, and thus LINGALA has become a p r e s t i g e language, the knowledge of which promises social and material advantages. The esteem held for this language is for instance demonstrated by the fact that many a tribal chief talks to his subjects not in the common tongue, but in LINGALA — irrespective of their agreeing to it or not. The chiefs see in this a means of impressing their tribesmen and of enhancing their own prestige (HULSTAERT 1950, 47).

132 Investigations carried out by L. B. DE BOECK in Kinshasa show that LINGALA enjoys great popularity also in the towns. Kinshasa, the former Leopoldville, has in particular become the melting pot of the various tribes and cultures. The growing together of the population is enhanced by the fact that the various ethnic groups have no separate dwelling places, but live at random amongst one another (BOECK 1953, 2).

133 The inhabitants of the town are divided into the following two groups:
a) *Congo.* To this group all those are counted who can reach Kinshasa overland from their home country, i.e. especially the members of the Bakongo tribes, who make up approximately three-quarters of the total population of Kinshasa [10].
b) *Ngala.* Among this group each person is counted who has reached the town over the Congo River (BOECK 1953, 1).
This division is not in the least the result of the linguistic situation in the capital of the Congo, for amongst the multiplicity of languages represented in Kinshasa, only two — apart from French — are of any notable importance: KIKONGO and LINGALA.

134 KIKONGO owes its spread in Kinshasa to the large number of *Bakongo* immigrants (see above). According to DE BOECK, however, it is not a lingua franca in the capital, but is only spoken amongst the members of the tribe in social contact [11]. A member of the *Bakongo* who comes to town can indeed make himself understood amongst his fellow tribesmen in one of the dialects of his mother tongue, but he soon will see himself forced to learn LINGALA in order to be able to mix with the rest of the population. After some years, when he has sufficient command of the language, he may well switch over to speaking LINGALA also with the members of his tribe (BOECK 1953, 2).

135 The importance that LINGALA has in Kinshasa is thus indicated. DE BOECK called Kinshasa a "LINGALA town". Apart from the *Bakongo*, all inhabitants of the town as a rule speak LINGALA. They mostly originate in distant regions and have already been able to acquire a certain knowledge of LINGALA during the journey to Kinshasa. For some time the immigrants in Kinshasa use LINGALA to speak to strangers, while within the family circle and in contact with their fellow tribesmen speaking their mother tongue. Later, i.e. after ten or more years, they change to using LINGALA

---

10 According to J. VAN WING the Bakongo represent 72% of the population of Kinshasa, according to A. DE ROP they represent 75–80% (WING 1953, 175; ROP 1953, 172). According to information supplied by Mgr. SIX the proportion of the *Bakongo* amounted to a total of 73% on 31 December 1950 (Probleem 1953, 8).

11 Suzanne COMHAIRE-SYLVAIN notes, however, that KIKONGO plays the role of a lingua franca in Kinshasa and is learnt as a second language by the *Yanzi, Mbala, Ngongo, Lari, Yaka,* amongst others (COMHAIRE 1949, 240). Most of these tribes, though, belong to the *Congo* group (cf. BRYAN 1959, 56–62).

with their children and fellow tribesmen, too, and only continue communicating in the mother tongue with their wives (BOECK 1953, 3/4).

136 The children born in Kinshasa grow up with LINGALA as their only language. Even when they learn other languages, even when their parents urge them to speak the vernacular language, LINGALA still remains their mother tongue, which they use primarily on the street in contact with their companions. Thus DE BOECK notes that in the fifties approximately 10% of the population of Kinshasa used LINGALA as mother tongue (BOECK 1953, 4/5).

137 The question as to how LINGALA became a prestige language has repeatedly been raised. A. DE ROP represents the viewpoint that it was the Europeans who made it into such. In addition he notes:

"In order to be able to make progress in life, school instruction seems to be suitable for the younger Bakongo, but they have no choice (even though they constitute 80% of the population) and they must be instructed in Lingala. The older generation looking for work in Leo have no choice either, because even in a position as auxiliary cook or auxiliary boy, they will be addressed exclusively in Lingala. What else remains for them to do but sooner or later to learn Lingala if they want to succeed in Leo." *

Because LINGALA is the official language of the administration, the court, the school and the church (WING 1953, 176), the knowledge of it has become an indispensable prerequisite for vocational advancement.

138 LINGALA is not the only African lingua franca in Kinshasa. Apart from it KITUBA, a lingua franca form of KIKONGO, and TSHILUBA, are primarily to be found. Both have achieved supra-regional importance in certain parts of the Congo, but in Kinshasa they succumb to the competition of LINGALA. The inhabitants of the town put them on the same level as the vernacular languages and consider it with them to be an expression of particularism and a limited tribal way of thinking. In contrast to this, LINGALA is deemed to have the standing of an "international" language, the knowledge of which professedly "grants a right to citizenship in the big town" (BOECK 1953, 4/5). Thus neither KITUBA nor TSHILUBA fulfil a clearly defined role as a lingua franca in Kinshasa. TSHILUBA only finds application amongst the *Luba* population, while KITUBA, though indeed mastered by some Europeans and non-*Bakongo,* is only used as communication medium with members of the *Bakongo* tribe (loc. cit. 4).

---

\* "Om vooruit te komen is, voor de jongeren onder de Bakongo, de school aangewezen, maar zij hebben geen keus (ook al maken se 80% van de bevolking uit) en moeten zich laten onderrichten in het Lingala. De ouderen, die werk zoeken in Leo, hebben ook geen andere keus, want zelfs in een betrekking als hulpkok of hulpboy zullen ze enkel in het Lingala toegesproken worden. Wat zit er dan voor de Bakongo anders op, als ze willen vooruitkomen, dan in Leo 'vroeg of laat het Lingala aanleren?' " (ROP 1953, 172).

139 The spread of LINGALA differs according to age, sex and ethnical origin. The younger generation learns the language quicker than the older one, and the men as a rule make faster progress than the women (BOECK 1953, 2/3). It is most widespread amongst the young male population. LINGALA has a greater importance amongst the tribes which live in the northern half of the Congo than in the south and south-west.

*Dialects*

140 The linguistic form of LINGALA is not consistent either. It boasts of countless dialects, depending on ethnical and social differences. Thus, for instance, the tongue spoken by the *Bakongo* stands out clearly from that of all other LINGALA users. A comparison of M. GUTHRIE's *Grammaire et Dictionnaire de Lingala* with the *Lingala Woordenboek* shows, furthermore, notable differences in vocabulary, as both authors collected their data in different districts of the LINGALA area (KNAPPERT 1958, 194). Not the least differences in the use of LINGALA are found in the mission stations. While, for instance, the Roman Catholic Mission in Kinshasa uses the LINGALA spoken around Nouvelle Anvers and Lisala, the Protestants have taken up the LINGALA tongue of Kinshasa, enriched by a number of words used further upstream (HULSTAERT 1950, 46).
The process of evolution of various dialects can be particularly illustrated by the example of *Bangala*, which arose as a result of the contact situation between Europeans and Africans and — firstly a LINGALA dialect — finally became a language in its own right (see par. 123).

141 In Kinshasa VAN WING came across two LINGALA dialects[12], one being the "school LINGALA", which is used in the church and in school, and the other "street LINGALA" (also called "river LINGALA" or "*lingala populaire*"); this latter is the language of the administration, the court and the street, and is reputedly made up of only a few hundred words (WING 1953, 176; HULSTAERT 1950, 46). That "street LINGALA" enjoys greater popularity than the "school LINGALA" can be shown by the fact that children use it as soon as they have left the school building.
LINGALA as a written language, which amongst other functions forms a basis for instruction in schools, differs considerably from the spoken language.

---

12 L. B. DE BOECK differentiates on the other hand between four dialects, as follows:
  1. spoken LINGALA *(gesproken of alledaags lingala)*,
  2. "bad" LINGALA *(slecht lingala)*,
  3. written LINGALA *(geschreven of letterkundig lingala)* and
  4. "exaggerated" LINGALA *(opgeschroefd lingala)*.
  In addition he mentions the LINGALA of the Whites as a further dialect; this stands out from all other LINGALA tongues by virtue of its own linguistic peculiarities – as, for example, the lack of distinction between open and closed e or between different pitches with a distinctive function (BOECK 1952, 117–132).

The written language can be viewed as an "invention of the Europeans" (REDDEN 1963, X), who attempted to make a "pure Bantu language" out of the incomplete pidgin language which they looked down upon. They did this by propping up its grammatical and in particular lexical substance with the languages of the lower and middle Congo. The result is that LINGALA users hardly understand the written language, even when it is spoken (op. cit. X).

*More recent developments in Kinshasa*

142 Since the fifties the linguistic situation in Kinshasa has gradually changed — not the least as a result of the demographic shiftings in the town. The number of *Bakongo*, who still in 1939 constituted less than 50% of the population of Kinshasa, rose by leaps and bounds thereafter, and in 1950 already made up 73% and occasionally overstepped the 80 per cent mark (Probleem 1953, 8).
On the one hand this development was the result of the relatively high birthrate amongst the *Bakongo* population, which from time to time exceeded 95% of the number of births in Kinshasa (WING 1953, 175/6). On the other hand it was favoured by a structural change in the labour migration in the Congo. Earlier a considerable part of the labour force in Kinshasa had come from far distant areas in the interior of the country, where the possibility of earning money scarcely existed. After these districts had been better developed and a demand for labour forces arose, the migrations to Kinshasa diminished considerably [13]. The lack of workers which came about in the capital as a result of this was off-set by a larger influx of people from the districts immediately in the neighbourhood — as a rule by the *Bakongo* (Probleem, 1953, 8/9; WING 1953, 176).

143 This new situation was of little advantage for the further development of LINGALA. By the fact that the stream of immigrants from the interior decreased the language was robbed of many supporters; for it was just the people from the interior who favoured the use of LINGALA in Kinshasa. KIKONGO, however, supported by the overwhelming majority of *Bakongo* inhabitants, could profit from this event. The Bakongo became aware of the value of their language; they were no longer ashamed to speak it in public. A certain "language nationalism" developed amongst them, and the inferiority complex towards LINGALA turned into an attitude of superiority (WING 1953, 175). A tendency could also be noticed amongst the educated

---

13 Those who continued to move to the capital were represented particularly by office workers, traders and such people who had come into conflict with the laws in their homeland and therefore desired shelter in the anonymity of the capital (WING 1953, 176).

Bakongo to promote their own mother tongue and shun the use of LINGALA.

144 But French is also becoming a competitor of LINGALA. Being taught from the first year of primary school on, it is gaining more and more importance as a result of the steadily increasing attendance at school. French is also spreading in the police force and amongst the soldiers and thereby penetrates into a domain of LINGALA (WING 1953, 177).

145 If the importance and prestige of LINGALA in Kinshasa has been reduced as a result of this, it has nevertheless not lost its function as a lingua franca. The new development in Kinshasa hardly seems to have had affected the situation in the interior of the country — in some districts LINGALA could even extend its influence.

## III. Eastern Africa

### a) SWAHILI

146 The name of the language occurs in various spellings, such as *Suaheli, Suahili* or *Swahili*. The stem of this word often appears in conjunction with the prefix *ki-*, which in this case means 'language'. *Kisuaheli, Kisuahili* or *Kiswahili,* therefore signify the 'Swahili language'. Whereas in German literature the spelling of Suaheli or Kisuaheli is preponderantly used, the French and British prefer Swahili, which is adopted in our present work as it most closely approaches the phonetic notation (swa'hili). This designation is derived from the Arabic word *sahil*, plural *swahil*, meaning 'coast' (REUSCH 1953, 21). *Kiswahili* therefore originally applied to 'coastal language'.

147 SWAHILI is divided into a large number of dialects. The written language has been based on UNGUJA, the dialect of Zanzibar, which thereby gained special significance. SWAHILI belongs to the group of *Bantu* languages, and, according to M. A. BRYAN, it is within this group closely related to the NYIKA dialects (GIRIAMA, DURUMA, etc.), which in the hinterland of the coast of Kenya are spoken to a larger extent (BRYAN 1959, 126–9).

*The development into a lingua franca*

148 In the development of SWAHILI, the three following stages in particular can be differentiated:
1. the spread along the coast;
2. its penetration into the interior of the continent;
3. development since the arrival of the colonial powers.

Map 3. *Eastern Africa*

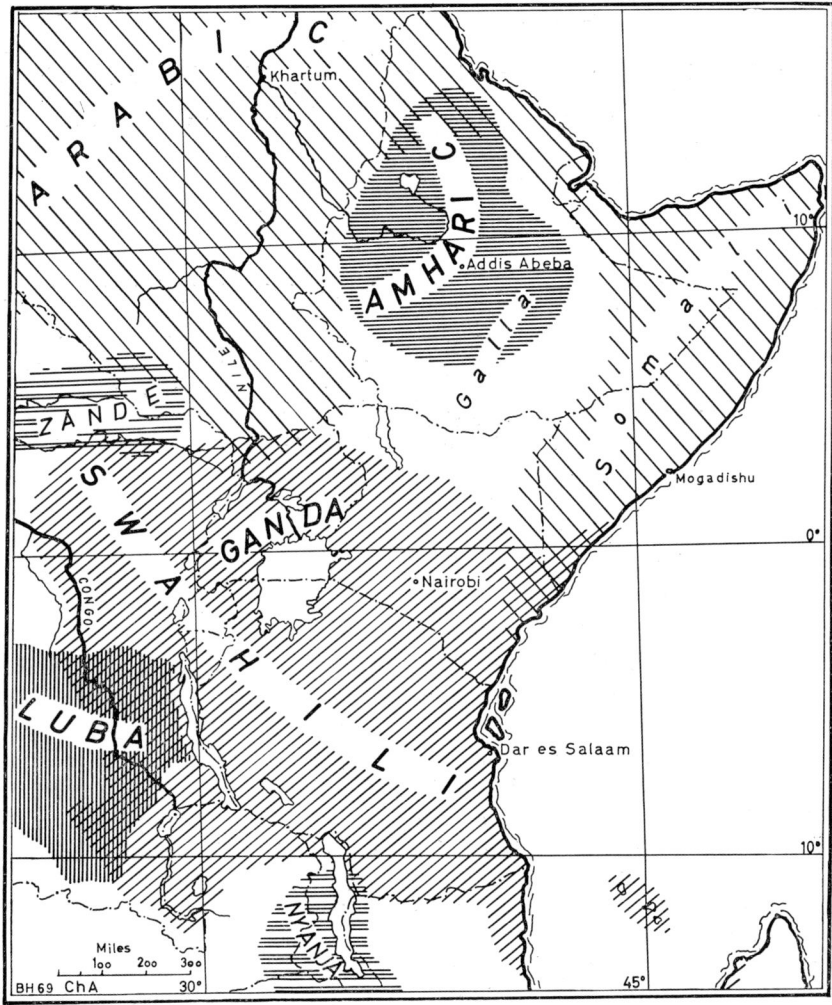

*Note:* The hatchings indicate the distribution of the different lingua francas.
*Source:* Author.

*Spread along the coast*

149 On the "origin" of SWAHILI, various opinions have repeatedly been voiced, which can be summarized as follows:
a) SWAHILI originated from a "mixture" of Arabic with one of the *Bantu* languages. F. JOHNSON, who has described the development of SWAHILI in the following way, for instance, represents this hypothesis:

"The Arabian immigrants of Lamu married Bantu women. Already they themselves adopted a number of Bantu words, forced to do this by their everyday life with their wives and by their trade with the natives. Their wives, on the other hand, learned from them a number of Arabic words. Their children, half-Arabs and half-Bantu, learned from their mothers Ki-Bantu and from their fathers Arabic, mixing both languages in the same way as their blood was mixed. With every new generation this process continued, until finally the present Kiswahili has grown up as a new language" (JOHNSON 1930, 24; quoted from REUSCH 1953, 22).

150 b) Other authors also base their studies on a "mixture" of the language, but maintain that not only one, but several *Bantu* dialects took part in it. Accordingly, for instance, BROOMFIELD notes:

"The Arabs lived in close touch with the natives, and they had numberless slaves. These African dependents of the Arabs were drawn from all the tribes with which the Arabs came into contact, and they spoke a variety of Bantu dialects. This was the origin of the 'Swahili' people, and among them the 'Swahili' language came into being. The Arab settlers, the children of their African wives, their African dependants and friends (representing a variety of Bantu tribes and dialects) evolved a common language to which both Bantu and Arabic contributed" (BROOMFIELD 1931, 80).

151 c) Pursuant to a further hypothesis, the immigrants from South Arabia and from the Persian Gulf adopted the language of the autochthonic population on the East African coast and enriched it with a number of new words and sentences. For this reason, a linguistic influence was exerted and no "mixture of language" occurred (KRUMM 1932, 19).

A linguistic examination proves that the latter hypothesis presumably most closely matches the historical reality. Although SWAHILI possesses a considerable number of borrowed words, most of them stemming from ARABIC, preponderantly cultured words are involved, whereas the basic vocabulary shows only few borrowings. Also in its grammatical structure, SWAHILI has been influenced only to a minute degree. The application of the comparative method indicates that on the basis of its regular phoneme and morpheme equivalents the language unequivocally proves itself to be a *Bantu* language, and that there exists no justification for calling it a "mixed language"[1].

152 The question as to where SWAHILI was first spoken, is not yet clarified with any degree of exactitude. Whereas F. JOHNSON and B. KRUMM assume that this language was first spoken in the area of the Lamu islands (JOHNSON 1930, 24; KRUMM 1932, 19), R. REUSCH represents the view that it originated between A.D. 700 and 800 simultaneously in various coastal places between Mombasa and Mogadishu (REUSCH 1953, 24).

153 Most likely, SWAHILI was first spoken in the area of the Tana River delta. Thus Bernhard STRUCK notes:

---

1 With the same justification, for instance, English could be designated as a "mixed language".

"... from the traditions, at least of the central and southern coastlines, we know that here in purely historical times former populations, who were foreigners to the language, adopted Suaheli, and for linguistic reasons we must presume the area of origin of Suaheli to be much further to the north, round about the region of the Tana River estuary ..." *

Amongst this population which now spoke Suaheli he counts the *wa-shomvi*, reported to have lived between Bagamoyo and Kilwa (REUSCH 1953, 20); the *wa-shupanga*, whose home country was Sadani, to the north; and the *wa-hadimu* living on the island of Zanzibar (STRUCK 1921, 178). According to the opinion of other authors, however, it is said that originally the *wa-shomvi* were *Swahili* (cf. REUSCH 1953, 20/1).

154 The development of SWAHILI into a lingua franca is presumed to have taken place as follows: during the second half of the post-Christian millenium there lived an African population on the East African coast to the north and south of the Tana River estuary, which spoke a former development form of SWAHILI. The brisk trade plying on the Indian Ocean at that time, brought a number of Arabs and Persians to the coast of East Africa, presumably at first into SWAHILI-speaking territory. They intermixed with the autochthonic population and adopted their language. By their continual expansion to the south, SWAHILI became the predominant language on the East African coast. It became the linguistic form of expression of a newly-created culture, which, emanating from the fusion of African, Arabian and Persian elements, was kept together by the common religion, the Islamic faith.

155 A special importance was attained by Swahili as a lingua franca of the Zenj Empire. In 975, Ali Ben Sultan al Hassan Ben Ali, son of a sultan in Shiraz and a female African slave, left his Persian home and sailed for East Africa. In exchange for a few bales of textiles he acquired the island of Kilwa, which soon became the blossoming imperial centre of the Zenj Empire[2]. When the Arabic traveller Ibn Battuta visited Kilwa in 1332, he met with native poets, who wrote lyric and epic poems in the SWAHILI language (BERTAUX 1966, 110/1). As the Zenj Empire governed the town of Sofala and its trade in gold since the beginning of the 12th Century, SWAHILI spread along the coast down to south of the Zambezi River. When, towards the end of the 15th Century, the Portuguese reached East Africa, SWAHILI

---

\* "... wir wissen aus den Traditionen zum mindesten von der mittleren und der südlichen Küstenstrecke, daß hier sprachfremde Vorbevölkerungen in rein historischer Zeit erst suahelisiert worden sind, und müssen aus sprachwissenschaftlichen Gründen das Ausgangsgebiet des Suaheli viel weiter nördlich um die Gegend der Tana-Mündung, vermuten ..." (STRUCK 1921, 178).

2 The designation Zenj (also spelt *Zendj*, *Zeng* or *Zindj*), which means as much as 'Country of Black', was already mentioned by Ptolemy during the 2nd Century (WESTERMANN 1952, 360).

was spoken in the coastal area between Sofala and Mogadishu (REUSCH 1953, 25/6).

*Penetration into the interior of the continent*

156 As a considerable number of merchants and seafarers crossing the western Indian Ocean in all directions were to be found among the SWAHILI-speaking population, the distribution of the language did not remain restricted for any length of time to the East African coast. Thus, Swahili colonies were established on the Comoro islands, on the north-western coast of Madagascar as well as on the southern tip of Arabia.

157 Although already at a very early date journeys were undertaken from the coast into the interior of Africa, it took centuries until SWAHILI found a foothold. The decisive breakthrough occurred only during the 19th Century. During their trading and slave-hunting journeys, which led them into the Central African lake district and the Congo, the Arabs did not use their own language, but SWAHILI, which became the predominant lingua franca along the caravan routes and at the trading posts. The spread of SWAHILI was allegedly made the easier because it took place in an area in which *Bantu* languages were almost exclusively spoken, and common characteristics with SWAHILI in structure and vocabulary could be observed (MEYER 1944, 259; LUKAS 1942, 18) [3].

158 The spread of SWAHILI followed three different directions corresponding to the major flow of traffic, i.e. along a southern, a central and a northern route (STRUCK 1921, 178; REUSCH 1953, 26).

159 The s o u t h e r n route had its point of departure at Kilwa and led via Liwale and Songea to Lake Nyasa. SWAHILI spread in particular amongst the *Ngoni,* who live near Lake Nyasa. These people transacted a lively trade with the coast, exchanging ivory and slaves, the booty carried off from countless campaigns, for textiles, powder and other wares (STRUCK 1921, 184).

160 The c e n t r a l route led from the town Bagamoyo, which lay opposite the island of Zanzibar, as far as Lake Tanganyika and into the upper Congo area. In 1830 Arab traders settled in Tabora [4], and ten years later in Ujiji on Lake Tanganyika. In 1850 they established the trading post Uvira on

---

3 In this connection, Emmi KÄHLER-MEYER notes: "Anyone having once occupied himself with the study of these languages will know that no difficulties will crop up in learning a second language once full command has been attained of the first one." ("Wer sich einmal mit diesen Sprachen beschäftigt hat, weiß, daß es keinerlei Schwierigkeiten bereitet, eine zweite solche Sprache zu erlernen, nachdem die erste einmal erfaßt worden ist" [MEYER 1944, 259].)

4 The town of Tabora was built on the foundations of an old settlement by the name of Kazikazi or Kazeh. It became the seat of a governor appointed by the sultan in Zanzibar (WESTERMANN 1952, 367).

the northern edge of the lake and after another ten years Nyangwe on the Lualaba River. At the same time they advanced in the south towards Katanga (LECOSTE 1954, 391).

As a result of this a narrow belt of SWAHILI-speaking areas originated between the Indian Ocean and the Central African Lakes. The language gained a large foothold in the area of the *Nyamwezi*, i.e. the area under influence of the trading centre Tabora.

161 The n o r t h e r n route ran from Pangani on the Indian Ocean via Usambara to the Kilimanjaro-massif and beyond that as far as the eastern bank of Lake Victoria. Bernhard STRUCK adds in this connection:

"The old caravans which, on the so-called Massai-routes, reached the eastern bank of Lake Victoria after the fifties, and even the southern end of Lake Rudolf at the end of the seventies, have always been composed entirely differently as compared to the steady and on the whole peaceful coming and going along the southern routes. In order to counter the inevitable menaces, robberies and attacks on the part of the tribes of the Masai and 'Masai apes'[5], who were tried fighters haughtily unmannered, the caravans were several hundred men strong, armed to the teeth, and organised into strictly military expeditions, which only left the coast at long intervals because of the danger; at no point in the deep interior could this lead to fixed settlements of the coastal people, and only at a late date were bases set up near the coast, at Taveta and Kiswani, for instance. Under these conditions and despite their great territorial expansion, contact of traffic and language was not very strong, and the users of Suaheli were only tolerated and for racial reasons as well as their modest fighting abilities treated as despised foreigners; it is significant that it was not the people of the steppes but the caravans travellers who had to learn the necessary elements of the people of the steppes but the caravans travellers who had to learn the necessary elements of the language of the 'Waschensi'[6]. Thus the *Masai* language was, apart from SWAHILI, the most important language in East Africa."*

---

5 The "Masai apes" were *Bantu*-speaking tribes, who, out of admiration of the success of the *Masai* in war, decided to imitate their way of life (author's note).

6 "Waschensi" (spelt *washenzi* according to Swahili orthography) means 'uncivilised people, barbarians' and is a pejorative designation of the *Swahili* people at the coast for the inland tribes, and includes the Masai, amongst others (author's note).

* "Die alten Karawanen, die auf den sog. Massairouten seit den 50er Jahren das Ostufer des Victoriasees, seit Ende der 70er Jahre selbst das Südende des Rudolfsees erreichten, sind von dem steten und im ganzen friedlichen Hin und Her auf den südlicheren Linien durchaus verschieden gewesen. Gegen die unausbleiblichen Bedrohungen, Räubereien und Überfälle seitens der hochfahrend auftretenden und kampfgewohnten Stämme der Massai und 'Massai-Affen'[5] waren sie zu viele hundert Mann starken, vollständig bewaffneten und straff militärisch organisierten Zügen zusammengeschlossen, die daher nur in großen Zeitabständen die Küste verließen, übrigens im fernen Innern nirgends zu festen Ansiedlungen von Küstenleuten führen konnten und näher der Küste erst spät z. B. in Taveta und Kiswani solche Stützpunkte fanden. Für diese Zustände, bei denen Verkehr und Sprachberührung, ungeachtet ihrer weiten räumlichen Ausdehnung, nur wenig intensiv sein konnten und die Träger des Suaheli nur geduldete,

This situation, however, changed completely when the rinderpest in 1890/91 annihilated two-thirds of the *Masai* population, whose economy up till today depends on cattle-breeding. New possibilities were opened up for SWAHILI as a result of this.

In the north-west SWAHILI made its way to the kingdom of Buganda, where thanks to the influence of the Arabs between 1860 and 1890 it became notably widespread and was even able to take over as court language (STRUCK 1921, 190). Later, however, it lost much of its importance.

162 Although the epoch of Arab slave-hunters and ivory-traders led to a considerable spread of SWAHILI in the interior, there were still large areas in East Africa where the language could find no entry. SWAHILI-speaking enclaves formed themselves only in the trading centres and in countries which had ties with the coast, whereas SWAHILI remained unknown in the areas lying in between them right up to the beginning of the 20th Century.

*NGWANA in the Congo*

163 In view of the distance between the coast and the centres in the interior where SWAHILI was gaining influence, as well as the lack of intercourse, language forms diverging from the coastal dialects arose in the inland territory, among which NGWANA *(Kingwana)* attained particular importance.

After the penetration into the eastern Congo of the Arabs and *Swahili* traders, a new stratum of population arose there, formed from the descendants of freed slaves[7] and the native inhabitants who had been converted to the Islamic faith. It called itself the *wa-ngwana (wa-ungwana)*, i.e. 'free people' and thereby opposed itself to the *wa-sengi*, meaning 'savages' (LECOSTE 1954, 391). They spread in the area between Lake Tanganyika and the Lualuba River from Kisangani (once Stanleyville) in the north as far as Katanga in the south (LUKAS 1942, 18)[8]. Referring to the *wa-ngwana*, Beaudoin LECOSTE notes:

"Just like their fellow believers on the eastern coast they adhere to the Chafélite rites of the Mohammedan Sumnite sect; the Bantu beliefs mixed with Arab mythology, however, play a great role. Their funeral, matrimonial

---

rassenmäßig und ihren bescheidenen kriegerischen Fähigkeiten entsprechend verachtete Fremdlinge waren, ist es bezeichnend, daß nicht die Steppenvölker Suaheli, sondern die Karawanenleute das Notwendige aus den Sprachen der 'Waschensi'[6] lernen mußten... (STRUCK 1921, 186/7). So war die *Masai*-Sprache lange Zeit abgesehen vom SWAHILI die wichtigste Sprache in Ostafrika."

7 Lyndon HARRIES doubts that former slaves were here involved (HARRIES 1955, 13).

8 According to G. HULSTAERT the soldiers, natives of Zanzibar, who reached the Congo under Herny Morton STANLEY, had a large part in this development (HULSTAERT 1950, 44).

and other customs form an imbroglio of Mohammedan practices and local habits; their jurisdiction is a kind of adapted law in which the sayings of the Koran exist alongside the customary rules of the country."*

164 The language of the *wa-ngwana*, NGWANA, is a SWAHILI dialect based on the Zanzibar tongue, but which was influenced by the different languages found in the Congo — in particular the languages of the *Luba* and *Mongo* group (LECOSTE 1954, 391; LIESENBORGHS 1942, 92/3).

The designation "Ngwana" is frequently defined in various ways by the various authors who have made a study of this dialect. The reason for this is presumably that in the eastern Congo several tongues derived from SWAHILI can be found between the designation of which no uniform differentiation is made by the local population (cf. HARRIES 1955, 13). Thus divergences can be found, for instance, in the usage of NGWANA, depending on whether it is spoken as a mother tongue or second language (LIESENBORGHS 1942, 93). LECOSTE gives his view as follows:

"The kiNgwana reveals two aspects: within the population which came under Arab influence it is very similar to kiUngudya[9]; used as lingua franca, it is less stable, varies according to the region and has a tendency to change till it becomes a sabir, the further one moves away from Mohammedan centres... This population, which desires to elevate themselves to the level of their fellow believers on the coast, seeks to attain purism, especially so in phonetics. But in their relations with the masses, they become less rigorous, but guard against falling into vulgarity."*

Up to the present there is no generally acknowledged standardised form of NGWANA. Lyndon HARRIES notes in this connection, that "... resulting translations embodied local provincialisms and faithfully reproduced grammatical errors and peculiarities of vocabulary as spoken by the people in the translators' vicinity" (HARRIES 1955, 13).

---

\* "De même que leurs coreligionnaires de la côte orientale ils appartiennent au rite Chaféite de la secte Musulmane Sumnite, mais les croyances bantoues mêlées de mythologie Arabe jouent un rôle considérable. Leurs coutumes funéraires, matrimoniales et autres, forment un imbroglio de pratiques mahométanes et d'usages locaux; leur justice est une espèce de droit adat où les prescriptions du Koran voisinent avec les règles coutumières du pays" (LECOSTE 1954, 391).

9 UNGUJA *(ki-unguja)* is the designation for the SWAHILI dialect spoken in Zanzibar (see par. 147).

\* "Le kiNgwana revêt deux aspects: chez les purs arabisés il reste assez proche du kiUngudya; utilisé comme langue véhiculaire, il est beaucoup moins stable, varie selon la région et tend à s'altérer jusqu'à devenir un sabir, à mesure que l'on s'éloigne des centres musulmans... Nos arabisés, aspirant à se hausser au niveau de leurs coreligionnaires de la côte, visent au purisme, specialement en matière phonétique. Mais, dans leurs relations avec la masse, ils se départissent de leur rigueur tout en se gardant de tomber dans la vulgarité" (LECOSTE 1954, 392).

## Development in Katanga

165 At the beginning of the 20th Century Katanga was still an economically poor country, populated by scarcely more than 4,000 people. The territory was travelled in by Arab traders, who exchanged ivory and copper for textiles and pearls. In their train went various groups of the *Sumbwa* from Unyamwezi, situated in the western part of the present-day Tanzania, which reached Katanga. Their tribal chief Msiri (Ngelengwa) built himself a new residence in Bukenya, a village north of Jadotville; this soon became an important centre of slave and copper trade with an ethnically and linguistically mixed population. In this area SWAHILI found favourable conditions of spreading as a lingua franca. The *Swahili* people having immigrated from the East African coast, found themselves in a privileged position under Msiri, who spoke SWAHILI himself in his contact with foreigners.

166 With the establishment of the *Union Minière du Haut Katanga* in 1906, a new period of development began. The mines of Katanga sparked off an interest which drew labourers from partly very distant regions. Among these the *Luba* people can be named in particular. Originating in the Kasai River area, they had at an early stage come under the influence of the Christian mission and as a rule had at their disposal a better school and vocational education than the rest of the groups within the population. By means of this they captured the most-coveted positions as office-workers, teachers, or artisans, and thus the middle class was formed in the majority by the *Luba*.

But also the spread of SWAHILI owes much to the *Luba*. They became the most zealous learners of this language, and played a great part in the formation of a new dialect form of SWAHILI, usually designated as K a t a n g a - SWAHILI.

The more recent position of SWAHILI in Katanga can be summarized as follows according to E. POLOMÉ:

At home, i.e. within the family circle, the use of the vernacular languages is still much in vogue. This, however, does not apply to families in which the spouses stem from different ethnic groups. Amongst the younger generation, however, can be detected an ever-growing tendency of giving up the use of the vernacular language and of adopting SWAHILI as first language. Even amongst youths belonging to the same tribe, SWAHILI is the predominant medium of communication. In the Katanga-SWAHILI, therefore, a process of C r e o l i s a t i o n has cropped up (POLOMÉ 1967).

Similar observations were made by Maria LEBLANC in Katanga in 1955. She ascertained that schoolchildren in 92% of the cases observed spoke amongst themselves in SWAHILI, and even brothers and sisters converse with each other in the lingua franca in between 63% and 88% of the cases. 23% of the children stated that they talked with their parents in SWAHILI, and only amongst the spouses themselves SWAHILI is of but modest importance: the portion of parents employing SWAHILI as language medium, is stated to amount to 3%. The process of S w a h i l i z a t i o n which can be observed in Katanga, has been characterized by LEBLANC as follows:

> "A newcomer (1) at first only knows his tribal language; then (2) he makes an effort to speak Swahili, and while maintaining relations with his racial brothers will still use his tribal language or combine the two. The second generation (3) born at the camp can no longer speak the tribal language but can understand it. We can even suppose that a member of the third generation (4) can no longer understand his tribal language and speaks Swahili exclusively while orientating himself to French." *

*Development since the arrival of the colonial powers*

167 In the second half of the 19th Century the Europeans took possession of the territory in which SWAHILI was in use. In the west, King Leopold II of Belgium, a clever businessman, founded an immense empire. During this enterprise, great services were rendered to him by the famous explorer STANLEY, who also was appointed first governor of the Congo Free State.

168 The Arab slave-traders resisted the foundation of the Congo Free State and were thereupon decisively beaten by Belgian troops. The *Swahili* people, who at that time happened be in the Congo, were not allowed to return to their homelands on the coast. They settled there, married women from the autochthonic tribes and predominantly pursued trade (HARRIES 1955, 12). The spread and importance of SWAHILI in the Congo was promoted by them to no inconsiderable degree.

The Belgian administrative officials became the successors of the Arabs in the further spread of SWAHILI (JONGHE 1933, 520). In the *Province Orientale* and in the Katanga area the soldiers were instructed in this language before World War I[10], and every effort was made to introduce SWAHILI as the educational language in the entire Congo (cf. KERKEN 1944, 265).

169 From the east coast of Africa Germans and British penetrated into the interior and took possession of the territory between the Indian Ocean and the Great Lakes (WHITELEY 1956, 343). In 1894/5, after the attempt had failed — with the exception of instruction in arithmetic — to carry out

---

\* "Un nouvel arrivé (1) ne connaît d'abord que sa langue tribale; dans la suite (2) il fait un effort vers le swahili et, gardant des relations avec des frères de race, emploiera encore la langue tribale ou combinera les deux. La deuxième génération (3) née au camp ne parlera plus la langue tribale tout en la comprenant. Nous pouvons même envisager que l'enfant de la troisième génération (4) ne comprendra plus sa langue tribale, fera un usage exclusif du swahili, et s'orientera vers le français ..." (LEBLANC 1955, 798).

10 Later on, amongst the armed forces, SWAHILI was replaced by LINGALA, the lingua franca of the northern Congo.

school teaching in German in the newly founded government schools of the then German East Africa, the administration once more turned to systematically promoting the use of SWAHILI in government administration, army and postal services as well as in other fields (STRUCK 1921, 168/9; WHITELEY 1956, 344; WRIGHT 1965).
This decision was made all the easier because already a number of SWAHILI-speaking Europeans was present. Even beforehand, the first white travellers had acquired a good knowledge of the language.
"Already at that time, it was a matter of course for the Europeans in Zanzibar and on the coast to speak Suaheli. And even if it was said that the actual speaking of the language was a little more halting than the jargon of the Indian traders finding themselves in the same situation, it deserves all the more mention that just as they did in contact with the Arabs, the Persians and Negros, the Europeans of different nationalities amongst themselves transacted their business in the Suaheli language." *

170 Whereas for a long time SWAHILI was written with Arabic letters, a change gradually took place around the turn of the century. The new orthography based on the Latin alphabet slowly gained the upper hand, and, in 1907, the German administration made Arabic spelling in all official papers as well as all documents under public law invalid (STRUCK 1921, 174)[11].

171 Especially through the increasing development of the interior, the spread of SWAHILI was considerably advanced. If during the period of Arab trade in the interior, a knowledge of it was chiefly restricted to the trading posts, such as Tabora, Mwanza, Ujiji which sprang up like islands along the caravan routes (see par. 160), the improved transport conditions led to the establishment of new centres, which became the meeting place of members of various tribes and languages. STRUCK additionally notes:

"The labour force, which had been hired from the interior for railway construction or for plantations, picked up some Suaheli expressions and during their service period in contact with the white overseers and the other coloured personnel learnt increasingly more of the language. Deeper in the interior, the assembly of great

---

\* "Suaheli zu sprechen war schon damals für die Europäer in Sansibar und an der Küste eine Selbstverständlichkeit, und wenn das tatsächliche Sprechen oft noch gebrechlicher gewesen sein soll als der Jargon der ja in gleicher Lage sich findenden indischen Händler, so verdient es um so mehr Erwähnung, daß wie mit diesen und den Arabern, Persern und Negern, und wie alle diese untereinander, die Europäer verschiedener Nationen auch unter sich ihre Geschäfte auf Suaheli abwickelten" (STRUCK 1921, 166/7).

11 Bernhard STRUCK mentions the reasons for this in that "for the East Africans who felt that the Islamic cultural superiority was much closer to them than the European one, ... the most essential stimulant towards learning European languages was missing", and that "on the part of the Europeans the acquisition of a Suaheli vocabulary sufficient for communication was always felt to be so easy ..." that they preferred communicating with the African population in SWAHILI (STRUCK 1921, 169).

numbers of natives especially during road building and bridge construction formed a strong opportunity for the spread of Suaheli, all the more so under the practical and social influence of the still necessary collaboration of the artisans from the coast." *

172 The Christian missions were of large importance in the further spreading of SWAHILI; they built a network of stations and schools throughout entire Africa. Most of all, they can take the credit for having created an extensive literature in this language, which included the translation of works of a religious nature as well as grammatical descriptions of the language.

At the beginning, however, there was no lack of opponents of SWAHILI amongst the missionaries. The close tie between this language and the spreading of the Islamic faith was stressed by them, and they saw the furtherance of SWAHILI as coincidental with a furtherance of the Islamic influence (cf. STRUCK 1921, 171).

Despite this, there was a growing opinion that the advance of the Mohammedans in East Africa could be halted just because SWAHILI was used within the Christian mission and one strived with increasing success to take away from SWAHILI the nimbus of an Islamic language.

173 In the Congo a difference of opinion arose between the two large Christian denominations as to which form of SWAHILI should be taken as a basis there. While the Catholic mission decided on the use of the s t a n d a r d SWAHILI, based on the Zanzibar dialect, the Protestants were of the opinion that, as the NGWANA, which had spread in the Congo, had already diverged so far from the standard form, it was right to treat this form as a language of its own and to make it the basis of instruction in the eastern Congo (HARRIES 1955, 13). Pursuant to the present stage of research it must appear doubtful whether the opinion of J. LUKAS and L. HARRIES is correct that standard Swahili in the Congo is making headway in comparison with NGWANA (LUKAS 1942, 18; HARRIES 1955, 14).

*Resistance to the spread of SWAHILI*

174 During the course of its history of development and growth SWAHILI has had to suffer in part from considerable setbacks. This, in one way, was caused by SWAHILI having been the predominant lingua franca in East Africa during slave-trading times and its use having frequently been

---

\* "Die Arbeitermassen, die aus dem Innern zum Bahnbau oder für die Pflanzungen angeworben wurden, schnappten unterwegs Suahelibrocken auf und lernten während ihrer Dienstzeit im Verkehr mit den europäischen Leitern und dem farbigen Personal immer mehr von der Sprache. Weiter im Innern bildete namentlich die Vereinigung großer Eingeborenenmengen bei Wege- und Brückenbauten eine starke Gelegenheit zur Ausbreitung des Suaheli, zumal unter dem praktischen und sozialen Einfluß der noch immer benötigten Mitwirkung der Handwerker von der Küste" (STRUCK 1921, 176).

shunned by the tribesmen of the interior, since this language provoked strong memories of the hated slave-hunters, who had used SWAHILI (cf. SUTHERLIN 1962, 70).

175 As has already been mentioned (par. 172), opponents of SWAHILI were also to be found amongst the circles of the Christian missions, who in this "language of the Mohammedans" saw a danger for their missionary work (cf. SUTHERLIN 1962, 75). Thus Julius RICHTER, the missionary scientist, pointed out during the German Colonial Congress in 1905 that "Islam was victorious everywhere where languages forming its vehicle were spreading, and that any check on it would have to be started by prohibiting SWAHILI as government language"*.

Colonial officials, especially those who were home from colonial service, also repeatedly disadvised the furtherance of SWAHILI.

176 Whereas the spread of SWAHILI was generally welcomed amongst the smaller groups, it met with resistance from the larger ethnic groups. The cause of this may be found in the fact that the minor tribes, by reason of the restricted spread of their languages, recognized the necessity of an intertribal medium of communication. Amongst the large tribes however — as, for example, the *Ganda* in Uganda, the *Kikuyu, Luo, Masai, Nandi* and *Kipsigis* in Kenya (see BRYAN 1959, 128) or the *Sukuma* in Tanzania — a pronounced ethnic consciousness can frequently be observed, a consciousness paired with remarkable pride in their own language and contempt for everything foreign. Such pride was encouraged by administration and the missions which granted special rights to the languages by applying them in schools and in radio broadcast, and by using them for the publication of books and newspapers (see SUTHERLIN 1962, 69). In Tanzania, amongst the *Haya, Nyamwezi, Sukuma* and *Chaga* — particularly in the years after World War II — a tendency became evident to repress the influence of SWAHILI in favour of their own languages and English (WHITELEY 1956, 349).

177 The situation in the kingdom of Buganda north of Lake Victoria is characteristic of this development. Thanks to the influential position of the Arabs, SWAHILI could gain a certain importance there between 1860 and 1890. After the beginning of the 20th Century, however, it lost influence to an increasing measure; not the least reason for this was that the caravan route which led along the west side of Lake Victoria via Karagwe and Bagamoyo to the coast and represented an important connection between the kingdom and the SWAHILI-speaking area in the east, were hardly used any more (STRUCK 1921, 190). At the same time a "language nationalism" awoke in

---

\* daß "der Islam überall siege, wo die sein Vehikel bildenden Sprachen vordringen, und daß bei seiner Eindämmung damit zu beginnen sei, das SWAHILI als Regierungssprache auszuschalten" (STRUCK 1921, 171).

Buganda, a circumstance which the English colonial powers accommodated themselves to, making LUGANDA the language of the *Ganda* population numbering over a million people, to the official language of the kingdom (WHITELEY 1956, 345).

Nevertheless, there was no lack of attempts to increase the influence of SWAHILI in Buganda. In particular during the beginning of the twenties there were efforts to help towards official recognition of the language in the entire Protectorate of Uganda, as it was then designated. In 1927, in a memorandum[12], W. F. GOWERS, the governor of Uganda, at that time, advocated the elevation of SWAHILI to an examination language for government officials and its further use in school education (loc. cit. 345/6).

As a result, disturbances broke out in Buganda and fears were vented that a furtherance of SWAHILI would have a detrimental effect on the continued development of LUGANDA. Thus the *kabaka*[13] Daudi Chwa, inter alia, declared in 1927:

"As it has now been understood that the Protectorate Government has adopted the Ki-Swahili language as the Native 'lingua franca' to be used and recognized as the Native Official Language throughout the Uganda Protectorate, I have considered it my duty as the Head of my Native Government of Buganda to record my objection against the adoption and use of this language in Buganda Kingdom as the official language of my people ... I feel ... that it is my duty to add here in conclusion, that it is quite unnecessary to adopt the Ki-Swahili language as the Official Native Language in Buganda, and I am entirely opposed to any arrangement which would in any way facilitate the ultimate adoption of this language as the Official Native Language of the Baganda in place of, or at the expense of, their own language, since I feel convinced that such a course will assuredly bring about the loss of our tribal status and nationality among the Native tribes of Africa, of which, as Head of the Native Government and Hereditary ruler, I hold myself the natural and lawful guardian, and which I naturally guard most jealously" (loc. cit. 346).

178 Whereas SWAHILI achieved great importance in the countries of Tanzania and Kenya as the language of instruction in schools, it is taught in Uganda only in police colleges (SUTHERLIN 1962, 75). A certain success was attained by SWAHILI outside the kingdom of Buganda particularly in the northern part of Uganda (WHITELEY 1956, 347).

Connected with the adverse attitude of the *Ganda* towards SWAHILI, however, is the recognition that their language has only a relatively small distribution and that Uganda would require another language which was spoken and understood in all its districts. SWAHILI is not considered suitable for this purpose, but rather the English language. A similar attitude can also be found amongst the larger tribes of East Africa, who, although

---

12 The memorandum carries the title "The Development of KiSwahili as an Educational and Administrative Language in the Uganda Protectorate" (WHITELEY 1956, 345).
13 *Kabaka* is the title of the ruler of Buganda.

resisting the adoption of SWAHILI, nevertheless readily learn the language of the former colonial powers, which was English [14].

179 A noteworthy parallel to the development in Buganda can be drawn in the interlacustrine states of Ruanda and Burundi. They also strongly opposed the spread of SWAHILI, although their territory was reached by SWAHILI-speaking groups at a very early stage [15]. Like Buganda at the time when SWAHILI set out to conquer East Africa, they boasted of strictly organized feudal systems of rule and a certain cultural individuality. Their reticence in the face of anything foreign prevented their acceptance not only of Islam, but also their adopting the SWAHILI language following in its wake (STRUCK 1921, 181).

180 The fact that SWAHILI could establish itself also in the area of larger tribes is demonstrated by the example of the *Chaga*, living around the Kilimanjaro massif. When, after centuries of rivalry between the various chieftainships led by their chiefs, the *Chaga* had gained political unity, the question arose as to which dialect should be used by the newly elected paramount chief. Finally, the choice did not fall upon one of the *Chaga* dialects, but upon SWAHILI, which had remained unaffected by the controversies between the various chieftainships. This was to prevent the possible preference given to a certain dialect and a reawakening of the half-forgotten rivalries between the chieftainships (SUTHERLIN 1962, 74/5).

*Standardization*

181 In East Africa after World War I, a need increasing year by year for a uniform language for school instruction arose. On the basis of its large distribution, SWAHILI seemed best suited for that purpose. Thus, opportunities were looked for which would lead towards the standardization of the language and bring its further development under control. In 1925, the governor of Tanganyika, as it was then called, convened a conference in Dar es Salaam, in order to examine this question. The result was the establishment of the *Central Publishing Committee,* with the avowed task of registering all profane schoolbooks published in SWAHILI. The committee's efforts were not to be restricted to Tanganyika, but should embrace entire East Africa (WHITELEY 1956, 345; WHITELEY 1957, 242). Two years later the attempt

---

14 The reason for this can presumably be found not only in the fact that the knowledge of English entailed greater prestige and better earning possibilities. It much rather seems that the advance of SWAHILI is looked upon as a menace to tribal unity — a fear which in the case of English appears to be far less pronounced.

15 Bujumbura (formerly Usumbura), the capital of Burundi, was already in the 19th Century an important trading settlement of SWAHILI-speaking Arabs and Africans (cf. WHITELEY 1956, 343).

was made in Kenya to introduce a standardized form of SWAHILI, and in 1928 an interterritorial conference was held in Mombasa, in which Carl MEINHOF, the German africanist, participated as linguistic advisor. All governments represented at the conference were in agreement on the necessity of close cooperation in the creation of new dictionaries, grammar and schoolbooks (WHITELEY 1956, 345).

182 On 1st January, 1930, the *Inter-Territorial Language (Swahili) Committee*[16] was established, the aim of which was the standardization and development of SWAHILI. After protracted indecision as to which of the SWAHILI dialects should be made the basis of a uniform written language, this problem was finally settled in favour of the Zanzibar dialect. Since the forties of the 19th Century, the Mombasa dialect (Mvita) — not the least on account of the work of KRAPF and REBMANN — had gained a predominant position, which later on was contested by the Zanzibar dialect (Unguja) (WHITELEY 1957, 243). All other dialects could not expect any further recognition.

183 In the years after the establishment of the *Swahili Committee* copious literature came onto the market, ranging from scientific description to reading matter for school lessons. Part of the task of the *Swahili Committee* was devoted to the problem of linguistic borrowing. In order to satisfy requirements of modern times, SWAHILI had to absorb a large number of new conceptual terminology. Differences of opinion thereby arose as to how this should be accomplished. Whereas, for instance Karl ROEHL objected to the adoption of borrowed words from foreign languages — more particularly from Arabic — other authors represent opposing views (WHITELEY 1957, 246).

184 In 1948 the *East African Literature Bureau* was founded, which independent of the *Swahili Committee* gave itself the task of publishing books in SWAHILI, and thereby gained a certain importance. Thereupon, the *Swahili Committee* concentrated more upon research and questions of orthography. This tendency was strengthened by the fact that in 1952 it transferred its headquarters to the Makerere College, Kampala (Uganda).

*More recent developments*

185 In spite of the close economic and political ties existing more particularly since the twenties of this century between the East African territories of Tanganyika, Kenya and Uganda – mainly conditioned by the presence of joint colonial power — the development of SWAHILI in accordance with the policy of education and language of the territory in question proceeded in diverse ways.

---

16 This organization, which in 1948 was given the more explicit name *East African Inter-Territorial Language (Swahili) Committee,* is often cited under the abbreviated style of *"Swahili Committee"*.

186 After the attempts in Uganda in the twenties to elevate SWAHILI to the position of official language in school instruction and administration had failed, this language was hardly able to make any noteworthy progress there. The language policy of the country was directed towards promoting the vernacular languages and to clear the way for English as lingua franca. In this programme, SWAHILI remained out of consideration. Nevertheless, it was able to maintain a modest position as lingua franca in some fields. Its usage is not only more widespread in the northern province of Uganda, but also in the police force. In particular, it is spoken in the urban centres such as Jinja and Kampala by members of various tribes, mainly, however, by immigrants from Ruanda and Kenya (WHITELEY 1962, 183).

187 In Tanzania, SWAHILI could not only retain the importance it had during the time of the German administration, but could even enlarge it considerably. It is the only African language which is employed in education. It is used in primary and higher grade schools up to the *Cambridge School Certificate* (WHITELEY 1962, 183). Moreover, it is the language used by the administration. It is the predominant language amongst politicians and trade unionists and thereby penetrates into domains reserved for a long time for English. There exists a large number of SWAHILI newspapers — Ruth E. SUTHERLIN has counted a total of 44 (SUTHERLIN 1962, 74) — and in the transmissions of Tanzania Broadcasting Corporation it occupies an eminent status.

188 The position of SWAHILI in Kenya can be rated as being approximately at a level between that occupied by SWAHILI in Uganda and Tanzania. A larger importance in education and administration was gained by SWAHILI in the forties and at the beginning of the fifties in this century (WHITELEY 1962, 183). Even today it is employed in district administration and in school instruction, more particularly in ethnically heterogenous areas. Pursuant to SUTHERLIN there exist 27 SWAHILI newspapers in Kenya SUTHERLIN 1962, 73), and in the programmes of the Voice of Kenya, SWAHILI is also one of the most important languages used. Politicians, who, during the voting campaign, are unable to use SWAHILI, have only little chance of success.

Nevertheless, serious obstacles impeded the growth of SWAHILI. The language policy of the country grants an important place to the vernacular languages. Altogether 19 vernacular languages have found employment in basic school education (SUTHERLIN 1962, 74). Thereby the resistance of the large ethnic groups such as the *Kikuyu, Kamba, Luo,* amongst others, to the lingua franca, is increased (see par. 176). English benefitted from this situation, which was similar to that in Uganda; by the mere fact that Kenya gave homes to a considerable number of British settlers, it has gained a remarkable position in comparison to Tanzania. In comparison with SWAHILI, English enjoys a far greater esteem in Kenya, and mastery of it is considered to be the *conditio sine qua non* for any social and vocational advancement (see WHITELEY 1962, 187).

WHITELEY gives another reason why a greater spread of SWAHILI in Kenya was prevented. In contrast to Tanzania, the standard form of SWAHILI, based on the Zanzibar dialect, could not establish itself in Kenya. This is because SWAHILI is split up into various dialects. Whereas in the coastal region the *Mvita* dialect predominates, in the interior pidgin forms of SWAHILI are mainly found, which essentially differ from the standard form and which are held in small esteem by the African as well as the European populations. Standard SWAHILI is to be found only in books and is in part employed in schooling (WHITELEY 1962, 186/7).

*Number of speakers and spread*

189 In 1921, STRUCK observed:

"As far as not only the German but the entire area of distribution ... M e i n h o f and I respectively, have assessed the number of Africans making themselves understood to a certain degree in Suaheli as being 2,000,000 and 1,900,000." *

Since then the number of SWAHILI-speaking people has multiplied [17]. There exist, however, important differences between the figures supplied by the various authors. Whereas, according to Ruth E. SUTHERLIN about seven million people speak SWAHILI (SUTHERLIN 1962, 70), it is used by thirty million people pursuant to M. J. TANGHE (TANGHE 1944, 180; cf. on the other hand MEYER 1944, 259). E. NATALIS gives the total number as 40 million, R. REUSCH even 44 million (NATALIS 1965, 14; REUSCH 1953, 22). It may be assumed that today approximately 20 to 25 million have mastered SWAHILI more or less well.

190 In the distribution of SWAHILI a distinction must be drawn between areas where it is employed as mother tongue and those where it constitutes the lingua franca.

Above all, SWAHILI is spoken as mother tongue in the small belt reaching from the estuary area of the Juba River in the north down to the Lurio River in the south. This belt, which is seldom wider than 10 miles, is, however, not exclusively inhabited by *Swahili* people, but also isolated islands of population speaking other languages can be found there, thus, for instance, *Digo* between Tanga and Mombasa.

SWAHILI is furthermore spoken as mother tongue on the off-shore islands,

---

\* "Für das gesamte, nicht nur deutsche, Verbreitungsgebiet ... haben M e i n h o f und ich die Zahl der sich in Suaheli einigermaßen verständigenden Afrikaner fast übereinstimmend auf 2 000 000 bzw. 1 900 000 geschätzt" (STRUCK 1921, 193).

17 Pursuant to Lyndon HARRIES it is spoken — in the Congo alone — by approximately four million people (HARRIES 1955, 12).

i.e. on the Lamu archipelago, the Bajun islands between Kisimayu and Lamu, Pemba, Zanzibar, the Mafia islands, the Kerimba islands, the Comoro islands as well as on the north west coast of Madagascar. Also in the interior of East Africa and in the eastern Congo, groups of population with SWAHILI as mother tongue can be found in particular in the trading centres. These groups frequently consist of descendants of coastal inhabitants, who during the time of the Arab expansion settled in the interior.

191 SWAHILI is spoken much more extensively as lingua franca. Pursuant to Bernard STRUCK it is employed in the south as far as Sofala in Mocambique as well as in the harbours of South Africa (STRUCK 1921, 189; cf. MEYER 1944, 259). On account of the brisk shipping traffic on the Indian Ocean it even reached Aden and Port Blair in India.

The largest area of SWAHILI-speaking people is to be found in Tanzania. The language is understood and spoken in all parts of the country, but according to the extent of its distribution important differences occur. Whereas SWAHILI is generally known, for instance, in the *Nyamwezi* area around Tabora, it is far less widespread in other districts, most of all in the area inhabited by the *Masai*. In Uganda it could hardly establish itself, not the least reason being the resistance on the part of the *Ganda* population. Speakers of SWAHILI, however, can be met in all parts of the country, particularly in the north. Likewise a knowledge of SWAHILI occurs only to a small extent in Ruanda and Burundi [18].

*Spread in western and central Kenya*

192 In Kenya, the language has also experienced a remarkable spread. Still more than in Tanzania, large areas can however exist here, too — chiefly in the north and north-east — where this language could attain but small importance. On the basis of my own investigations I was able to collect some more exact material on the rating of SWAHILI in western and central Kenya [19]. In this connection, a questionnaire was employed, containing 32 questions on the knowledge and use of languages. A total of 1,350 interviews took place in 45 different localities of Kenya. Thereby, information was gathered on 15,541 persons. Moreover, 616 children in primary school Standards VI and VII were interviewed on the basis of a similar questionnaire.

18 H. KITUMBOY, on the other hand, notes: "In Ruanda-Urundi only in Government School in Usumbura Township Swahili and French are being taught: in the rest of the schools which are run by missionaries they teach Vernacular; but outside the school Swahili is nearly everywhere spoken freely" (KITUMBOY, 1961, 65/6).
19 This material was gathered during a field research journey from August to December, 1968. I would hereby like to extend my deeply felt gratitude to the "Deutsche Forschungsgemeinschaft" (German Research Association), which generously aided this research.

193 Of the 15,541 persons investigated in this sample test, 10,141 or 65.3% spoke Swahili. On the basis of a classification according to age and sex the following percentages of SWAHILI-speaking population resulted:

*Number of users of Swahili in percentage*

| Age | Male | Female | Total |
|---|---|---|---|
| 0–19 years | 69.0% | 54.6% | 62.5% |
| 20–39 years | 84.7% | 66.7% | 76.6% |
| 40 years and over | 63.3% | 40.2% | 51.9% |
| Total | 74.1% | 54.9% | 65.3% |

According to these figures, Swahili is more widespread amongst the male population (74.1%) than under the female population (54.9%). Also in respect of age essential differences are shown in the knowledge of the language. SWAHILI has found its largest spread amongst the people between the ages of 20 and 39, the least, however, amongst persons over 40 years of age.

Differences also exist in the knowledge of SWAHILI with regard to the tribal membership of the population. In respect of the separate tribes the following percentage figures of SWAHILI speakers resulted:

| Tribe | Proportion of SWAHILI users | Tribe | Proportion of SWAHILI users |
|---|---|---|---|
| Kamba | 61.0% | Nandi | 76.9% |
| Embu | 53.3% | Kipsigis | 76.6% |
| Kikuyu | 49.2% | Tugen | 45.5% |
| Luhya | 58.0% | Keyo (Elgeyo) | 75.1% |
| Gusii | 53.4% | Marakwet | 71.8% |
| Nubi | 93.7% | Terik (Nyang'ori) | 81.7% |
| Masai | 39.1% | Sabaot (Kony, Lako | |
| Njemps (Tiamus) | 39.6% | and Sebei) | 80.4% |
| Teso | 62.0% | Pokot (Suk) | 30.6% |
| | | Luo | 57.2% |

It is surprising in this connection that SWAHILI — apart from *Nubi* — is most widespread amongst the tribes which in more recent years have become known under the designation of *Kalenjin*. More particularly the *Nandi, Kipsigis, Terik* and *Sabaot* may be mentioned in this respect. On the other hand, however, the Pokot tribe — also to be counted amongst the *Kalenjin* group — makes up the smallest proportion of SWAHILI users. Amongst the Bantu tribes, the variations are less considerable. The extreme values lie between 61.0% in respect of the *Kamba* and 49.2% with regard to the *Kikuyu*. (This, however, does not apply to the Kikuyu living in the diaspora; see below.) Remarkable – and indeed hardly expected — is the low percentage in respect of the *Kikuyu* tribe. Various reasons can be attributed to this; here only one of them shall be mentioned. The *Kikuyu* form the most numerous tribal group in Kenya. As has already been mentioned, a relationship can frequently be observed between the size of an ethnic group and its attitude towards lingua francas; the larger the tribe, the stronger the resistance to adoption of a lingua franca. This hypothesis is supported by the other above-mentioned percentage figures. Whereas for example the *Luhya,* one of the largest ethnic groups in Kenya, make up a proportion of 58% of SWAHILI users, the proportion in the case of the relatively smaller neighbouring tribes *Teso* and *Sabaot* at 62% and 80.2% are higher. In a similar way, the knowledge of Swahili seems to be considerably more widespread in the small group of *Terik* than in the case of the large neighbouring tribes *Luo, Luhya* and *Nandi.*

194 Differences in the spread of SWAHILI, however, cannot only be detected amongst the individual tribes, but also considerable variations frequently occur within the tribe itself. As a rule, the number of SWAHILI users becomes larger the further one moves away from the centre of a tribal territory and the nearer one gets to its periphery. Some examples may act as an illustration:

*Percentage of SWAHILI users*

|  | Centre of tribal area | Periphery of tribal area |
|---|---|---|
| Luo | *57.2%* | *61.7%* |
| Luhya | *58.0%* | *84.6%* |
| Njemps | *39.6%* | *54.4%* |

Similarly pronounced differences furthermore reveal themselves between the rural and urban parts of a tribal area. Thus, for instance, in Kisii Town the proportion of SWAHILI users is 20% higher (73.6%) than in rural parts of the GUSII-speaking area (53.4%), and in Narok the percentage of the SWAHILI-speaking population is even almost double (77.6%) of that of the rural *Masai* areas (39.1%).

195 Particularly significant are the contrasts between those who have left their homeland to search for work in other parts of the country, and those remaining within the tribal territory. The analysis of the interviews justifies the assumption that the labour migrations influence to a considerable degree the linguistic and sociolinguistic attitudes of the persons in question. The following comparison may serve as an example:

*Percentage of SWAHILI users*

|  | Within the tribal area | Outside the tribal area |
|---|---|---|
| Kikuyu | 49.2% | 87.4% |
| Kamba | 61.0% | 76.8% |
| Luhya | 58.0% | 79.8% |
| Luo | 57.2% | 75.8% |
| Teso | 62.0% | 88.7% |
| Sabaot | 80.4% | 87.3% |
| Nandi | 76.9% | 81.8% |
| Kipsigis | 76.6% | 81.6% |

This clearly demonstrates that the labour migrations serve as an important stimulus for the spread of SWAHILI. This can be noted especially amongst the *Kikuyu:* outside the tribal area the knowledge of SWAHILI is 38% higher than in the Central Province, the home land of the *Kikuyu*. In the case of those tribes, however, which indicate higher percentages within their home territory, the differences are less distinct. This applies in respect of the *Sabaot, Nandi* and *Kipsigis*.

196 Hitherto, only the relative distribution of SWAHILI in western and central Kenya has been considered. SWAHILI, however, is not the only lingua franca used in this territory. Pursuant to the statements made by the people interviewed a larger number of languages is spoken as second language, of which the most important can be taken from the following table:

*Second languages*

| Name of language | Spoken as second language by %[20] |
|---|---|
| Swahili | 85.4% |
| English | 27.8% |
| Luo | 4.6% |
| Kikuyu | 3.3% |
| Luhya | 3.2% |
| Gusii | 1.4% |
| Ganda | 1.3% |
| Masai | 1.0% |
| Nandi | 1.0% |

Accordingly, apart from SWAHILI, English is also of special importance, in that it overshadows all other languages. It is surprising, however, that GANDA, the lingua franca of the southern part of Uganda, is spoken by

---

[20] These statements are based on the answers of the 1,350 persons questioned — they therefore do not relate to the entire sample test, which included 15,541 persons.

some 1.3% of the people questioned as second language, although as a first language it carries no importance in Kenya.

A problem presenting itself relates to the combinations in which the foreign languages occur amongst the individuals questioned. In order to arrive at a typology of the combinations, the languages are classified according to the following categories: (a) mother tongue, (b) lingua francas and (c) languages not being lingua francas, or, v e r n a c u l a r languages, as they are called here. (b) is further subdivided into SWAHILI and English. In combining these categories with each other, eight possible types of language combinations are obtained. The frequency of the occurrence of these types is exhibited in the following table. The following abbreviations are used in this connection: M = mother tongue, V = vernacular language, S = Swahili, and E = English.

*Types of language combinations*

| Language combinations | Frequency of occurrence (by percentage) |
|---|---|
| 1. M | 13.3% |
| 2. M + one or several V | 0.6% |
| 3. M + S | 48.2% |
| 4. M + S + one or several V | 10.1% |
| 5. M + E | 0.4% |
| 6. M + E + one or several V | 0.2% |
| 7. M + E + S | 19.9% |
| 8. M + E + S + one or several V | 7.3% |
| Total | 100.0% |

The types (2), (5) and (6) occur in such small numbers that they are of no statistical importance. The predominant type, employed by almost half of all persons questioned, is (3) Mother tongue + SWAHILI. Less frequent, but comprising nevertheless one fifth of the population, is the type (7) Mother tongue + English + SWAHILI.

In summary, it may be stated: in the case of a second language being learned, this predominantly applies to SWAHILI — possibly together with one or several other languages. Only 1.2% of those who speak a second language, have no command of SWAHILI, and approximately 98% of the English-speaking population use this language as an alternative. It is therefore almost predictable that anyone who speaks English also masters SWAHILI. This language is, therefore, by far the most important linguistic medium of communication in western and central Kenya.

197 SWAHILI also attained a denser spread in the eastern Congo. The dialects in use there, however, differ considerably in part from the SWAHILI spoken at the East African coast. In the west, SWAHILI has advanced

across the Lualaba River to the Lomami River. In the north it is spoken as far as the Uele River, where it penetrated into the sphere of influence of another lingua franca, that of LINGALA (LAMAN 1928, 377). In the south it has spread in Katanga and to an increasing measure is conquering the Kasai Province. The advance mostly follows the railway line (HULSTAERT 1950, 44).

Less importance was attained by it, however, in the countries on the other side of the southern border, Zambia and Malawi, and also in Mocambique it seems to have spread only in the north and along the coast.

*Dialects*

198 A number of dialects are gathered together under the designation "SWAHILI", showing considerable differences not only in their linguistic structure but also in their sociolinguistic position. More particularly, the following dialects can be discerned [21]:

1. *Mbalazi*. It is mainly spoken by the Amarani, fishermen from the village of Brava (Barawa) in the Somali Republic. It is furthermore used in the towns of Merca, Afgoi and Mogadishu, situated further to the north (PRINS 1961, 25).
2. *Bajuni* (Bajun). BAJUNI, also called *Tikuu, Tikulu* (i.e. 'big country'), *Gunya* or *Faza Swahili*, is spoken by approximately 20.000 people along the coast between Mogadishu and Zanzibar, most likely even down to Mocambique (PRINS 1961, 26). Whereas in this large territory it is used by some widely dispersed groups, it is spread more densely in the stretch of coastline between Pate and Kisimayu.
3. *Siu* (Siyu). It is spoken in the town of Siyu on the island of Patta (Pate) and on the mainland opposite.
4. *Pate*, used on the island of Patta.
5. *Amu* [22], the language of the island Lamu. As language of poetry, AMU has achieved a certain panache.
6. *Mvita*. It is spoken in the harbour town of Mombasa and its surroundings. MVITA is one of the most important SWAHILI dialects. German missionaries, who had already arrived in the middle of the

---

21 The enumeration of the SWAHILI dialects is essentially based on the data compiled by TUCKER (1958), PRINS (1961) and BRYAN (1959). The prefix *ki-* in combination with the dialect names (*chi-* in the case of the *Mbalazi* and the *Fundi* dialects), which in this case means 'language', is uniformly left out.

22 The dialects of SIU, PATE and AMU show only minute differences. Their separate treatment is based less on linguistic criteria than on the fact that a distinction is drawn between them by the speakers themselves (BRYAN 1959, 127). To this group also belongs SHELA, which is spoken in the village of the same name in the south of the island Lamu (PRINS 1961, 26).

19th Century in the area around Mombasa, employed this dialect as the basis of religious and linguistic work (WHITELEY 1956, 344/5). As a written language MVITA carries little importance today. Through the railway connection leading from Mombasa to Uganda, MVITA has attained a certain spread as lingua franca in the area between Lake Victoria and the Kenyan coast, most of all in the focal points Voi, Kibwezi, Nairobi and Kisumu (STRUCK 1921, 190).

7. *Fundi*, spoken in the north of Vanga, in the southernmost part of Kenya.
8. *Vumba*. Distributed on the island of Wasin and in Jimbo, and additionally along the coastal strip between Shimoni and Vanga.
9. *Tanga*. It is used between Vanga in the north and the Pangani estuary in the south.
10. *Mtang'ata*, between Tanga and Pangani. It may possibly also be found in the surroundings of the village Sadani, situated further to the south (BRYAN 1959, 127).
11. *Mrima*. Its distribution embraces the entire coast of Tanzania as far as Kilwa in the south. There is little difference between it and the UNGUJA dialect.
12. *Mgao*, spoken to the north and south of Kilwa. Along the southern caravan route leading from Kilwa to Lake Nyasa (par. 159), MGAO advanced far into the interior of East Africa and is also spoken on the banks of Lake Nyasa today (PRINS 1961, 26).
13. *Phemba*, the dialect of the island Pemba with the exception of its southern tip (cf. *Tumbatu*).
14. *Tumbatu*. It has spread in the northern part of the island of Zanzibar, on the Tumbatu island and in southern Pemba.
15. *Hadimu*, used in the southern part of Zanzibar.
16. *Unguja*. Pursuant to R. REUSCH, UNGUJA is a derivation of SWAHILI, i.e. the one spoken in Kilwa, the centre of the *Zenj* Empire (REUSCH 1953, 27). It is the dialect of the town of Zanzibar and of the central area of the island of the same name. Of all SWAHILI dialects it has attained the largest spread and importance. As "standard" SWAHILI it became the language of education, administration and literature.

Three further SWAHILI dialects can be discovered on the Comoro islands (see HEEPE 1920):

17. *Ngazija*, on the island Grande Comore;
18. *Nzwani*, on the island of Anjouan (Johanna);
19. *Mwali*, on the island of Mohéli.

199  Moreover, a great number of dialects, as a rule undifferentiated by name, occurs in the East African interior. The use of SWAHILI differs from tribe to tribe, and it is therefore not unjustified to speak of the dialect of *Kikuyu*,

*Luo, Sukuma,* etc. Amongst the dialects of the interior special importance has been acquired by (20) NGWANA in the eastern Congo (par. 163/4).

200 Of these dialects some differ as a result of their special linguistic form and sociolinguistic position, i.e.:

21. *ki-Vita* ('war language'), the language of the army, which, pursuant to M. A. BRYAN, is dying out (BRYAN 1959, 128).
22. *ki-Setla* ('settler language'). This dialect is predominantly used by the Europeans in contact with their servants and farm labourers;
23. *ki-Hindi,* the SWAHILI as used by the majority of the Indian population in East Africa;
24. *ki-Shamba* ('plantation language'). It is used in large parts of the interior. The English designation of *up-country Swahili* is often applied to this form of dialect.

The dialects (21) to (24) have undergone a process of p i d g i n i z a t i o n, whereby they lost structural characteristics such as class concord which prevail in the other SWAHILI dialects.

## b) GANDA

201 GANDA *(Luganda),* the predominant language of Uganda, belongs to the group of *Bantu* languages.

The fact that this language — even though to a more modest degree — attained the status of a lingua franca, is chiefly the result of two factors. The Kingdom of Buganda came under British influence earlier than other parts of the state of Uganda. Roads and schools were built and soon there grew up amongst the *Ganda* population an increasing number of people who not only could read and write but had familiarized themselves with other achievements of European culture. From Buganda, the British extended their rule towards the west, north and east and set up their systems of administration similar to those in their Kingdom. In pursuance of this policy they frequently made use of the *Ganda* people as administration officials. GANDA thereby gained a certain importance as language of administration also beyond the former area of use — more particularly in the neighbouring territories such as Busoga, Toro or Ankole. In addition GANDA obtained an important function as language in the schools and in religious instruction (FALLERS 1960, 31). Thus, for example, Margaret Chave FALLERS reports on the development in the area of the *Soga* east of the Victoria Nile:

"As administrative and mission activity expanded from Buganda into Busoga at the end of the nineteenth century, Ganda were used, as we have seen, as assistants and as teachers, in some places as administrators. They used Luganda as the official language and taught Luganda as the written form. Today, the *Bible* is the Luganda *Bible,* the elementary school language is Luganda, and the official administrative and judicial language is Luganda, whenever English cannot be used. So for the Soga, the Lusoga dialects are the languages of the villages; the language of the press, radio and the administration is Luganda" (FALLERS 1960, 32).

Thus, in the thirties, the knowledge of GANDA was already widespread in the southern and central part of the Protectorate of Uganda, as it was called then (cf. THOMAS/SCOTT 1935, 286).

202 The labour migrations, the history of which can be traced back to early colonial times, served as a further impulse for the spread of GANDA. For road construction, public buildings and the railway, the British hired a considerable number of labourers from the district of the western Nile, amongst others, and the Kingdom of Buganda since then has become an important destination for hired labour forces from all parts of the country and neighbouring lands. The census of 1948 proved that members of 21 foreign tribes were dispersed all over Buganda, and their number in some parts of the Kingdom exceeded that of the autochthonous *Ganda* (RICHARDS 1955, 1; FALLERS 1960, 24/5). They were working chiefly on the cotton and coffee plantations.

Amongst those who had immigrated into Buganda, GANDA became widespread as a lingua franca. Thus A. W. SOUTHALL notes that mainly amongst the Nilotic *Alur*, originating in the western Nile district, a certain knowledge of GANDA had generally been acquired (SOUTHALL 1955, 156); and A. I. RICHARDS, during her investigations amongst these immigrants ascertained that the majority of them had a command of GANDA (RICHARDS 1955, 15).

203 The fact that GANDA has not acquired special importance as a lingua franca is presumably due to its having to share this function with two other languages, English and SWAHILI. The attempt by the British administration in the twenties to elevate SWAHILI to the official language in Uganda, admittedly failed on account of the determined resistance of the *Ganda* population, which in this plan perceived a danger to the status of their own language.

The sphere of influence of GANDA includes today the entire southern part of Uganda — in the north, however, it has scarcely come into use. The number of its users amounts to 1.5–2 million people [23].

204 The triumphal march of SWAHILI presumably played a decisive part in the East African area which has up to today remained relatively poor in lingua francas. It can be assumed that the spread of SWAHILI was connected with the decay of one or the other lingua franca. Thus for instance Bernhard STRUCK reports that MASAI held an important position up to the

---

23 Whereas, pursuant to M. A. BRYAN, the number of speakers in Uganda amounts to 836,091 and in Tanzania approximately 5,500 (BRYAN 1959, 109), the figures supplied by other authors are as a rule higher. J. ROBERTS estimates the total number even to be 2.5 million (ROBERTS 1962, 120).

time of the rinderpest in 1890/1, by which two-thirds of the *Masai* population was wiped out. The *Swahili* traders were not infrequently forced during their trading journeys in the interior of East Africa to use Masai as a lingua franca, since the knowledge of their own language had not sufficiently spread there (STRUCK 1921, 187).

205 KAMBA, in southern Kenya, also seems formerly to have enjoyed a certain prominence as a lingua franca. As late as in 1925, Gerhard LINDBLOM reports "that Kikamba is one of the most widely spread languages in East Africa. I would even go so far as to assert that, next Kisuaheli, the "lingua franca" of East Africa, Kikamba is the best language to know for the traveller in the parts of East Africa above referred to. It is understood and spoken by a great number of Akikuyu and Masai, the immediate neighbours of the Akamba to the west and south-west. Also among the tribes living upon and around Kilimandjaro (wataita, wataveta, wadjagga, wakahe etc.) my knowledge of the Kamba language was sometimes very useful to me ... the Akamba were the principal trading people of the interior of the present British East Africa ..." (LINDBLOM 1925 5/6).

### c) AMHARIC

206 AMHARIC belongs to the Semitic languages forming a branch of the so-called *Hamito-semitic* — according to Joseph H. GREENBERG called Afro-asiatic — family of languages.

207 The development of this language is closely tied up with the history of the North East African empire of Ethiopia. The earlier epoch of this empire is connected with the name of another language, the GE'EZ. GE'EZ – sometimes also called "Ethiopian" — was the language of a group of people which, originating in southern Arabia, emigrated to North-East Africa during the last centuries before the Christian era and founded a kingdom there (PRAETORIUS 1886, 3). GE'EZ became the language of literature — evidenced by inscriptions dating as far back as the 4th Century. Around the turn of the millenium it died out as a vernacular language, but retained further importance as the language of the Orthodox Ethiopian Church and of the savants. The classical epoch of GE'EZ as literary language falls into the period between the 13th and 17th centuries, i.e. after it had declined as language of the people already several centuries previously (ULLENDORFF 1960, 121).

208 AMHARIC became the successor to this language. It is presumably one of the "daughter" languages i.e. a later development form of GE'EZ, and even took on its alphabet — though enlarged by some letters (KLINGENHEBEN 1966, 11). The first written documents in AMHARIC date from the 14th Century and contain songs composed in honour of the kings (ULLENDORFF

1955, 16). AMHARIC spread south of the ancient metropolis of Aksum and already during the first half of our millenium embraced the provinces of Lasta, Damot and Simien (Semien). In 1681, H. LUDOLF reported that AMHARIC had spread as far south as Shoa, i.e. into the vicinity of the present capital city of Addis Ababa. It thereby was able to considerably enlarge its original area of usage in the Amhara province north of Lake Tana and with its help a medium of communication was established in the entire empire of that day (ULLENDORFF 1955, 17/8; 23).

209 During the 16th and 17th centuries AMHARIC challenged the predominant position of GE'EZ as the literary language. In his attempt to win the Christian empire of Ethiopia over to the Roman Catholic faith, the Pope then in power sent a group of Portuguese Jesuits to Africa around the middle of the 16th Century. They received a friendly reception in Ethiopia and gained many adherents amongst the local population. In 1622 they even succeeded in converting to Roman Catholicism the Ethiopian ruler Susneos (SOCINIANUS). His attempt to replace the monophysitic form of the Ethiopian Church with Roman Catholicism as state religion failed on account of the strong resistance of his subjects, and under his son and successor Basilides (FASILADES, 1632–1666) the Jesuits were expelled from the country and Roman Catholicism was prohibited (WESTERMANN 1952, 291).

During their fight against the Ethiopian Church the Jesuits did not employ the GE'EZ language, the history of which was strongly tied up with that of this church, but used AMHARIC. They made this language the medium for propaganda in order to win the favour of the people, and took it as the basis for a copious religious literature. Upon the expulsion of the Jesuits, however, GE'EZ regained its leading role as language of literature and was able to retain this status up to the middle of the 19th Century (ULLENDORFF 1960, 123/4).

210 The development of AMHARIC into the official language in Ethiopia only took place in more recent times, although as the language of the courts it had already for some years acquired an important function (ULLENDORFF 1960, 124). This development started under the rule of Theodore II (1855—1868), who carried out an administrative reform and conceived a programme for the unification of the empire in which AMHARIC was also taken into consideration (ULLENDORFF 1965, 1). The language gained in influence and in 1886 F. PRAETORIUS was able to report that AMHARIC as lingua franca was spoken far beyond the frontiers of Ethiopia (PRAETORIUS 1886, 4). Its use was extended particularly by the fact that as an official language it was spread throughout all parts of the country by the administration and school education. According to Johannes LUKAS it has furthermore "as a consequence of the wars of the Ethiopian kings expanded not only all over entire Abyssinia but also beyond that to the places wherever

it was carried by the Amharic arms; it spread particularly under the warlike Menelik II."*

Since the end of the Second World War AMHARIC has in increasing measure been penetrating into the domain of the church, which so far was reserved to GE'EZ. Thus Sylvia PANKHURST reports that a tendency exists in Ethiopia to conduct religious service in AMHARIC, and to employ Amharic even for the sermon, the ritual for which so far GE'EZ was used (PANKHURST 1955, 283).

211  The spread of AMHARIC has not been concluded even today. Edward ULLENDORFF, one of the foremost experts on this language, notes:

"As Amharic is the only recognized language of the Ethiopian Empire, it is not only essential for all official purposes, but the distribution of Amharic speaking administrative officials throughout the country affords it considerable prestige — not rarely supported by a moderate degree of compulsion. How far the present Ethiopian Government has succeeded in its policy of encouraging Amharic at the expense of other languages, is not at present easy to gauge, but there can be little doubt that Amharic is slowly gaining ground" (ULLENDORFF 1955, 24).

AMHARIC is spoken today almost within entire Ethiopia. No records are available on the exact extent of its application as lingua franca. As mother tongue it is spoken mainly on the plateau between Addis Ababa in the south up to the Angareb River north of Lake Tana. The total number of its speakers may be taken to be approximately five million [24]. In spite of the large size of the area where it is in use AMHARIC shows only slight differences in its dialects. In this connection August KLINGENHEBEN writes: "More apparent than the differences of dialect are the differences of language of the educated — more or less influenced by Geez — and the vernacular language of the people."**

---

\* "infolge der Kriege der äthiopischen Könige nicht nur über ganz Abessinien, sondern darüber hinaus auch noch bis dorthin ausgebreitet, wohin es die amharischen Waffen trugen, dehnte sich daher besonders unter dem kriegerischen Menelik II. aus" (LUKAS 1942, 20).

24  In this connection, ULLENDORFF wrote in 1966: "It is very difficult to give a reliable estimate of the number of Amharic speakers ... The best estimates range between 3–5 millions" (ULLENDORFF 1955, 23). Ten years later, however, he presumes that "they may now range between five and ten millions" (ULLENDORFF 1965, 11).

\*\* "Auffälliger als dialektische sind oft Unterschiede der mehr oder weniger vom Geez beeinflußten Sprache der Gebildeten und der Umgangssprache des Volkes" (KLINGENHEBEN 1966, 11).

# IV. Central Sudan and North Africa

## a) ZANDE

212 The linguistic position of ZANDE has not been finally established up till today. Pursuant to J. H. GREENBERG it belongs to the "*Adamawa-Eastern* sub-family" of *Niger-Congo* languages (GREENBERG 1963, 9).

213 Around 1800 a group of battle-ready immigrants, known under the name of Avongara (Vungura) crossed the Mbomu River west of Shinko and penetrated into the territory between the Uele and Mbomu rivers. They conquered the entire area between Bangassou in the west and Maridi in the east and occupied all positions of power. They imposed their culture and language on the conquered tribes. Through this, the language spread as a lingua franca all over the entire territory of the *Avongara* rulers, and it was also learned by tribes who did not belong to the Zande nation, such as the *Amadi* on the upper Uele River (BAXTER/BUTT 1953, 14). A large number of tribes relinquished their language and adopted ZANDE as mother tongue.

Map 4. *Central Sudan*

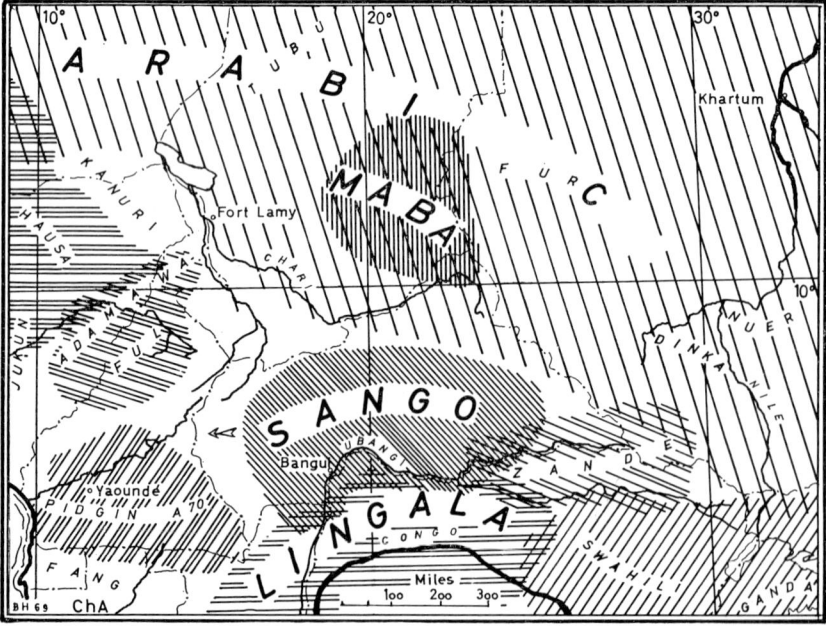

*Note:* The hatchings indicate the distribution of the different lingua francas.
*Source:* Author.

214 During the course of the colonial age, the territory of *Zande* was divided up between the Belgians, British and French. The Zande nation lost its former importance, and the influence of ZANDE receded simultaneously. Languages, which by the expansion of ZANDE had been driven to the brink of extermination, regained in part their former spread (TUCKER 1940, 16). Nevertheless ZANDE still today enjoys an expansion which is not reached by many African languages. It is spoken in the largest part of the territory between the latitudes 3° and 6° N. and the longitudes 23° and 29° E. (cf. LUKAS 1942, 20). On account of the thinly populated area where this language is spoken the total number of ZANDE users is relatively small — it may scarcely amount to one million [1].

## b) SARA

215 SARA belongs to the group of *Bongo-Bagirmi* languages [2], the interrelationship of which has already been pointed out by Georg SCHWEINFURTH in 1872. Under the designation of "SARA" a large number of dialects is comprised, which are spoken in the south-western part of the Chad Republic, particularly between the rivers of Logone and Chari. After the arrival of the French in Central Africa, the *Sara* people developed a remarkable mobility. Thus Louis CHABRELIE ascertained:

"From Pointe-Noire... the Sara labourers, occupied with work in the port or with the railway line of Congo-Ocean as far as the most remote posts in desert regions where they are employed as labourers, shooters or militiamen, one has occasion to see Saras and to hear their language..." [*]

216 It is not known to what extent SARA fulfils the function of a lingua franca (cf. LUKAS n.d., 48). The inhabited area of the Sara themselves has in recent decades to an increasing measure been penetrated by other lingua francas. Thus, from the north, the TURKU or CHAD-ARABIC has advanced as far as Fort Archambault, and from the south SANGO, the predominant language of the Central African Republic, is spreading (CHABRELIE 1935, 130).

---

1 In 1940, A. N. TUCKER stated the number of *Zande* as amounting to 750,000, of which it is said that 500,000 are living in the present Congo-Kinshasa State, 231,000 in the Sudan and approximately 21,000 in the Central African Republic (TUCKER 1940, 16/7). Earlier estimates, which surely were too high, describe the total number to be three to four millions (see PHILIPPS 1926, 24).

2 Pursuant to the present stage of research to what extent the supposition by J. H. GREENBERG that this group can be classified amongst the "Nilo-Saharan" family discovered by him is justified, must still be allowed to remain unclarified.

* "Depuis Pointe-Noire... des travailleurs Sara, occupés aux travaux du port ou de la ligne du chemin de fer Congo-Océan, jusqu'aux postes les plus reculés de la région désertique, où ils servent comme tirailleurs ou miliciens, on a l'occasion de voir des Sara et d'entendre leur langue..." (CHABRELIE 1935, 125).

## c) KANURI

217 Together with KANEMBU, TEDA, DAZA, ZAGHAWA and BERTI, KANURI is counted amongst the group of *Saharan* languages[3]. Today the concept "Kanuri" (*kanurí* designating the language and *kanúri* the population), originally the name for the inhabitants of the region Kanem situated to the east and north-east of Lake Chad (WESTERMANN/BRYAN 1952, 47) comprises in a larger sense the KANURI-speaking population of the northern Nigerian province of Bornu (LUKAS 1937, IX).

218 The development of KANURI as lingua franca is closely connected with that of the *Kanem-Bornu* empire, which occupies an important place in African history. This empire, situated in the area around Lake Chad can presumably be traced back as far as the 8th Century A.D. In the second half of the 11th Century the Islam and oriental culture found its way into *Kanem-Bornu* and became of decisive importance for its further development. The empire achieved an extent which temporarily stretched from Niger in the west to Wadai in the east and Fezzan in the north; it entertained trade relations with Egypt and other North African countries (WESTERMANN 1952, 152/3). Towards the end of the 14th Century, on account of the perpetual threats on the part of the *Bulala* tribe the centre of the empire gravitated towards the province of Bornu on the western side of Lake Chad and thereby the *Kanuri* living there became the governing class of the population in the empire. At the end of the 19th Century the *Kanem-Bornu* went into a decline and in 1893 were conquered by the adventurer Rabeh, who came from the eastern Sudan (op. cit. 154—8).

219 The spread of KANURI was a result of the expansion of the *Kanem-Bornu* empire. The conquered tribes around Lake Chad used it as lingua franca, and many of them finally relinquished their own language and adopted KANURI as first language[4] (cf. WESTERMANN/BRYAN 1952, 47). As language of the conquerors KANURI won greater importance particularly amongst the ruling classes of the conquered peoples. Thus, Adolf von DUISBURG notes that "in the formerly tributary vassal states of Logone, Wandala, Baghirmi, Kanem, Damagherim and Wadai, KANURI belongs to the languages spoken

---

3 This terminus originally appeared in the publications of Joseph H. GREENBERG, who at first called this group the *Central Saharan* group (see GREENBERG 1955). Johannes LUKAS on the other hand employed the designation of "East Saharan" (cf. LUKAS 1952). Pursuant to GREENBERG, the *Saharan* language belongs to the "Nilo-Saharan" family postulated by him, whose genetic position has not yet satisfactorily been defined.

4 J. LUKAS writes: "The political development of Bornu was the cause of the breaking down of the old tribal divisions, so that now all the old tribes are fused into the larger group, viz. the Kanuri Nation. Of the old tribes, who are treated in detail by Nachtigal, nothing but the names can be given here..." (LUKAS 1937, X).

by the upper classes still today; there it occupies the rank of a court language and that spoken by diplomats"*.

KANURI became widespread more particularly during the second half of the 16th Century under the rule of the Bornu prince Idris Aloma (1571 to 1603). Through him the empire became extremely powerful. "Envoys of the Bornu ruler kept up political contact with foreign states; active-minded teachers and busy traders settled in most of the larger towns, particularly in the capital cities, and furthered the spread of the highly respected Bornu customs and culture. Thus it also occurred that KANURI was accepted as language of nonautochthonous educated people and as medium of communication in trade, which position is in part still enjoyed today."** Moreover, KANURI as language of the soldiers was carried by the Bornu armies into the conquered territories (LUKAS 1942, 22).

220 Up to the 19th Century, KANURI predominated "in the entire interior Sudan as lingua franca" (DUISBURG 1913, 1). With the collapse of the *Kanem-Bornu* empire the importance of KANURI as lingua franca also gradually dwindled; up to the beginning of the 20th Century it was, however, still spoken by approximately two million people, and DUISBURG was to ascertain: "With the help of Kanuri, communication is possible practically everywhere, be it with the Sudan Arabs, the Schoa, or the Makari, Gamerghu and Wandala; even with the northern Adamaua-Fulbe, the Musgu on the Middle Logone and with the heathen tribes of the Mandara Mountains this idiom can be used for communication..."*** J. LUKAS notes as late as 1937 that KANURI extending beyond the tribe bearing the same name is understood by some tribes in the north-east, north, and south-east of the Bornu province (LUKAS 1937, IX). Eighteen years later, however, GREENBERG states that KANURI is only rarely spoken any more by "non-*Kanuri*" (GREENBERG 1965, 53).

---

* daß "in den ehemals tributpflichtigen Vasallenstaaten Logone, Wandala, Baghirmi, Kanem, Damagherim und Wadai das Kanuri auch heute noch zum Sprachschatz der oberen Schichten gehört; es hat dort den Wert einer Hof- und Diplomatensprache" (DUISBURG 1930, 114).
** "Gesandte des Bornuherrschers hielten politische Verbindung mit den fremden Staaten; rührige Lehrer und Händler ließen sich in den meisten größeren Orten, vor allem in den Hauptstädten, nieder und sorgten für Verbreitung der hochangesehenen Bornusitten und -kultur. So kam es auch, daß das KANURI als Sprache der fremdstämmigen Gebildeten und als Verständigungsmittel im Handelsverkehr angenommen wurde und stellenweise noch heute diese Geltung hat..." (DUISBURG 1930, 116).
*** "Mit Hilfe des Kanuri ist eine Verständigung fast überall möglich, sei es bei den Sudan-Arabern, den Schoa, oder bei den Makari, Gamerghu, Marghi und Wandala; sogar bei den nördlichen Adamaua-Fulbe, den Musgu am mittleren Logone und bei den Heidenstämmen des Mandara-Gebirges kann man dieses Idiom zur Verständigung gebrauchen..." (DUISBURG 1930, 114; s. DUISBURG 1913, 1).

221 The shrinking of the area of spread of KANURI can in part be connected with the expansion of the lingua francas HAUSA (in the west) and FUL (in the south), as well as ARABIC (in the east). Although the *Kanuri* have consistently and strongly resisted the advance of HAUSA in particular (GREENBERG 1965, 53), it seems that HAUSA as official language of northern Nigeria is constantly advancing within the Bornu province inhabited by the *Kanuri* (cf. DUISBURG 1930, 114).

222 Even today, KANURI is used as lingua franca, if only to a small degree. It is said to be used as a second or third language by "many" *Tubu* and *Buduma*, by Arabs and Tuareg as well as by some tribes in the south of *Maiduguri*, amongst others the *Mandara* (Wandala), *Higi*, and *Margi* (WESTERMANN/BRYAN 1952, 48; MEEK 1931, 215/252; DUISBURG 1930, 114). Moreover, pursuant to LUKAS it has spread in the west amongst the *Ngizim, Bolewa, Bade* und *Ngamo* between Gashua and the Gongola River and more particularly amongst the *Kotoko,* living to the south of Lake Chad (LUKAS n.d. 44). The present number of people understanding and speaking KANURI, may well amount to approximately one million[5] (WESTERMANN/BRYAN 1952, 46). The predominant part of them speaks KANURI as mother tongue (cf. DUISBURG 1930, 114).

223 KANURI is divided into a number of dialects, to which, amongst others, the *Manga, Lare* and *Kagama* belong (see LUKAS 1937, IX; WESTERMANN/BRYAN 1952, 47/8). Also the *Kanembu* — at least those living to the west of Lake Chad — are alleged to speak a dialect of KANURI. "Standard" KANURI as being employed in Nigeria in school education and administration is based on the dialect of Maiduguri (Yerwa), capital of the Bornu province and centre of social life of the *Kanuri* people (WESTERMANN/BRYAN 1952, 47).

## d) MABA

224 MABA, by its users called *bura mabang,* consists of a group of dialects spoken in the eastern part of the Chad Republic. Its genetic position among the African languages must up to today be deemed undefined[6].

---

5 In 1942 von DUISBURG noted: "Data compiled by me in the Lake Chad area, led me to assume that Kanuri is still today understood by approximately 2 million people and employed by them partly as mother tongue and partly as medium of communication." ("Berechnungen, die ich im Tschadsee-Gebiet vorgenommen habe, lassen mich annehmen, daß die Kanurisprache heute noch von ungefähr 2 Millionen Menschen verstanden und teils als Muttersprache, teils als Verständigungsmittel gebraucht wird" [DUISBURG 1942, 31; s. a. S. 65].) According to LUKAS KANURI is spoken as first or second language by even four million people (LUKAS n. d., 45).

6 Although by using insufficient comparative linguistic material, J. H. GREENBERG counts MABA amongst his "Nilo-saharan" family (GREENBERG 1963, 130 ff.).

225 At the beginning of the 17th Century, Abd el Kerim (Abdulkerim), of Arab descent, founded an Islamic empire in Wadai, which during the following centuries played an important role in the history of the Central Sudan. The fact that MABA became the lingua franca of this empire, is attributed by Georges TRENGA to the following reasons:
a) The establishment of the empire took place in the territory where MABA was spoken. Not only the old capital of Wara (Ouara) but also the later capital city of Abéché were erected on the soil inhabited by *Maba* tribes.
b) The Maba population constituted the class of people leading in number as well as politically within the empire (TRENGA 1947; 16; see WESTERMANN 1952, 174).
Thereby MABA attained special importance in comparison with the other languages spoken in Wadai (with the exception of ARABIC; see below). It was the vernacular language of the upper social classes and was spread by the government officials and their subalterns in all parts of the empire. Thus, next to Arabic, it had already become the language of administration and trade in Wadai during the 17th Century (cf. LABOURET 1947, V). It expanded particularly greatly amongst the tribes of *Kajanga, Kashmere* and *Mararit* (LUKAS 1939, 343).

226 MABA was learned as lingua franca not only by the African tribes but also by the Arabs. On the other hand, ARABIC forms a rival lingua franca which is almost of the same importance as MABA in Wadai.
Pursuant to Johannes LUKAS, the expansion of MABA has up to today not yet come to a standstill (LUKAS 1936, 341). It is spoken by the majority of the population in Wadai as well as in the parts of the Sudan State bordering to the east. The number of speakers is given by TRENGA as being 250,000 to 300,000 (TRENGA 1947, 16).

## e) ARABIC

227 With the victorious advance of Islam the Arabic language also penetrated into North Africa and started a development rendering it the most widespread language in Africa. Already in 640, eight years after the death of Mohammed, his adherants crossed the Suez isthmus and began their conquests in Africa. In 683 they destroyed Carthage and in the west advanced as far as the Atlantic coast, so that at the end of the 7th Century they ruled the entire North African coast. Since the 8th Century, the Mohammedans attacked the southern areas more and more often. Considerable resistance was encountered by them on the part of the *Berbers* in the mountainous regions of North-West Africa. They succeeded in forcing the *Berbers* further and further into submission and in converting various groups of them to the Islamic faith apart from winning their support for their aims. Thus the assistance of the Berbers is not the least cause of the Mohammedans crossing

the Straits of Gibraltar in 711 and advancing as far as France. Other Berber groups successfully resisted the onslaught of the fanatical adherents of Mohammed by taking shelter in inaccessible parts of the Atlas Mountains. Other Berbers again finally evaded the attacks and migrated towards the south into the Sahara Desert. The Christian empire Ethiopia above all served as a further bastion against the advance of the Mohammedans. Whereas the likewise Christian empire of Nubia on the Nile was finally overrun and Islamized by the Arabs in the first half of the 14th Century, Ethiopia has been able to defend itself against the Mohammedans up till today.

228 By this development, the linguistic map of northern Africa was decisively altered. In the shadow of Islam, ARABIC spread almost everywhere where Mohammedans set foot. At first it had as a rule the function of a lingua franca until it became mother tongue as a result of the dying out of the local languages. The situation in Egypt offers an example of this. When the Arabs penetrated there in 640, COPTIC — a later development form of the Egyptian language — was the language of the predominantly Christian population. COPTIC also obtained prominence as a literary language; the script was based on the Greek alphabet which had been enlarged by seven letters — by six, according to other statements — of the demotic script. For some centuries COPTIC was able to maintain its position vis-à-vis ARABIC, which had taken on the role of a lingua franca. After the turn of the millenium, however, the influence of COPTIC became more and more restricted, until it only fulfilled one final function, namely that of church language, which it has been able to maintain up to today. Otherwise it has been replaced by ARABIC[7].

Also BERBER has been repressed in many places by the ARABIC since the 8th Century, but even today some districts can be found in South Morocco, in the Middle Atlas and the Tell Atlas in which the influence of Arabic has remained relatively small.

229 According to Charles A. FERGUSON, the language which became the lingua franca of the Islamic world is not '*Arabiyyah,* the classic ARABIC, preserved for us in remnants of pre-Islamic poetry and in the Koran. This form of ARABIC was the language of the poets and orators and today, inter alia, constitutes the basis of the script. Next to '*Arabiyyah* there existed a dialect which in imitation of the designation of the Greek vernacular language in the Hellenistic world, FERGUSON calls K o i n e, and to which the majority of modern Arabic dialects can be traced back (FERGUSON 1959, 616/7). Most likely during the early times of Arab expansion Koine developed amongst the soldiers and town dwellers and its spread during the first centuries of Islamic chronology largely coincided with that of the Arab-

---

7 According to Georg STEINDORFF, however, last remnants of COPTIC are still spoken today in some communities in Upper Egypt (STEINDORFF 1951, 1).

Mohammedan town culture. It is probable that the Koine was primarily the vernacular language of the resident population. Amongst the nomadic bedouin tribes, however, dialects of ARABIC can be found, which cannot be traced back to the Koine (loc. cit. 618).

230 If northern Africa through the triumphal advance of ARABIC became one of the big linguistic ally homogeneous areas of the world, it can be said that the expansion of this language in the south of the Sahara was less successful. The advance of Islam did not come to a standstill here either, it still continued to make headway — a development which seems to persist into present times. The primary part of the medium of communication, employed in the spread of Islam, however, no longer consisted of ARABIC. This role was taken up by other languages, such as MANDINGO, FUL, SONG'AI, HAUSA, KANURI or SWAHILI. ARABIC was frequently able — though not as a lingua franca — to gain a certain importance as the language of theologians and savants in the area where these languages were spoken (cf. TAESCHNER 1964, 21).

231 In some parts of sub-Saharan Africa, however, ARABIC became more widespread as lingua franca. Thus, Diedrich WESTERMANN remarks that in the West a dialect form of ARABIC under the designation of *Hassani* is spoken (WESTERMANN 1940, 402). Mainly in the area between Lake Chad and the Nile it spread far towards the south. Its use was not restricted to the nomads only, but ARABIC — more particularly amongst the Islamized tribes — became the lingua franca. Georges TRENGA observes:

"This language spoken in the Ouadai since more than 500 years perhaps owed and still owes its expansion mainly to the Arab nomades who, thanks to their mobility were able to travel all over the regions of the country and could initiate friendly relationships with the population, teaching them their language simultaneously while being introduced to theirs." *

232 The spread of ARABIC during colonial times was as a rule hardly impeded, but was frequently even furthered. In this connection General DE RENDINGER states in respect of the development in the area east of Lake Chad:

"The peace of the French which brought calmness into these troubled regions and encouraged the negros to descend to the planes and promoted all kinds of exchanges, tends gradually to wipe out the differences between the various parts of the population; an Arabic dialect penetrating into all circles as the lingua franca effaces more and more all other languages: some of them, as I could ascertain in 1934, are about to vanish completely." **

---

* "Cette dernière langue parlée au Ouadai depuis plus de 500 ans peut-être, a dû et doit encore son expansion principalement aux Arabes nomades qui, grâce à leur mobilité ont pu parcourir toutes les régions du pays, nouer des relations amicales avec les sédentaires et leur apprendre leur langue en même temps qu'ils s'initiaient à la leur" (TRENGA 1947, 16/7).

** "La paix française, ramenant le calme dans ces régions troublées, encourageant les noirs à descendre dans les plaines, favorisant maintenant les échanges de toute

In some districts, some special forms of ARABIC emerged, which underwent a process of p i d g i n i z a t i o n.

233 One of these pidgin forms is TURKU in Central Africa. It is the leading lingua franca of the Chad Republic and is furthermore spoken in the north of the Republic of Cameroon and the Central African Republic. According to Johannes Lukas its sphere of influence reaches in the south as far as the river Ubangi (Lukas 1943, 123). A special lingua franca form of ARABIC seems to have been derived from TURKU, which was called a "barrack and market gibberish" by G. J. Lethem. It is spoken in the area around Lake Chad and is used particularly in the towns of Fort-Lamy, Dikwa and Maiduguri (Lethem 1920, XIII).

234 The ARABIC of southern Sudan constitutes another pidgin form also called *Mongalese* or "*Bimbashi* Arabic". It was carried by Egyptian troops into southern Sudan and spread as lingua franca in the area between Malakal and the north of Uganda. Later on its expansion was promoted by the construction of roads and the increasing development of the country. Although efforts were made to replace the South Sudan ARABIC with English, it retained a certain importance mainly with the administration. A language of the police force, army, Arab traders and administration officials it enjoyed a remarkable esteem. Thus A. N. Tucker observes:

"It also had — and still has in some areas — a great prestige as being the language best calculated to win favour with the police, for the native police are not, as a rule, recruited from the tribes, speaking totally different languages. Ultimately, of course, it was a useful language to know, should one's case come before the District Commissioner, since it enabled the plaintiff to evade the court interpreter, who was not always to be trusted to translate fairly unless well bribed" (Tucker 1934, 28).

By groups of Sudanese soldiers South Sudan ARABIC was carried even into the countries of East Africa, where, however, it did not achieve the function of a lingua franca. Thus, for instance, in southern Uganda a population group can be observed, which has become known under the designation of *Nubi*. They are the descendants of soldiers from the Sudan, who served under the government of the Protectorate of that time and who had settled in Uganda. The *Nubi* are strong adherents of Islam and speak the South Sudan ARABIC as mother tongue (Thomas/Scott 1935, 88).

235 ARABIC, however, could gain little influence in the Christian Empire of Ethiopia, Sudan's neighbour to the east. But this does not apply to Eritrea, situated in the north. Amongst the *Tigre* settled there for example it has become widespread (Leslau 1956, 125). ARABIC, furthermore, is employed

---

nature, tend peu à peu à effacer ces différences entre les diverses peuplades; un patois arabe, s'introduisant dans tous les milieux comme langue véhiculaire, désagrège de jour en jour toutes les autres langues: certaines d'entre elles, comme il m'a été donné de le constater en 1934, sont en voie de disparition totale" (Rendinger 1949, 144).

as second language along the East African coast as far down as south of the Equator.

236 In the Somali Republic it is understood in all parts of the country. The position of ARABIC in this country is in some points characteristic of its use in other areas situated on the southern edge of the Sahara. As a second language, ARABIC is especially widespread in the towns of the Republic. Within the family circle, however, its use is shunned. According to B. W. ANDRZEJEWSKI the reason for this must be looked for in the fact that the *Somali* are reluctant to enable their daughters to learn foreign languages. Thus it happens that the Somali women hold but little truck with ARABIC. At home the children only talk SOMALI, and the grown-ups are of opinion that the use of ARABIC should be restricted to public life and religion (ANDRZEJEWSKI 1962, 179).

237 The development of ARABIC in the Somali Republic — just as in other parts of the area of expansion of this language — was closely connected with that of Islam. Through itinerant Koran and other colleges the knowledge of ARABIC together with that of religion was carried into the most distant villages. All religious teachers and preachers had to learn ARABIC, and success in their profession as well as social prestige was to a large extent determined by the degree of knowledge of this language (ANDRZEJEWSKI 1962, 178). Special importance has been attained by ARABIC as language of literature. During their official contacts with the *Somali* the European colonial powers at first used ARABIC, and all protective agreements were worded in this language, too. Today it is one of the three literary languages of the country, together with English and Italian, and is employed in documents, periodicals, government communications, as well as in private and business correspondence, etc. (loc. cit. 177).

## V. Western Central Africa

### a) BULU

238 BULU belongs to a group of *Bantu* languages spoken in the Republic of Cameroon, Gabon and Rio Muni; they are subsumed by Malcolm GUTHRIE under the designation A 70 (GUTHRIE 1953, 40). ETON, YAUNDE and FANG are counted amongst these languages, which are closely interrelated.

239 It is not known when the development of BULU as lingua franca commenced. It is, however, certain that this development received considerable impulse at the beginning of the 20th Century. G. T. VON HAGEN reports:

Map 5. *Western Africa*

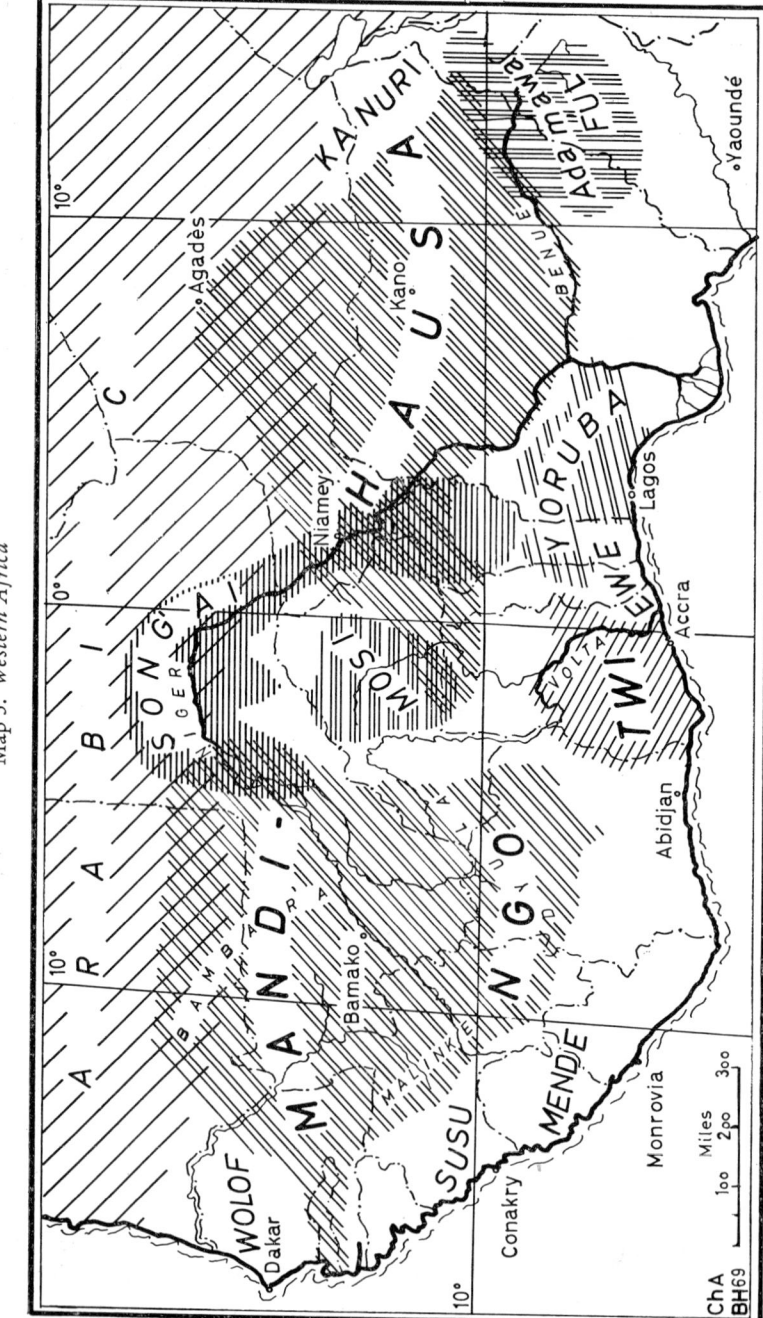

*Note:* The hatchings indicate the distribution of the different lingua francas.

Source: Author.

"They (i.e. the *Bulu* people, author's note) advance closer and closer to the coast, expand towards the south and absorb the local Fang population; across the Dia River they now have almost completely populated the dead bush between their former borders and the Njem. Ahead of them goes the victorious march of their language. In Fang villages in which in 1907 I experienced difficulties in finding a Bulu-speaking inhabitant, I met with Bulu in 1912 as leading lingua franca from the line of Kribi-Kampo up to the line of Jukaduma-Molundu (but in no case — as can always be heard — Jaunde). In a few decades there will hardly exist a native inhabitant in the protectorate including its new acquisitions south of the Njong and Dume Rivers who will not be able to communicate verbally in Bulu." *

240 The spread of Bulu as lingua franca was to no small extent furthered by the work of the American Presbyterian missionaries. A number of textbooks and the Bible were translated into BULU, and BULU was employed as language of education and religious instruction (NIDA 1955, 157).

BULU attained special importance as language of the schools established by the missionaries; such schools were founded not only in the *Bulu* area, but also in areas where other languages such as KAKA, MAKA, NJEM, BAJUE and NGUMBA were spoken. The thirst for knowledge drove many Africans into the mission schools. In order to be able to follow the lessons they had to learn BULU which as a result spread troughout the sphere of influence of the Presbyterian mission in South Cameroon.

241 A certain resistance to the predominance of BULU could be observed already at that time. Thus the *Ngumba* (Mvumbo), living near the coast, made efforts to repel the influence of BULU in favour of their own language. They attempted in vain, to cause the mission to translate the religious literature into NGUMBA, too. This controversy led to the *Ngumba* leaving the Presbyterian Church and forming their own association (NIDA 1955, 157).

242 The subsequent development led in increasing measure to a lessening of importance of BULU as lingua franca. Already for some time it had to defend itself against the competition of YAUNDE, a further language of supra-regional expansion in southern Cameroon. Not for the least reason that the town of Yaundé, belonging to the area of spread of YAUNDE, was developed into an important centre of administration and trade and was

---

* Sie (d. h. die *Bulu*-Leute, Anm. Verf.) dringen immer weiter zur Küste vor, dehnen sich nach Süden aus und saugen die dortigen Fang auf; über den Dscha hinweg haben sie jetzt fast völlig den toten Busch zwischen sich und den Njem bevölkert. Ihnen voraus geht der Siegeszug ihrer Sprache. In Fangdörfern, in denen es mir 1907 schwierig war, einen Bulu sprechenden Menschen zu finden, fand ich 1912 das Bulu von der Linie Kribi-Kampo bis zur Linie Jukaduma-Molundu die herrschende Verkehrssprache (keineswegs — wie man immer hört — das Jaunde), und in wenigen Jahrzehnten wird es im Schutzgebiet einschließlich seiner Neuerwerbungen südlich des Njong und Dume kaum noch einen Eingeborenen geben, der sich nicht in Bulu verständigen kann" (HAGEN 1914, 4/5).

made capital of the Cameroon Republic, the YAUNDE language obtained a radiating influence, to which BULU could not offer a comparable alternative.

243 Still more important for the further development of BULU as lingua franca was French, which gradually spread in the interior of the Cameroon Republic. High social prestige and economic benefits could be attained by learning it. Mainly in the field of education it gained considerable importance, and even amongst the *Bulu* population the desire was expressed to replace BULU with French as language used in the schools.

244 In addition, a third reason must be stated. During the course of the colonial age — and chiefly after World War II — in various parts of Africa national consciousness developed which often transferred itself to the level of the tribe. Such development occurred for instance in southern Cameroon. The smaller ethnic groups, which for a long time had been under the cultural and linguistic influence of the large tribes, became aware of the value of their own culture and took up arms against any impingements from outside. In this way, the use of BULU as lingua franca was increasingly rejected. Tribes such as the *Kaka, Maka, Njem,* amongst others, voiced the opinion that their languages "were no worse than BULU" and made efforts to get the Bible translated into their own languages (NIDA 1955, 158).

245 Because BULU was taken on by some tribes as first language, it was able to maintain certain importance. In 1962 Pierre ALEXANDRE ascertained that the *Ntum* and *Fang* below the age of fifty and resident in the Cameroon Republic, speak BULU dialects. The use of NTUM and FANG is predominantly restricted to older people (ALEXANDRE 1966, 13).

246 BULU, therefore, is spoken today not only by the 120,000 members of the tribe of the same name[1] in the districts ("Départements") of Ntem, Dja-et-Lobo and Kribi in South Cameroon. Moreover, it is spoken as first language by some other tribes such as *Zaman, Yengono, Yelinda* and *Yembama* (ALEXANDRE 1966, 12). BULU dialects are furthermore spoken today by about 80,000 to 100,000 people, i.e. by *Fang, Mvae* and *Ntum* living in the districts of Djoum, Ambam and Ebolowa, as well as by the *Fong* in Sangmélima and Ebolowa.

### b) YAUNDE

247 YAUNDE (Ewondo)[2] is the language of the approximately 100,000 members of the tribe of the same name which lives in the surroundings of Yaoundé,

---

1 According to G. T. VON HAGEN, the BULU tribe consisted of even 150,000 members in 1913 (HAGEN 1914, 4).
2 The designation "Yaunde" (Jaunde) was taken over by the early European travellers from members of the coastal tribes who accompanied them on their first expeditions into the interior of the country. The name of "Ewondo", which

the capital city of the Cameroon Republic, and more particularly in the south-west of the country. According to M. GUTHRIE it belongs to the A 70 group of *Bantu* (GUTHRIE 1953, 40).

248 The development of YAUNDE into one of the predominant lingua francas in southern Cameroon is most of all the result of the colonization of the country by the Germans and later by the French. After the occupation of the coastal region of (what is now called the Republic of) Cameroon by Germany in 1894, the development of the interior still took a few more years. The trading post Yéundo (later on called Jaunde) was established, by which it was intended to link up the coast with the Adamawa plateau. The *Yaunde*, living round about Yéundo, thereby came into closer contact with the colonial masters, to whom they were soon to prove very useful. They hired themselves out as farm labourers, porters and soldiers (NEKES 1912, 469) and together with the Whites or under their orders travelled into far distant parts of the country.

249 Thereby their language soon spread also outside their settlements and it became the lingua franca in large parts of the southern Cameroon. Thus, Hermann NEKES noted already in 1911:
"With the exception of the coastal area communication by means of the Jaunde language is possible between the Sanaga River and the southern border of the Republic of Cameroon until far into the east. Even the Sudanese Wuti on the left bank of the Sanaga River understand Jaunde. The coloured soldiers, whether they are Sudanese or Bantu negros, communicate with each other in broken Jaunde. Jaunde has so to speak become lingua franca of the south of Cameroon and is still further spread by the Jaunde, who are very fond of travelling." *

250 The spread of YAUNDE was presumably considerably furthered by the fact that it took place in a territory where the languages differ only in minor degrees. The adoption of YAUNDE as lingua franca therefore frequently demanded nothing but the familiarization with the peculiarities differing from one's own dialect. Outside the Yaunde tribe the language is spoken by the *Bene, Enoa, Fong, Mvele*, the majority of the *Eton, Mengisa, Bamvele* and many *Bafia* (GRAFFIN/PICHON 1930, 6). It could however not gain a foothold in the coastal area, i.e. in the sphere of influence of DUALA. On the other hand, the attempts already undertaken during the time of German

---

has established itself mainly in French works, represents the name given to their language by the *Yaunde* themselves (cf. GRAFFIN/PICHON 1930, 6).

* "Mit Ausnahme des Küstengebietes kann man sich in der Jaundesprache zwischen dem Sanaga und Südgrenze Kameruns bis weit im Osten verständigen. Selbst die sudanischen Wuti auf dem linken Sanaga-Ufer verstehen Jaunde. Die farbigen Soldaten ob Sudan- oder Bantuneger verständigen sich auf gebrochen Jaunde. Das Jaunde ist gleichsam Verkehrssprache des Südens von Kamerun geworden und wird durch die reiselustigen Jaunde immer weiter verbreitet" (NEKES 1911, 2).

administration to assist DUALA (NEKES 1911, VI) in its greater spread in the *Yaunde* territory, also remained without success.

The expansion of YAUNDE does not seem to have come to a close even today. Pierre ALEXANDRE thus states: "Ewondo tends to become lingua franca within the whole *béti* area, replacing non-codified idioms, such as the Bané, Fong, Eton, Mangisa etc."*

### c) Pidgin A 70

251 Pidgin A 70 has become known under several designations such as *bulu bediliva*, i.e. 'BULU of the motorists', *ewondo populaire* or *pidgin ewondo*. The designation of "Pidgin A 70" was introduced by Pierre ALEXANDRE in 1962. Under "A 70" Malcolm GUTHRIE subsumed a group of *Bantu* languages, spoken in southern Cameroon, Gabon and Rio Muni, i.e. the *Eton, Yaunde, Bulu, Fang*, inter alia (GUTHRIE 1953, 40). Pidgin A 70 is a lingua franca which originated in the territory of these languages and spread from there. It is derived from the two predominant languages of this group, YAUNDE and BULU (ALEXANDRE 1967a, 1)[3].

252 The origin of Pidgin A 70 presumably falls into the time after the First World War. The building sites along the railway line between Eséka and Yaoundé or Otélé and Mbalmayo, respectively, became collecting points for people of different origins and different languages. Soon the necessity of a common linguistic medium of communication between the labourers on the railway became evident. *Pidgin English*, the lingua franca of the Cameroon coast, experienced only a small spread in this territory. In such a situation, Pidgin A 70 emerged as intertribal medium of communication.

The spread of the language took place along the large traffic routes, in the market places and in the urban districts. Pidgin A 70 is today spoken in the entire southern part of the Cameroon Republic. It is less widespread in the hinterland of Duala, but is extensively used in the town Duala itself by the population coming from the interior (ALEXANDRE 1963, 578). In the north Pidgin A 70 is spoken as far as Yoko, and it is alleged also to be used in the towns of North Cameroon (BRYAN 1959, 16; ALEXANDRE 1963, 578). In the south it penetrated as far as Congo-Brazzaville, into the region of Ouesso-Souanké.

253 Pidgin A 70 is the language of all those who either have no command of French or do not want to speak it. It is particularly widespread amongst

---

\* "L'éwondo tend à devenir langue véhiculaire dans toute la zone béti, remplaçant les idiomes non codifiés, tels le Bané, le Fong, l'Eton, le Mangisa etc." (ALEXANDRE 1956, 2).

3 It would be very interesting to examine the proportion to be attributed to each of these two languages in the development of the lingua franca.

the lorry drivers and traders. Differences in use of this language can be observed in accordance with the age and sex of the people speaking it. Men use it to a much greater extent than women; people at an age of vocational activity much more frequently than old people or children. Whereas Pidgin A 70 is hardly used in areas off the main traffic routes, it has gained certain importance in the centres of trade and traffic.

An examination of its vocabulary proves that Pidgin A 70 is particularly the language of modern African life. Thus it can express distinct conceptual differentiations in the fields of trade (weights, prices, goods), of travel and of the administration (office, police force, jail, taxes, etc.) (ALEXANDRE 1963, 580).

## d) DUALA

254 DUALA belongs to the north-western branch of *Bantu* languages.

When, in 1884, the German explorer Gustav NACHTIGAL signed a protective treaty with the *Duala* ruler Bell, the *Duala* already looked back on a tradition as a trading nation on the northern Cameroon coast, which presumably dates from as early as the close of the 18th Century. After that time a close contact existed between the British and the tribes of the Cameroon coast (ARDENER 1956, 18). The *Duala* undertook journeys into the interior of the country and along the coast as far as Calabar and entertained an important position as go-betweens in the trade between the interior and the European ships on the Atlantic coast. Thereby, their language attained the position of a lingua franca amongst the neighbouring tribes, particularly that of a t r a d i n g  language (MEYER 1944, 277; ARDENER 1956, 36).

255 Upon the commencement of the German rule, a change made itself felt in the status of DUALA as a lingua franca. The interest of the Germans concentrated itself primarily on trade and the *Duala* saw their hegemony as trading power threatened. Thus tensions arose between them and their new colonial masters, which between the years 1891 and 1895 took on the form of warlike disputes. The Germans were able to establish themselves and the *Duala* trade lost its former importance. As could be expected, the influence of Duala as lingua franca also receded.

256 On the other hand, DUALA received a remarkable fillip through the work of ecclesiastical institutions, particularly that of the Basle mission. It was made the basis of school and religious instruction and thereby was able to gain a certain importance outside the *Duala* territory. It became more widespread in the districts of Victoria, Kumba and Mamfe. The history of DUALA is thus characterised by a development from a t r a d i n g  language into a  s c h o o l  and  c h u r c h  language (MEYER 1944, 277). It became thereby the first African language of literature in the coastal area of (the present Republic of) Cameroon — a circumstance which contributed towards

DUALA being made, inter alia, the basis of the official spelling of tribal and place names in the coastal region (ARDENER 1956, 37).

257 The fact that DUALA, in spite of the efforts on the part of the mission, gradually lost its function as lingua franca, must primarily be traced back to the presence of a rival lingua franca. The contact of the Europeans with the tribes of the Cameroon coast, which had started already towards the end of the 15th Century with the appearance of the first Portuguese ships, not only led to important consequences in cultural and linguistic fields. After Portuguese had at first spread to some extent on the coast, the English language started to gain a foothold as second European language after the close of the 18th Century. Throughout the 19th Century it served as medium of communication between Africans and Europeans, and thus even the agreements between the Germans and the *Duala* in 1884 were concluded in English (ARDENER 1956, 37). With the dwindling of *Duala* trade in the nineties of the previous century, English took on more and more the role of DUALA as t r a d i n g language. In its lingua franca form, which had become known under the designation "pidgin English", it had thereby become the predominant language of the Cameroon coast. It ousted DUALA to an increasing extent and became the language of the market place and plantations. Neither pidgin English nor DUALA obtained official recognition by the German colonial power. Whereas, however, the use of DUALA was hardly encouraged by the German administration, pidgin English was deemed to be a little valued, but nevertheless necessary idiom of communication, which had to be used because the spread of the German language was very slow (ARDENER 1956, 37).

258 Thus DUALA is of very restricted importance today. Its established area of distribution consists mainly of the town of Duala and its immediate hinterland. The number of people speaking DUALA as mother tongue is stated to be 22,927 (see ARDENER 1956, 15), and if the number of those people speaking it as second or third language is added, this amount would not be appreciably larger [4].

### e) BALI

259 BALI presumably belongs to the family of *Niger-Congo* languages. Its position within this family, however, has not finally been clarified.
The *Bali* form a division of the *Chamba*, who live further to the north in the

---

[4] Contrariwise, the data supplied by Emmi KÄHLER-MEYER in 1944 can hardly be looked upon any longer as correct: "The area where D u a l a is spoken, i.e. the districts of Duala, Nkongsamba, Victoria, Kumba and Mamfe, comprise 12,500 sq. miles with 290,000 inhabitants..." ("Das Sprachgebiet des D u a l a, d. s. die Bezirke Duala, Nkongsamba, Viktoria, Kumba und Mamfe, umfaßt 32,000 qkm mit 290,000 Bewohnern..." [MEYER 1944, 281].)

Adamawa territory. When the *Ful* (Fulbe, Peul) advanced in the 19th Century to the plateau of Adamawa, the *Bali* fled towards the south into the grassland of the (present) Cameroon Republic. In the majority they relinquished their language and adopted the language of a population settled there (MEYER 1944, 278). Upon the colonization of the Cameroons by the Germans this language soon attained prominence. It received considerable impulse from the administration and even to a much greater extent by the mission. Thus Emmi KÄHLER-MEYER observes:

"This new *Bali* language has become the church and school language of the Basle mission, which maintains schools in most towns and villages. As a result, and through the preeminent position bestowed upon the Bali among the more than twenty splinter tribes of the Bamenda district, the language is gaining ground." *

260 This development, however, gradually receded, and BALI lost more and more its function as lingua franca. The reason for this is not known, but the spread of a rivalling lingua franca, i.e. pidgin English, may well have contributed towards this process. Pidgin English, which already during the 19th Century had maintained the role as a lingua franca on the Cameroon coast, spread amongst the labour forces on the plantations started up after 1900 (SCHNEIDER 1960, 12), and it influenced the decline of another lingua franca, i.e. DUALA. Not the least contributory cause of the penetration of pidgin English into the Cameroon grassland were the countless labourers who learned it in the south on the plantations and carried it into their homeland in the Bamenda district.

### f) Adamawa-FUL

261 FUL — by the French called *Peul* (Peulh, Poular) and in the anglophone language area often known under the designation of *Fulani* — is spoken by more than four million people in entire West Africa between Senegal and the Chad Republic (see WESTERMANN/BRYAN 1952, 18/9). The language presumably belongs to the family of *Niger-Congo* languages, and within this family must be counted among the "West Atlantic" languages (GREENBERG 1963, 8), a group, whose status as a histroric unit is problematical.

262 In spite of the great dispersion and the distinction which the *Ful* had in respect of the history of West Africa, their language could not achieve an important role as a lingua franca. The reason for this in part must probably be looked upon in the fact that the *Ful* dispersed in a territory where

---

* Diese neue Balisprache ist Kirchen- und Schulsprache der Basler Mission geworden, die in den meisten Städten und Dörfern Schulen unterhält. Dadurch und durch die Vorrangstellung, die die Bali unter den anderen über zwanzig Splitterstämmen des Bamenda-Bezirks einnehmen, gewinnt die Sprache an Boden" (MEYER 1944, 278).

important lingua francas such as MANDINGO (MALINKE, BAMBARA, DYULA) and HAUSA[5] were already existing. Only in eastern Nigeria and northern Cameroon, more particularly in the mountainous region of Adamawa, FUL acquired prominence as lingua franca among the multitude of various ethnic groups, as will be shown later.

263 During the course of this millenium the *Ful* coming from the most distant part of West Africa in their search for grazing grounds for their herds of cattle had moved still further towards the east. It is maintained that already towards the end of the 13th Century some groups had reached the area of Lake Chad. In the 18th Century there existed in Adamawa numerous *Ful* settlements, which as a rule had to pay tribute to the tribes already settled there. This changed towards the beginning of the 19th Century, when the *Ful* Osman dan Fodio founded a powerful empire east of the Niger River in the territory of the Hausa states. Amongst his henchmen was the *Ful* Adama, stemming from Adamawa, who was sent to his homeland in order to Islamize the country named after him later on, and to subordinate it to the rule of Osman.

264 Upon his arrival, Adama met with favourable conditions for the planned enterprise. The *Ful* at that time lived in a tense relationship with their neighbours and willingly supported their fellow tribesmen. Already in 1805, Adama had subjected numerous tribes and became the ruler of the emirate of Adamawa. Some of the freedom-loving tribes, however, escaped from his rule by seeking refuge in the inaccessible mountains. Despite various setbacks under the successors of Adama, the *Ful* rule expanded in the Cameroons temporarily to the Sanaga River, but the *Wute* for example living to the south of Tibati, could flee successfully from their rule (MEYER 1944, 268).

265 Up till today the *Ful* represent a privileged social stratum in the northern Cameroon, although their power was considerably reduced by the French

---

5 Maurice DELAFOSSE notes on the spread of FUL in western Sudan:
"It can be said that within that vast area the Ful language or language of the Toucouleurs and the Ful has gained a certain importance, but even this importance is by far surpassed by that of 'mandé': except perhaps in the Fouta-Diallon and certain Soninke areas, the Ful language is in fact only spoken and understood by the Toucouleurs and Ful people, while 'mandé' constitutes the habitual language which is understood and spoken by all the inhabitants of the whole area and also the Toucouleurs, when they converse with foreigners."
("On peut dire que, dans toute cette vaste région, le foulan ou langue des Toucouleurs et des Peuhls, a seul une certaine importance, et encore cette importance est-elle de beaucoup dépassée par celle du mandé: le foulan en effet, sauf peut-être dans le Fouta-Diallon et certains pays soninké, n'est parlé et compris que par les seuls Toucouleurs et Peuhls, tandis que le mandé est la langue usuelle que comprennent et parlent toutes les peuplades de la région et les Toucouleurs eux-mêmes lorsqu'ils ont à converser avec des étrangers" (DELAFOSSE 1901, 217).

administration. A cultural exchange took place between the *Ful* and the so-called "heathen tribes of Adamawa", the *Ful* being mainly on the giving side. Although they learnt hoeing from the Adamawa tribes, they influenced on the other hand the lives of the latter to such an extent that it seems justified to speak of a "*Ful*ization" of Adamawa. Chiefly, they helped two cultural assets to large expansion: Islam as well as their own language.

266 According to expectations *Ful* has gained greatest importance as lingua franca in places where their political influence is at its strongest. In spite of the latent animosity and mistrust still to be met with amongst the mountain tribes today, they put up but little resistance to the spread of FUL. This expansion was given tremendous fillip through trade. FUL conquered the market-places of north Cameroon and thereby penetrated into the rural districts (PODLEWSKI 1966, 13/4). Moreover, it was learnt by the members of the mountain tribes who had hired themselves out to the plantations of the *Ful* and who carried it to their homeland.

267 FUL is today the leading lingua franca in the northern part of the Cameroon Republic. In the south, its sphere of influence reaches as far as Tibati, MBUM acquired a certain distinction there (see below). To the north FUL was able to expand via Maroua to the vicinity of Lake Chad and there penetrated into the area where another lingua franca, i.e. KANURI, was spoken. Even in south-eastern Nigeria, between the Benue River and the frontier of the Republic of Cameroon, FUL is widespread.

268 As demonstrated by Pierre-Francis LACROIX, the linguistic formation of the Adamawa FUL is not consistent. It rather is divided into a multiplicity of dialects. The *Ful* themselves distinguish between the following three forms:

a) "East Ful" (fulfulde funaangere), spoken in the north of the Cameroon Republic, particularly in Diamaré;

b) "West Ful" (fulfulde hiirnaangere), to which, inter alia, the dialect of the Ngaoundéré belongs;

c) *Kambariire*, a p i d g i n form of Adamawa FUL, alleged to be used by the non-*Ful*. This word is derived from the HAUSA *kambari*, and was originally the designation of Mohammedans who had for a long time lived amongst non-Mohammedans (LACROIX 1962, 78).

269 Moreover, in the territory between the Atlantic coast and Lake Chad some languages are spoken which are said to have the function of lingua francas. To these belongs, for example, JUKUN, presumably a *Niger-Congo* language (see GREENBERG 1963, 9), which is spoken on both banks of the Benue River in eastern Nigeria. It is maintained that, inter alia, it is used as lingua franca by the *Wurbo*, a tribe of fishermen living along the Benue between Lau and Abinsi, and by the *Kentu* in the southern area of the Benue River (WESTERMANN/BRYAN 1952, 141).

270 In this connection MBUM must also be mentioned, which, according to J. H. GREENBERG, must be counted to the *Adamawa* branch of the *Niger-Congo* family (GREENBERG 1963, 9). It is spoken on the *Adamawa* plateau between Tibati and Ngaoundéré and further to the east as far as the source of the Benue River. Although used in the centre of the area of spread of a significant lingua franca, the Adamawa FUL, MBUM also seems to have acquired the function of a lingua franca. It is said that the *Ful* in Ngaoundéré have a good command of it, and Franz THORBECKE noted on the situation in the town of Tibati: "Everyone speaks and understands Mbum; apart from that one person will speak Wute as an additional language, a second person will communicate in Fullah, and a third person will have a command of both additional languages, but the lingua franca, the language of the market-place, remains Mbum." \*

271 Far to the east, GBAYA (Baya, Baja) is spoken, which most likely is also part of the *Niger-Congo* family (GREENBERG 1963, 9) and is made up of a multiplicity of dialects. It is chiefly spoken in the western part of the Central African Republic. As a lingua franca it is probably spread in the southwest of this state as well as in the adjoining parts of the Republic of Cameroon. Julius LIPPERT remarks in this connection:

"Baya is widespread as a lingua franca. I first heard it in Nola on the Sanga River, and then, during the journey along the Kadei, I had with me an interpreter with a knowledge of Baya, who was understood everywhere. To the Kaka, Baya is more familiar than their mother tongue. To the south, the boundary of use of this Bantu dialect [6] is approximately the border of the homogeneous primeval forest south of the Kadei River, to the east most likely the Sanga River." \*\*

Pursuant to NAUMANN, GBAYA is understood in the south partly by the *Yangere, Kaya,* and *Bum* and even as far as Ngaoundéré, to which place the *Gbaya* formerly frequently were taken as slaves, a communication in this language is maintained to be possible (NAUMANN 1915, 42).

---

\* "Jeder spricht und versteht Mbum, der eine außerdem Wute, der andere Fullah, der dritte alle beide Sprachen, aber die Verkehrssprache, die Sprache des Marktes ist Mbum" (THORBECKE 1914, 171).

6 Contrary to this statement, GBAYA cannot be counted to the *Bantu* group (author's note).

\*\* "Das Baya ist als Verkehrssprache weit verbreitet. Ich hörte es erst in Nola am Sanga, und habe dann während der Kadeireise einen des Baya kundigen Dolmetscher gehabt, der immer verstanden wurde. Den Kaka ist das Baya geläufiger als ihre Muttersprache. Im Süden ist die Verbreitungsgrenze dieses Bantudialektes ungefähr die Grenze des geschlossenen Urwaldes südlich des Kadei, im Osten wohl der Sanga" (LIPPERT 1907, 204).

## g) SANGO

272 The SANGO lingua franca — also called *Sango commercial* or *Pidgin Sango* — is derived from a dialect of the same name, which is spoken on the banks of the Ubangi River in the vicinity of the small town of Mobaye. Not only the lingua franca but also the dialect of Mobaye belong to a group of dialects subsumed under the designation of NGBANDI (TUCKER/BRYAN 1956, 40; SAMARIN 1955, 256; JACQUOT 1961, 158).
The NGBANGI group shares in a closer relationship with the majority of languages which are spoken in the area covered by the Ubangi River and its tributaries, more particularly so with the widespread languages BANDA and GBAYA. Together with these languages, NGBANDI, according to J. H. GREENBERG, is counted to the *Adamawa Eastern* branch of the Niger-Congo family (GREENBERG 1963, 9).

*Development into a lingua franca*

273 Doubtlessly, the prominence and the large spread enjoyed today by the SANGO lingua franca is the result of a more recent process, which could hardly have commenced before the arrival of the Europeans. It is, on the other hand, reported that already at the time of the intrusion of the French colonial troops in the Ubangi territory, SANGO enjoyed a — though modest — supra-regional importance. In this connection it is said that the *Buraka* and most likely also the *Gbanziri*, the western neighbours of the *Sango,* who just like the latter primarily derive their livelihood from fishing, have used SANGO already in pre-colonial times, i.e. prior to 1890 (SAMARIN 1955, 256).

274 In 1889 the French established a stronghold in Bangui, the later capital of the Central African Republic. Thence they advanced upstream on the Ubangi River into the interior of the country as far as Rafai in the Mbomu territory and between 1890 and 1894 they founded a number of posts along the river.
It was to be expected that the French, during their journeys on the Ubangi River employed mainly members of the tribes living along the river banks as crews for their ships and as soldiers. Amongst them a lot of *Sango* people were represented, who thereby carried their language into distant parts of the Ubangi region. Of significance is the name received by the spreading language: *sango tí tulúgu,* i.e. "SANGO of the soldiers". The ship crews were more particularly recruited from the *Gbanziri* and *Buraka*, who — as has already been mentioned — were said to have spoken SANGO as second language already before the arrival of the French (SAMARIN 1955, 257).

275 The question as to why SANGO amongst the many languages along the Ubangi River became the predominant lingua franca, cannot be answered

with any degree of certainty from the material available [7]. It is possible that the fact that some neighbouring tribes had used the language of *Sango* already in early times, contributed to its general recognition as an interethnic medium of communication.

On the other hand, the development of SANGO, as soon as it had become a lingua franca, is better known. Together with the French, members of the tribes of the Upper Ubangi penetrated as soldiers, sailors or traders' assistants to the north as far as the Chari River territory. Already in 1897 Fort Crampel was erected on the Gribingui, a tributary of the Chari River.

276   There were presumably several reasons for the groups of populations encountered during these conquests deciding also on their part to learn SANGO. The first reason was that there hardly existed anywhere in this territory a lingua franca which was already in use throughout; the contacts then established, however, demanded a general medium of communication. Through the fact that it was spoken by people who already for some time were in touch with Europeans and had taken over several of their cultural assets, SANGO had acquired a certain esteem. By learning it, it was hoped to acquire social and material advantages. The prerequisites for a larger spread of French were at that time not yet available — the French themselves were often forced in their contact with their subjected peoples to employ SANGO.

Secondly, linguistic viewpoints possibly furthered the spread of SANGO. I took place in a territory in which mostly closely related languages were used as means of communication amongst one another. These languages differ from SANGO partly only dialectically, and thus it was generally quickly adopted and easily learned. In addition, according to Benjamin LEKENS, SANGO underwent at an early stage a process of p i d g i n - i z a t i o n, whereby it is maintained it became easier to learn (cf. SAMARIN 1955, 258).

277   Thus the sphere of influence of SANGO was steadily increased. Everywhere in the Ubangi territory where the Europeans had gained a foothold SANGO was spoken. Even the Senagalese, who had been brought to Central Africa in order to occupy the country, learnt this language. William J. SAMARIN, one of the foremost experts on SANGO, writes:

"Every African who desires to share in what the new way of life has to offer, which is found mostly outside the 'bush' villages, must always necessarily learn Sango in order to communicate with those Africans who represent the government or the various commercial firms" (SAMARIN 1955, 258).

---

7 William J. SAMARIN points to the favourable geographic, cultural and linguistic conditions prevalent in respect of the creation of a lingua franca in this territory. He cannot, however, convincingly prove why it was SANGO and not any other language which established itself (SAMARIN 1955, 257/8).

In this way, SANGO became the language of all those who left their home villages in order to look for work and riches in towns like Bangui. The designation *sango tí salawísi*[8], under which the language also became known, reflects the importance attributed to the lingua franca by the countless migrant labourers. This designation has the approximate meaning of: "the language of those who leave the village in order to take up gainful employment".

278 Although the Roman Catholic and Protestant missionaries in the Ubangi territory had not without reservations welcomed the spread of "Pidgin Sango" and would often have preferred as medium of religious tuition the vernacular languages which they felt to be the "cultural" languages, it was they who gave a special fillip to the growth of SANGO. As these missionaries recognized that it was not possible to acquire a sufficient knowledge of this multiplicity of languages and turn them to useful advantage — a fact which was aggravated by their frequently being transferred from one tribal territory to another — they were forced to use SANGO, which was understood everywhere.

Thus, the learning of SANGO was stimulated, and many an African first came into contact with this language there. The missionaries made efforts to regularize the language as far as orthography was concerned; it is due to them that SANGO was elevated to a written language and that the initial literature of any volume came into being[9].

279 The fact that the interest in the learning of SANGO has not flagged up till today and that the spread of this language in the Central African Republic has not yet come to an end, can be attributed especially to the following reasons[10]:

a) SANGO — together with French — is looked upon as a p r e s t i g e language, as it is spoken by the leading social stratum of the country[11]. Anyone not having learnt SANGO is branded as uneducated or as "somebody from the bush" (SAMARIN 1955, 262/3).

b) In a corresponding way, the knowledge of SANGO forms a hardly avoidable prerequisite for social and vocational advancement.

c) Moreover, significance of SANGO as a unifying factor in the development into a national state is stressed. It does not infrequently happen that

---

8 *salawísi* is derived from the French word *service* (SAMARIN 1955, 257).
9 Inter alia, the New Testament, some parts of the Old Testament, the mass-book as well as the catechism, were translated into SANGO. Moreover, the Protestant mission in Bossangoa edits a monthly periodical in SANGO under the title of "La Trompette Evangélique" (JACQUOT 1961, 163).
10 These reasons have already in part been mentioned, in as far as they were of importance for the early development period of the lingua franca.
11 SAMARIN, on the other hand, notes that the so-called *évolués*, i.e. those Africans, who have received a fundamental education in French, stand out from the rest of the population by speaking French amongst one another (SAMARIN 1955, 265).

people, who understand one another in dialects of the same language turn to SANGO for conversation (cf. SAMARIN 1955, 264). Not much sympathy is bestowed on the vernacular languages, the reason being that they do not contribute towards unification, but towards the division of the population.

d) Finally SANGO often seems to be looked upon as the language of Christianity. An illustration of this is given by the reported dream of a *Kare* man, in which he had been addressed by the devil in his mother tongue[12] and by God in SANGO (loc. cit. 264). It is hardly surprising, therefore, that a close contact is considered to exist between SANGO and Christianity as the Word of God was conveyed as a rule by means of SANGO to the native population (see par. 278). For the sole reason of being able to follow religious tuition the numerous Christians in the Central African Republic felt it their duty to learn SANGO. Little change in this situation has occurred up till today.

280 In 1965, the importance of SANGO was officially acknowledged — the language was declared the n a t i o n a l language in the Central African Republic (ALEXANDRE 1967, 22).

*Present extent of use*

281 The total number of users of SANGO amounts to approximately one million (VOEGELIN 1964, 70), according to Pierre ALEXANDRE even to 1.5 million (ALEXANDRE 1967, 22). No exact data can be given on the spread of the lingua franca. Pursuant to André JACQUOT it is widespread in the entire territory of the Central African Republic (JACQUOT 1961, 158), and this statement has been confirmed by other authors (cf. for example, SAMARIN 1955). It must, however, be surmised that areas exist in which its use is very limited. It may be assumed that it is far less used in the north and north-east of the country than in the south, where it is spoken beyond the left bank of the Ubangi River as far as Congo-Kinshasa (JACQUOT 1961, 158). In the south-west SANGO has advanced along the Ubangi River as far as Dongou (HAUSER 1954, 25).

282 It seems that the spread of SANGO is essentially restricted to the Central African Republic. The reason may be found in the economic isolation of the country (SAMARIN 1955, 260) and the lack of contact with the neighbouring countries. In addition, a feeling of national antagonism seems to have developed between some states. On account of their higher standard of living, the Cameroon people, for instance, consider themselves superior to the inhabitants of the Central African Republic (loc. cit. 260). In the north, however, it must be said that the sphere of influence of SANGO reaches

---

12 The *Kare* or *Kari* live in the territory of the Mbomu River, in the south-east of the Central African Republic and in Congo-Kinshasa. Their language is counted among the *Bantu* languages.

as far as the *Sara* area, in part even beyond the frontiers of the Republic of Chad, to which region it was carried by native labourers having found employment in the Ubangi territory (CHABRELIE 1935, 130).

In the south, SANGO was confronted by LINGALA, another lingua franca, by which it was possibly prevented from spreading further. In similar manner, in the north, TURKU or Chad ARABIC, another lingua franca, opposed SANGO.

*Dialects*

283 In consideration of the wide spread achieved by the lingua franca, and additionally of the heterogeneous population speaking it, it is hardly surprising that a number of different dialects grew up.

Thus already differences exist in the use of SANGO between the youngsters and the grown-ups, in whose case the language is interlarded with many borrowed words from the own mother tongue (JACQUOT 1960, 174). Beyond that there exist dialectal variations corresponding to social differences. SAMARIN discovers a widespread dialect, inter alia, of which he maintains: "... it is that of the displaced or 'evolved' population: the *métis*, the truck-drivers, the roadworkers, the travelling merchants, etc." (SAMARIN 1958, 63). This dialect, which must be defined sociologically and not geographically, approximately constitutes the standard form of SANGO. Chiefly through the fact that borrowed words from French are passed out it has an influence on the other SANGO dialects which should not be underestimated (loc. cit. 63).

284 Dialectal differences can also be found within the mission. Pursuant to JACQUOT there is not only one Protestant and one Roman Catholic SANGO orthography (cf. SAMARIN 1955, 267), but also two corresponding dialect forms conforming to these orthographies. Whereas the Protestant SANGO is built up on the basis of the dialect of Bossangoa, its Roman Catholic variation has been formed by the dialect of Mbaiki (JACQUOT 1960, 173).

285 Finally, the sub-division into dialects is especially distinguished through its having an ethnic basis. In the use of SANGO, almost every tribe has particular phonological and lexical characteristics (cf. SAMARIN 1958, 63; JACQUOT 1960, 173) so that it is not entirely unjustified to maintain that there are as many dialects as there are tribes making use of SANGO. Here, however, further studies are required in order not only to investigate the number and spread of the various dialects, but also the linguistic and sociolinguistic differences between them.

*Sociolinguistic situation*

286 The extent of the use of SANGO fluctuates not only within the separate regions of the Central African Republic, but is also quite different in respect

of age and sex. Thus SAMARIN ascertained that SANGO in the interior of the country is not spoken by children up to the age of ten nor by grown-ups over forty (SAMARIN 1955, 263); it is therefore the predominant language of the working population there. This does, however, not apply everywhere and in particular in the capital city of Bangui an entirely different situation exists. There it is the children who have an excellent command of SANGO. At school, the melting pot of various ethnic groups, SANGO has established itself as lingua franca. According to JACQUOT the children frequently have a better mastery of SANGO than of the language of their parents (JACQUOT 1961, 163). Here the tendency of the development from the p i d g i n language to c r e o l e becomes evident by the fact that the SANGO lingua franca becomes the first language of some people.

287 SANGO is also not in the same way as widespread amongst men as it is amongst women. In this connection SAMARIN notes that the knowledge of it is more widespread amongst men than amongst women (SAMARIN 1955, 263). This can be explained in the best way by taking into consideration the larger male proportion in school attendance (see below) and the greater mobility of the male population, which often can leave the territory of their own tribe and away from home quickly learns SANGO.

On the other hand, the knowledge of SANGO is more widespread amongst the women than it may appear at first sight. Thus SAMARIN, for instance, observed that women, who had a command of SANGO, denied understanding the language, and also their husbands in spite of facts pointing to the contrary stated that their womenfolk could not communicate in SANGO (loc. cit. 263). Possibilities for women to learn SANGO are offered above all in the market-place. There they meet women from other tribes and thus the market-place presents fertile soil for the spread of SANGO. It is therefore not surprising, that JACQUOT — in contradistinction to SAMARIN — ascertained in the case of the women vis-à-vis the men a frequent superiority of knowledge of the lingua franca (the garrulousness of women being given by the latter as the reason; JACQUOT 1960, 174).

288 Thanks to the investigations by André JACQUOT we have an intimate knowledge of the importance of SANGO in the capital city Bangui. His data rely on the results of a system of interviews which he carried out at the request of the *Ministère des Finances et du Plan (Territoire de l'Oubangui)* in 1958 (JACQUOT 1961). In this case he approached altogether 1,412 persons living in ten villages of the northern district of the town [13].

The investigation renders possible a review of the multiplicity of ethnic groups and languages represented in Bangui. Accordingly, the 1,412 persons

---

13 It is subject to question whether this sample test, in consideration of the limited area of residence of the persons questioned, is deemed to be representative for the entire population of the town of Bangui.

interviewed belonged to 26 various ethnic groups; this review, however, also demonstrates that the individual tribes were represented in very different ways and numbers. Thus 96.4% of all persons questioned professed to belong to five tribes, i.e. *Mandjia* 36.7%, *Mbakamandjia* 34.3%, *Gbaya* 10.5%, *Gbanu* 9.2% and *Banda* 5.7%, whereas the remaining 3.6% were divided up amongst the other 21 ethnic groups[14].

289 The results of these interviews prove that SANGO is undoubtedly the predominant language in Bangui. With the exception of one twenty-two year old woman, who had lived in Bangui but for a short time, all persons questioned confirmed their knowledge of SANGO (JACQUOT 1961, 160).

It is certain that the urban surroundings essentially contribute towards the spread of SANGO. It is, however, astonishing that 90.5% of the people interviewed who were not born in Bangui[15] maintained that they had learnt the language already during childhood, i.e. as a rule b e f o r e their arrival in the capital. The remaining 9.5%, who accordingly had learnt SANGO not in their homeland, but in Bangui, are made up of 31.9% men and 68.1% women. As the number of new arrivals in Bangui shows a slight preponderance of male population (53.1% vis-à-vis 46.9% of the female population), SAMARIN's statement that the spread of SANGO amongst the women in the country is smaller than amongst the men (cf. sect. 232) is thereby supported.

290 JACQUOT, like SAMARIN, also ascertained that the use of SANGO is not tied up with a certain social context, but is practically unlimited (SAMARIN 1955, 262; JACQUOT 1961, 163). In increasing measure, people of the same origin and language are using the lingua franca in daily life[16], and also within the family SANGO is spoken more and more. Whereas amongst the 1,412 persons interviewed in Bangui, 15.8% declared that within the family circle they exclusively employed their mother tongue, 74.6% stated that they used SANGO to the same degree as the mother tongue, and for 2.5% SANGO was the sole means of communication within the family[17]. All of the persons questioned, however, unanimously maintained[18] that during their visits to their homelands they conversed in their mother tongue (loc. cit. 163).

291 In JACQUOT's records data are furthermore found on the spread of SANGO

14 *Mandjia* (Manja), *Mbakamandjia* (Ngbaka Manja), *Gbaya* (Baya) and *Gbanu* (Banu) presumably speak dialects of o n e a n d t h e s a m e language (cf. TUCKER/BRYAN 1956, 37–39).
15 Only 12.9% of all persons interviewed stated to have been born in Bangui.
16 Thus SAMARIN observed, for example, a group of people in Mbaiki, whose mother tongue was ISUNGU (Lissongo, Mbati) a *Bantu* language, who in discussing some local affairs did not, however, use their own language, but conversed in SANGO (SAMARIN 1955, 262).
17 JACQUOT supplies no data on the remaining 7.1%.
18 Apart from a 22 year old office clerk, who was born in Bangui and stated to be able to speak only SANGO and French.

as w r i t t e n language. Altogether 32.2% of all persons questioned were able to read SANGO, but only 11.8% were also in the position to write it.

In this connection a marked discrepancy shows up between the two sexes. Whereas SANGO is hardly spoken less by the women and girls in Bangui than by the male population, the number of women able to read or read and write the language is disproportionately smaller. Thus the female section of the population group able to read SANGO amounts to 33.7% vis-à-vis 66.3% of the male population; and within the group in the position to read and write SANGO the female population is far more unfavourably represented with 6.6% in comparison to 93.4% of the male population. These unbalanced figures are the result of the low school attendance on the part of the female population (cf. par. 289). For a long time having been the prerogative of the male youths, school attendance by the girls up to today has by no means become a matter of course.

SANGO has chiefly remained a s p o k e n language. Its use as a written language has achieved greater importance only at the Christian missions (JACQUOT 1961, 163/4).

## VI. West African Coast

### a) YORUBA

292 YORUBA, presumably a *Niger-Congo* language[1], belongs to the most important African languages if measured by the number of its speakers. According to more recent statements it is spoken by about 12 million people (BAMGBOSE 1966, 2)[2]. It is sub-divided into approximately twenty in part very different dialects, but has a so-called standard form, used in school instruction, in literature and during contact between people who speak different dialects. This standard form is based on the dialect of Oyo; it contains, however, also characteristics of other YORUBA dialects. YORUBA is spoken not only in south-western Nigeria, but also far in the west by sizeable groups in Dahomey and Togoland.

293 The importance of YORUBA as lingua franca is relatively small[3]. Johann

---

1 Within the *Niger-Congo* family YORUBA is counted amongst the *Kwa* group. Whether this group actually forms a genetic unity as branch of the *Niger-Congo* family, as has been assumed so far, has not yet satisfactorily been investigated and must therefore remain contentious.
2 Former estimates resulted in essentially smaller figures between three and five million (see FORDE 1951, 3; WESTERMANN/BRYAN 1952, 84; ROWLANDS 1963, 208).
3 Pursuant to E. C. ROWLANDS, a prominent expert on this language, it is not used as lingua franca at all (ROWLANDS 1963, 209).

LUKAS notes: "In the Warri province the Yoruba dialect of the Yekri, a trading people, plays a specific role. Yoruba is second language also for a number of users of small sub-divisions of languages in the north of the Owo district in the Ondo province, for instance, in Ikaramu" (LUKAS n.d. 21/2). It is furthermore said to be lingua franca in the northern and north-western part of the Auchi district of the Benin province.

294 Earlier statements point to the fact that YORUBA formerly had been widespread as lingua franca in Dahomey, Togoland and even in the north-eastern territory of the present state of Ghana. Ernst HENRICI reports in 1891:

"In a similar way Yoruba, as far distant as the Fullah tribes, occupies the position of a general lingua franca, which it attained through the brisk trade of the Yoruba people, who extend their trading expeditions not only to Yendi, to the Moschi and Grussi as well as to the Middle Niger River, but who have also settled amongst them. Between the Salaga River and the Niger River Yoruba enjoys the same communication value as Haussa, and also in Adeli, people can be found in almost every place, with whom one make oneself understood in Yoruba." *

Also Diedrich WESTERMANN ascertained that YORUBA is widespread as a t r a d i n g language, particularly in the north-east of Togoland (WESTERMANN 1905, 32*).

## b) EWE

295 The EWE language is counted amongst the *Kwa* group of the *Niger-Congo* languages. It is sub-divided into a number of dialects which in part differ so greatly from one another that a communication between the speakers of some dialects is hardly possible, or even impossible. The most important of these dialects are:
ANG'LO (phonet. aŋlɔ, also called *Awuna*). It is mainly spoken in the area near the coast between the Volta River and the Togo border.
Western interior (occasionally called aŋfɔɛ). It is composed of several dialects, which differ but little from one another and are spoken north of ANG'LO.
WATYI, spoken in south-eastern Togo with the exception of the coastal strip.

---

\* Desgleichen hat Yoruba weit hinaus bis zu den Fullahstämmen die Stellung einer allgemeinen Verkehrssprache, zu welcher es durch den regen Handel der Yorubaleute gelangt ist, die nicht nur ihre Handelsreisen bis Yendi, zu den Moschi und Grussi und zum mittleren Niger ausdehnen, sondern sich auch unter diesen Völkern niedergelassen haben. Zwischen Salaga und dem Niger ist die Yorubasprache eine fast ebenso gültige Münze wie Haussa, und auch in Adeli findet man fast an jedem Ort Leute, mit welchen man sich auf Yoruba verständigen kann" (HENRICI 1891, VII).

MINA or GE *(gɛ̃)*[4]. It serves as a means of communication chiefly in Togo along the coast as well as in south-western Dahomey. Its centre of spread is Anecho, and for this reason this dialect is occasionally also called *Anecho-Ewe*.

ADYA *(Aja)* is a language spoken on both sides of the Togo-Dahomey border to the north and south of 7° latitude.

GU (phonet. *gū*), spread in south-eastern Dahomey, inter alia, in Porto Novo.

FO (phonet. *fɔ*), often called *Dahoméen* by the French. It is the predominant language form of southern Dahomey.

MAHI (phonet. *maxé*), spoken in and east of Savalou (WESTERMANN 1905, 27/8\*; WESTERMANN/BRYAN 1952, 83/4).

In the following, the eastern, i.e. the EWE dialects GU, FO and MAHI spread preponderantly in Dahomey, shall be left out because they take up a certain special position linguistically and sociolinguistically.

296 The boundary of expansion of the *Ewe* population is formed in the southwest by the Volta, but some EWE settlements are still to be found on the other side of the river, such as Tefle, Vume (Wume), Bakpa or Mefe (Mafi). Thence EWE is employed on the right bank of the Volta River by the *Adang'me* population living there, and serves as lingua franca upstream along the Volta from the Atlantic coast up into the region of Anum (WESTERMANN 1905, 11\*).

297 Even in the north-western part, north of Hohoe, EWE is used by some Togo Remnant tribes as lingua franca. To these mainly belong the *Santrokofi, Akpafu-Lolobi,* the southern *Balemi* and the *Likpe* in Ghana, as well as on the other side of the border the *Ahlo, Kposo* and *Kebu* in Togoland. Apart from those, it is particularly widespread in the area of the *Avatime, Nyangbo-Tafi* and *Logba,* which forms an enclave in the *Ewe* country. If the function of EWE as medium of communication amongst the southern and eastern Togo Remnant tribes can be traced back as far as the early 19th Century, it may be said that it received its decisive impulses through the arrival of the German colonial power on the Slave Coast. Up till then, TWI was the leading lingua franca in this area. Already for some considerable time lively trade between the Gold Coast and the Togo Remnant tribes living east of the Volta River had taken place. This trade was mainly carried on by TWI-speaking merchants, who thereby were able to spread their language in the area of these tribes. But "by the German government, the border traffic to the British Gold Coast was rendered more difficult as this government had a natural interest in diverting the trade route of the inhabitants of the hinterland to the German coastal places... In addition

---

[4] *gɛ̃* is the designation applied by the speakers of this dialect themselves. MINA and *gɛ̃* are often employed in a complementary sense in Togo: the latter in respect of the basic form and MINA for the lingua franca form.

the influence of the mission must be mentioned, which had elevated Ewe to a written language and had already created a sizeable amount of literature" (WESTERMANN 1905, 12*). Thereby EWE spread towards the north, but it could only in part oust the influence of TWI.

Today three EWE dialects are used as written languages, i.e. ANG'LO, MINA and GU (WESTERMANN/BRYAN 1952, 84). The ANG'LO dialect has thereby gained considerable importance and prestige in south-eastern Ghana and in the south of Togo. It is used in school, in the church and in various publications.

298 Although the literature of MINA in comparison appears to occupy a very modest place, this very dialect seems to be on the way to becoming the dominating African lingua franca in Togoland. Towards the end of the 17th Century and during the 18th Century groups of GA- and TWI-speaking inhabitants of the Gold Coast left their homeland and settled on the eastern Togo coast in the vicinity of the present town of Anecho. They relinquished their languages and adopted EWE as first language. The use of EWE amongst these immigrants led to a formation of a special dialect, i.e. MINA (see HENRICI 1891, 4/5). MINA spread along the coast. It penetrated in the west as far as Lome, the capital of Togo, and became there the language of the street and market place by slowly reducing the influence of the other dialects, particularly that of ANG'LO. Thence MINA was carried along the railway line into the interior of the country and in the centres of trade and traffic, such as Atakpamé and Sokodé, took on the function of a lingua franca.

### c) TWI

299 TWI, often also named *Akan*[5], is the dominating language of the state of Ghana. It is included in the group of *Kwa* languages, which, in turn, belongs to the *Niger-Congo* family (GREENBERG 1963, 8).

300 The large spread of TWI is to a major part due to the political development on the Gold Coast in precolonial times. At the end of the 16th Century Osai Tutu (1695–1731) founded the *Ashanti* empire, as capital of which he

---

* Aber "durch die deutsche Regierung wurde der Grenzverkehr nach der englischen Goldküste erschwert, da sie ein natürliches Interesse hatte, den Handelsweg der Hinterlandbewohner in die deutschen Küstenorte zu lenken ... Hierzu kommt der Einfluß der Mission, die das Ewe zur Schriftsprache erhoben und in derselben schon eine ansehnliche Literatur geschaffen hat" (WESTERMANN 1905, 12*).

5 The terminus *Akan* has been used in different ways. Whereas some authors employ it as designation for a single language, it serves others as the name for a group of closely-interrelated languages to which, next to TWI, GUANG and ANYI'BAULE belong (see WESTERMANN/BRYAN 1952, 78 ff). But even the use of the terminus TWI is not uniform. With some authors it does not comprise the FANTE dialect, which is mentioned as a separate language.

designated Kumasi. Under his successors the empire expanded even further in spite of several setbacks. It reached the zenith of its power under Osai Osibe Kwamina (1800–1824), who extended the rule of the *Asanti* as far as the coast and who, shortly before his death, was able to inflict a serious defeat of the British troops in occupation there. The *Ashanti* empire at that time reached as far as Kong and into the *Mosi* territory in the north. Around the middle of the 19th Century, the hostilities between the *Ashanti* and the British became more and more aggravated and finally led to the capture of Kumasi by the British Governor WOLSELEY in 1874.

301 As language of the Ashanti empire, TWI spread to all those places where the Ashanti armies gained a foothold. Many tribes adopted TWI and gave up their own language. Amongst them were some sections of the *Guang*, who once had made up the leading population group in the territory of present-day Ghana. Thus, the formerly powerful *Wasaw* in the north and east of Ahanta presumably relinquished their language in favour of TWI (CHRISTALLER 1875, X), and it is maintained that also the *Fante*, living on the coast west of Accra, originally spoke a GUANG dialect before taking on TWI (RAPP 1955, 229).

302 It was not only the political development which helped towards the spread of TWI as a lingua franca, but the religion of the TWI-speaking population gained in importance beyond their boundaries and became the language of r e l i g i o n amongst the neighbouring tribes. "The language of the fetish priests, even with the Ga, is Twi, and the religious terminology of the peoples of South and Central Togo as well as of the Gold Coast is Twi to a large extent. All religious hymns and cult songs of the Guang people, with the exception of the Gondja, consist of Twi texts . . ." *

303 The colonial times gave fresh impulse to the spread of TWI. In the south of the territory of the Gold Coast, as it was then called, schools were established and in the comparatively underdeveloped north there soon arose a stratum of officials from the south, in the majority members of the TWI-speaking population, who carried TWI into those areas.

The Gold Coast was given a network of motor roads and new markets were opened to trade in areas which hitherto had hardly been accessible. As lorry drivers and traders, TWI people penetrated far into the north and spread their language in the market-places. Thus, E. L. RAPP, for instance, remarks on the situation in north-eastern Ghana:

"The men of the Dagomba speak Haussa mostly as second language; the women, however, and chiefly the market women (and which woman there is not a market woman?) in the towns have quite a good command of Twi

---

\* "Die Sprache der Fetischpriester, auch bei den Ga, ist das Twi, und die religiöse Terminologie der Völker Süd- und Mitteltogos wie der Goldküste ist zum großen Teil Twi. Sämtliche religiösen Gesänge und Kultlieder der Guang-Völker, außer den Gondja, sind Twi-Texte . . ." (RAPP 1955, 229).

already today."* Beyond the Volta River in the east, where TWI could in part already gain a foothold before the Pax Britannica after the Ashanti wars, it was adopted more and more by the Togo Remnant tribes.

The expansion of TWI on the left bank of the Volta River received a tremendous fillip through the arrival of the Europeans on the Gold Coast. TWI-speaking traders crossed the Volta River and carried on trade with the tribes resident there, more particularly with the *Nkunya, Bowili, Balemi*, and the western *Kebu, Adele* and *Ewe*. The products acquired there they sold to the European trading posts on the coast. Thereby, TWI spread as lingua franca amongst these tribes. The influence of the language, however, was restricted by the arrival of the German colonial power towards the end of the 19th Century. The Germans attempted to repress the trade with the Gold Coast, then under British administration. In addition, a rivalling lingua franca, i.e. EWE, was introduced there particularly through the work of the German missionaries (see WESTERMANN 1905, 11/12*). Only after the First World War, when the western part of Togo had become British mandatory territory, the situation changed again in favour of TWI.

Also among the *Adang'me* and *Ga*[6], living on the south-east coast of Ghana, Twi spreads further, and most of the men and the market women have a command of it.

304 TWI is spoken today by approximately 2.9 million people as mother tongue and by a further million as lingua franca (REDDEN 1963, IX; GIL 1964, table 1). Accordingly, about 58% of the total population of Ghana has a command of it[7]. The nuclear territory of TWI lies between the Volta and Tano Rivers, and the area of spread as lingua franca reaches beyond that up to the border of Togoland and the Ivory Coast, and from the Atlantic Coast in the south to beyond the Volta towards the north.

---

* "Die Männer der Dagomba sprechen als zweite Sprache meist das Haussa als Lingua franca, die Frauen dagegen und vor allem die Marktfrauen (und welche Frau ist dort keine Marktfrau) in den Städten können schon heute das Twi recht gut gebrauchen" (RAPP 1955, 229).

6 The spread of TWI amongst the *Ga* is especially remarkable in as far as these people prossess a pronounced "language nationalism". The German missionaries who arrived at the Gold Coast in 1826, settled in the territory of the *Ga* and created a wealth of literature in GA, mostly of religious content. They were presumably not in a position at that time to recognize and take into consideration the limited importance of GA and the large spread then already gained by TWI. When in the second half of the 19th Century a more specific knowledge of the interior of the country revealed the prominence of TWI, the Ga people had, on the basis of the preference extended by the Europeans, already become convinced that their language was superior to the others. Attempts to introduce TWI as "auxiliary language" into the Ga territory met with impassioned resistance on the part of the *Ga* population and had little success (RAPP 1955, 222).

7 According to the census of 1960, the total population of Ghana amounted to 6,727,000; in 1968 approx. 8 million according to estimates.

*Dialects*

305   TWI is sub-divided into a number of dialects, of which, pursuant to CHRISTALLER, there exist presumably more than twenty (CHRISTALLER 1875, X–XIV). The most important of these dialects is ASANTE, being spoken by almost one million people in and around the town of Kumasi, capital city of the *Ashanti* empire. AKUAPEM is spoken in the north of Accra. It served as a basis for the first large publications in TWI, thus, for instance, in the translation of the Bible, and presumably enjoys for this reason the highest esteem amongst the TWI dialects (REDDEN 1963, IX). AKYEM is spoken in the area between ASANTE and AKUAPEM.

A special position within the TWI area is occupied by the FANTE dialect, which is used along the coast from Accra in the east about as far as Sekondi in the west[8]. By reason of their spread on the coast the *Fante* — in a similar manner to the *Ga* — already came into early contact with the Europeans, and their dialect was elevated by the missionaries to a written language. Not the least because of this there developed amongst the *Fante* a pride in their language, together with a depreciation of other languages, for instance, also of other TWI dialects.

### d) GA

306   GA (phonet. gã) together with ADANG'ME and KROBO forms a group of dialects which are spoken in the south-east of Ghana. Traditionally, the so-called *Ga-Adang'me* group is counted amongst the *Kwa* branch of the *Niger-Congo* family.

In 1826, German missionaries settled in the part of the Gold Coast which at that time was under Danish administration. As language for school instruction they chose GA, which was spread in the area of their work. Thus it came about that this language today, in spite of its limited number of users, boasts of a rich literature, amongst which there is a Bible translation. GA was furthermore able to draw advantage from the fact that Accra, the capital of the state of Ghana, is situated in the territory of its use. Pursuant to E. L. RAPP, GA is "spoken by somewhat more than 50,000 people as mother tongue and understood by about 100,000 others as lingua franca and school language". The Ghana census of 1960, on the other hand, states the total number of the GA population as amounting to 236,210 (GIL 1964, 2).

---

[8] In 1933 Ernst SCHULTZE reported on a lingua franca which he called "Fanti", and which is said to be used on the Guinea Coast, more particularly on the Gold Coast (SCHULTZE 1933, 395). It can hardly be doubted that this name is derived from that of the above-named TWI dialect; it is, however, used by SCHULTZE in an entirely different sense. SCHULTZE apparently designated with this a pidgin form of English spread in West Africa, an application which is entirely unjustified and presumably is the result of a misunderstanding.

## e) MENDE and TEMNE

307  MENDE belongs to the group of *Mande* languages, which, according to Joseph H. GREENBERG, are counted amongst the *Niger-Congo* family (GREENBERG 1963, 8).
The *Mende*, living in the interior of Sierra Leone, advanced in the direction of the Atlantic coast already at an early date. Thus J. F. SCHOEN reported as early as 1882, that "it seems that the nation is pressing on to the seashore, as they occupy at present the country where, in 1839, the slave-dealers had their depôts of slaves in the Sherbro country. Their baracoons were destroyed on the banks of the great river Bum by Capain DENMAN, of the British Navy, in 1840 or 1841, and since that time the country is open to British commerce and missionary operations, and the Mende are the principal occupants of the place, and their language has all but superseded, and will ere long supersede, the Sherbro altogether" (quoted from MIGEOD 1908, V).

308  Today, MENDE is spoken everywhere in the southern half of Sierra Leone. It has spread along the coast among the *Bulom* (Sherbro), *Banta, Bum, Krim* and *Vai*, and is also used in the interior as a lingua franca by the *Gola, Kissi* and *Kono* (cf. DALBY 1962, 63). MENDE is still on the advance and thereby contributes towards the recession of the languages spoken in the coastal area. Thus BANTA is already dying out and MENDE is becoming more and more the predominant language of the *Banta* population — only a few old people still speak BANTA. Not very much different is the situation amongst the *Bum* and *Krim*. Also amongst the *Vai* living in Sierra Leone a sizeable group can be detected, speaking MENDE as mother tongue. A growing spread can also be ascertained amongst the *Gola, Kissi* and *Kono* (DALBY 1962, 64—6).
Pursuant to the census of 1948, MENDE is spoken by 586,000 people (WESTERMANN/BRYAN 1952, 37). Including those people who use it as a lingua franca, the total number today may well approximate one million[9] (cf. HAIR 1962, 40).

309  TEMNE, next to MENDE the most prominent African language in Sierra Leone, has also spread to some extent as lingua franca. Just as MENDE it presumably belongs to the *Niger-Congo* family, but within this family belongs to the so-called "West Atlantic group". TEMNE is spoken as second language amongst the *Loko* (*Landogo* and *Logo*), *Limba, Bulom,* and in part also amongst the *Susu* in the north-west of Sierra Leone (DALBY 1962, 64). The area of its spread therefore comprises the central part as well as large areas in the north of Sierra Leone. The number of its speakers, stated in the census of 1948 to be 505,000 (WESTERMANN/BRYAN 1952, 13), may well amount to 600,000 (cf. ROBERTS 1962, 119).

---

9 Thus Janet ROBERTS, for instance, estimates the number to amount to 900,000 (ROBERTS 1962, 119).

## f) SUSU

310 As in the case of MENDE and MANDINGO, the predominant lingua franca of the western Sudan, SUSU (Sosso, Soussou) belongs to the group of *Mande* languages, which Joseph H. Greenberg includes in his *Niger-Congo* family (Greenberg 1963, 8). SUSU is so closely related to the neighbouring DYALONKE, that both of them are treated as dialects of one language only in the *Handbook of African Languages* (Westermann/Bryan 1952, 36).

311 Already in the 18th Century SUSU had achieved a temporary prominence. P. E. H. Hair remarks in this connection:
"Susu appears to have been in fairly widespread use in the Sierra Leone estuary, possibly as a lingua franca, at the time of the settlements there around 1790, but its use in this locality thereafter receded" (Hair 1965, 38).

312 The area of influence of SUSU as lingua franca today includes more particularly the western part of the state of Guinea, i.e. the territory between the Fouta Djalon and the Atlantic coast. Especially in the area adjacent to the coast, SUSU is still gaining in importance. Various smaller tribes live there, such as *Mani* (Mmani), *Baga*, as well as the *Nalu* and *Landuma*, who in increasing measure relinquish their linguistic and cultural characteristics and are steadily being absorbed by the *Susu*, advancing towards the coast. The concomitant sociolinguistic process seems to take a similar course in the individual cases: At first SUSU is used as a lingua franca in the communication outside the own ethnic group. The youngsters acquire a deficient knowledge of the language of their parents and grow up with SUSU as p r i m a r y language, which during the course of the coming decades will increasingly displace the other language. This one will eventually only be spoken by the older generation and in extreme cases will die out.
Maurice Houis thus reports that the language of the *Mani* in the Kabak province of Guinea is already extinct and is only still used in some villages of the Samu province near the border of Sierra Leone (Houis 1963, 2). A similar situation arose in the case of the *Landuma* and *Nalu*, on which Houis reports:

"Now in the zone situated on the left side of the Rio Nunez River (up-stream, the Tinguilita), the Landuma and Nalu population practically completely gave up their respective language, at least in the more active part of the population; even if this is not the case, the Susu language represents for them the language affording them the best means for communication." *

---

\* "Or, dans la zone située du côté de la rive gauche du Rio Nunez (en amont, la Tinguilita), les Landuman et les Nalu ont pratiquement abandonné leur langue respective, du moins dans les couches actives de la population; même quand ce n'est pas le cas, le susu représente néanmoins pour eux la langue qui leur permet le plus de communications" (Houis 1963, 1).

In the area of these tribes around the town of Boké a dialect grew up, which possibly represents a lingua franca form of SUSU.

The influence of SUSU has certainly made itself felt most amongst the *Baga*. The preponderant majority of the *Baga* population living in the coastal strip between the Bay of Sangaréa and Cape Verga, speaks SUSU as a second language, and the importance of this language is still rising (Houis 1963, 1). SUSU, however, is less widespread amongst the *Baga* of Sitemu and Monchon.

313 On the peninsula of Kalum and in the province of Tabunsu further to the north, the influence of SUSU may well be at its strongest. Also in Conakry, the capital city of Guinea, SUSU is the leading lingua franca. The autochthonous population of the city, the *Baga,* increasingly prefer using SUSU. On account of the strong influx of people, the *Susu* in some parts of the city have already reached a proportion of 40 to 57% of the total population of Conakry, and even 84 to 94% of the inhabitants have a command of the language (Skalnikova 1964, 288/9).

314 The spread of SUSU amongst the neighbouring tribes of the interior, such as the *Ful, Dyalonke, Limba* and *Temne*, is unknown, as is the case with the exact total number of users of SUSU. As first language it is spoken by approximately 400,000 people, according to figures given by Houis[10] (Houis 1963, 10). Together with those who speak it as lingua franca the total number, however, may well not exceed considerably half a million. The sphere of influence of SUSU in the north reaches into the vicinity of Boké, in the east to Mamou and in the south includes a part of Sierra Leone.

## g) WOLOF

315 WOLOF (Volof, Ouolof), often called Dyolof (Jolof)[11] by the Europeans, probably belongs to the family of *Niger-Congo* languages. Within this family it is counted with the "West Atlantic languages" (Greenberg 1963, 8), a designation, the linguistic value of which must be considered doubtful.

316 WOLOF owes its development into a lingua franca, on the one hand, to the fact that it is the language of an ethnic group which is very large in number. With a proportion of 35%, the *Wolof* constitute by far the largest ethnic group of the state of Senegal (Crowder 1962, 85). On the other hand, the *Wolof*, on account of their early contact with the Europeans, have

---

10 In 1953, de Lavergne de Tressan stated the number of *Susu* speakers as follows: 243,877 in Guinea, 54,000 in Sierra Leone and 1,689 in Portuguese Guinea (Tressan 1953, 195).

11 Dyolof (phonet. dyɔlɔf) is the designation of the *Wolof* for their country (Westermann/Bryan 1952, 18).

gained a certain degree of prominence. In this connection Abdoulaye DIOP remarks:

> "Owing to their economic position the Wolof impose themselves as model on the other groups. They occupy the privileged social situations and are relatively prevalent in the other higher social categories. Thus they enjoy a prestige which they gained not through a brilliant past but through their actual success; this, however, is explained by the fact, as we have seen, that they have an ancient contact with the colonization." *

Contact between the WOLOF-speaking population and the Europeans in fact began at a relatively early time for sub-Saharan Africa. Thus P. E. H. HAIR reports that the Portuguese, during their travels along the West African coast in the second half of the 16th Century, considered it the best thing to take with them, next to the MANDINGO-speakers, WOLOF interpreters as well (HAIR 1966, 15).

WOLOF has become known particularly as the language of trade and is used as such beyond the *Wolof* territory in the trading centres by Libanese, Mauritanians and Moroccans, amongst others (GAMBLE 1957, 22). Apart from this, it seems to be widespread on the coast amongst the labourers coming from the interior. Thus A. DIOP ascertained during his investigations in Dakar that of the FUL-speaking *Tukuleur* who had immigrated, almost 95% (91 of 96) speak WOLOF (DIOP 1960, 414).

317 Today WOLOF is said to be spoken in the entire territory of Senegal as well as in Gambia (WESTERMANN/BRYAN 1952, 18; GAMBLE 1957, 22). It has spread along the railway line from Kaolack as far as Tambacounda and is spoken by a not inconsiderable number of *Tukuleur, Serer, Dyola, Balante, Mandyak, Mankanya, Banyun* (Banyuk) and even *Malinke* as lingua franca (SAUVAGEOT 1965, 1). In Gambia it is used particularly to the north of the river of the same name as well as in and around the capital city of Bathurst.

Altogether, approximately 1,150,000 may speak WOLOF as mother tongue (SAUVEGEOT 1965, 1), whereas it is presumably used by a further 500,000 as lingua franca. The total number of users of WOLOF accordingly amounts to over 1.6 million [12].

---

\* "Par leur position économique, les Wolof s'imposent comme modèles aux autres groupes. Ils détiennent les situations sociales privilégiées, et sont relativement plus nombreux dans les catégories sociales supérieures. Ils ont donc un prestige qui leur vient non d'un passé brillant mais de leur réussite actuelle; ce fait s'explique d'ailleurs, comme nous l'avons vu, par l'ancienneté de leur contact avec la colonisation" (DIOP 1965, 190).

12 This statement approaches the figure of 1.5 million, reported by Pierre ALEXANDRE (ALEXANDRE 1967, 24). In earlier works, however, much lower figures are given; for example, in the *Handbook of African languages* 668,510 (WESTERMANN/BRYAN 1952, 18), and according to de Lavergne DE TRESSAN 843,559 (TRESSAN 1953, 150).

*Present-day situation in Senegal*

318 Thanks to an investigation by François WIOLAND and Maurice CALVET we are in possession of more detailed data on the present situation of WOLOF in Senegal (WIOLAND/CALVET 1967). It is based on the evaluation of questionnaires sent out to all public schools in Senegal in 1963/4. Altogether the statements of 35,434 pupils from 360 schools in the country were taken into consideration. This sample test proved that Senegal in conformity with the spread of WOLOF can be divided into two zones:

1. Zone with a strong majority of WOLOF users;
2. Zone with a minority of WOLOF users.

319 Zone 1 comprises the administrative regions Cape Vert, Thiès, Djourbel and the district (Département) of Dagana. To this must be added the Sine Saloum region, inhabited by the *Serer,* in which WOLOF is also spoken by the preponderant majority of schoolchildren. In this zone WOLOF is used by between 96% and 99% of inhabitants according to the character of the administration unit, and only in west Kaolack, the heart of the *Serer* country, the proportion is smaller with 86.21%. In the town of Kaolack itself, however, the percentage of the users of WOLOF amounts to 97.57%.
In Dakar, 72.23% of the schoolchildren speak WOLOF as first language (lit. *"en famille"*) and a further 24.39% as second language. Accordingly, only 3.38% of them have no command of WOLOF. Remarkable is the importance of WOLOF within the family. 3,501 of the schoolchildren in Dakar declared speaking WOLOF at home, but only 66.2% of them have parents of *Wolof* descent. In the case of the remaining pupils, in 17.4% of the cases one parent is of *Wolof* descent and in respect of 16.4% of the children neither father nor mother is a member of the *Wolof* tribe. Especially the ethnically mixed marriages are contributing towards the spread of WOLOF. If any one of the spouses — be it husband or wife — is of *Wolof* descent, then as a rule the WOLOF language becomes the generally understood medium of communication within the family. But even if none of the spouses is a member of the Wolof tribe, their children not infrequently learn WOLOF as their first language — thus approximately 11.82% in Dakar and 14.58% in Ziguinchor, the capital of the Casamance. In this respect, WOLOF occupies a unique position amongst the languages in Senegal. It is possible that French can become the mother tongue of a child representing the issue of an ethnically mixed marriage, but in this case one of the parents belongs to an ethnic group not represented in Senegal (WIOLAND/CALVET 1967, 609). The importance of WOLOF in Senegal is furthermore illustrated by the fact that the zone with a strong majority of users of WOLOF includes the part of the country best developed and most

densely populated. Of the nine largest towns in Senegal, eight are situated in this zone, i.e. Dakar, Kaolack, Thiès, Rufisque-Bargny, Saint-Louis, Djourbel, Louga and M'Bour.

320 Zone 2, in which WOLOF is used by a minority of people, more particularly lies in the area of spread of the languages FUL, BAMBARA and DYOLA, i.e. in the north-east, east and south (south of the Gambia River in the Casamance) of the country. In the BAMBARA-speaking district (département) Kédougou in the extreme south-east of Senegal WOLOF seems not to have spread at all. The centre of resistance to the spread of WOLOF can further be found along the Senegal River in the districts Matam and Bakel. Whatever the case, every tenth inhabitant (10.19%) speaks WOLOF, however, in the district of Bakel, and every third inhabitant in the district of Tambacounda (35.63%).

But even in this zone WOLOF is steadily increasing the extent of its use. In Ziguinchor it is not only spoken as lingua franca but also as first language by more persons than any other language. 33.93% of the schoolchildren stated that they spoke WOLOF at home; in comparison to this figure, 25.07% speak BAMBARA and 19.84% DYOLA, the autochthonous language of this territory.

321 The increasing urbanization is not the least reason for the furtherance of the spread of WOLOF. As the following table shows, the proportion of WOLOF users in the city is in part more than five times as great as in rural areas:

Percentage of WOLOF users

|  | City | District (département) |
|---|---|---|
| Ziguinchor | 80.04% | 17.33% |
| Podor | 80 % | 12.75% |
| Vélingara | 47.81% | 7.19% |
| Sédhiou | 40.72% | 9.33% |
| Bignona | 37.15% | 6.75% |
| Kolda | 27.81% | 5 % |

According to this WOLOF is the most widespread language in Senegal, and its expansion has still not come to an end. WIOLAND and CALVET give three reasons for this:

a) "The fascination of the capital city,
b) The urban phenomenon,
c) The mixed marriages".

The importance of the ethnically mixed marriage for the spread of WOLOF as a mother tongue as well is seen in the fact that in the case of almost one third of the schoolchildren (31.08%), who use WOLOF with their parents at home, only one of the parents, or neither of them, belongs to the *Wolof* tribe. With regard to non-*Wolof* parents it can be said that 80% of the cases treat of *Ful, Serer* or *Bambara*.

Outside the *Wolof* territory WOLOF is mostly spoken in the area inhabited by the *Serer*. In some areas there the proportion of WOLOF users, which makes up in part more than 97%, is not much smaller than that in the *Wolof* territory itself.

WIOLAND and CALVET are of opinion that the status of French is not endangered by the expansion of WOLOF; but that both lingua francas fulfil complementary functions according to their own fields, in which French represents the official language of the country, particularly as medium of communication in school, university, in administration, technology and in international affairs. As first language, however, French is used only to a very limited extent: the investigation showed that only 0.87% of the persons questioned in Dakar and 0.22% in the whole of Senegal admitted to speaking French as mother tongue. In these figures, however, the pupils of private institutions are not taken into consideration; amongst these French is much more widespread than amongst those in public schools.

## VII. Western Sudan

### a) HAUSA

322  HAUSA belongs to the group of *Chad* languages, which presumably form a branch of the *Afro-Asiatic* language family[1]. The languages of this group are spoken in the area around Lake Chad.

*Development into a lingua franca*

323  The spread of HAUSA was originally restricted to the so-called seven "pure" *Hausa* states of Biram, Daura, Rano, Kano, Zazzau (Zaria), Gobir

---

[1] The designations *Chad* and *Afro-Asiatic* are used in the sense applied by J. H. GREENBERG (GREENBERG 1963, 42–65). There is a lack of unanimity as to the designation of these language groups. According to Johannes LUKAS HAUSA belongs to the *Chad-Hamitic* languages, to which he contrasts the *Chadic* languages (BURA, BATA, TERA, etc.), calling them a group on their own (cf. WESTERMANN/BRYAN 1952, 153–177). GREENBERG's *Chad* comprises both of LUKAS' different groups. Afro-Asiatic, according to GREENBERG, corresponds to the designation Hamito-Semitic of other authors, a terminus which GREENBERG had previously used himself (GREENBERG 1955, 43–61). A. N. TUCKER and Oswin KÖHLER have recently suggested the designation *Erythraic* as a replacement for this.

and Katsena, the area of which — apart from a small strip in the north — lay in the territory of the present Northern Nigeria. The spread of HAUSA in the seven so-called "impure" *Hausa* states, such as Kebbi, Nupe, Yoruba, Jukun, inter alia, already characterizes its development as lingua franca.

324 It was thanks in particular to trade that HAUSA became the leading lingua franca in the Western Sudan. The *Hausa* territory with its favourable geographic situation for trade between the Rain Belt in the south and the Sahara in the north was already in early times made the starting point for big caravans and the place of transshipment for wares of the most different sorts. In addition, the *Hausa* people proved themselves as clever and passionate traders. Johannes LUKAS notes in this connection:

"...the H a u s s a no doubt belong to the most e f f i c i e n t t r a d e r s in the world. Always on the move, radiating in all directions, buying and selling, patient, eloquent and efficient in business, and yet firmly rooted in their national heritage, friendly and obliging in their manner even far away from their homeland, superior to heathenism by their Mohammedan culture, almost fanatical in their faith, they establish their trading posts everywhere, which soon became a centre of economic life which is not only tolerated but also held in esteem." *

Through trade, HAUSA became one of the most widespread languages in Africa. Almost the entire northern half of the African Continent was visited by *Hausa* traders[2]. *Hausa* colonies sprang up in some North African cities such as Tripoli, in the eastern Sudan as far as the Red Sea and in the larger cities of entire West Africa.

Thus, for instance, M. BANTON reports in his study of Freetown, the capital city of Sierra Leone:

"One other tribe which deserves mention is the Hausa, composed of immigrants from Nigeria who are mostly traders and who enjoy a high status on account of their Muslim orthodoxy. They have taken the initiative in opening new lines of trade — such as peddling drinks and pieces of bread and butter among the vendors in the markets — while some blind Hausa beggars come from Nigeria to Freetown to sing in the streets and gather pennies from the curious" (BANTON 1957, 158).

325 This development, however, did not in every case lead towards HAUSA in the diaspora also becoming a lingua franca. Frequently its use remained

---

* ...die H a u s s a gehören ohne Zweifel zu den t ü c h t i g s t e n H a n d e l s - v ö l k e r n dieser Erde. Ewig in Bewegung, nach allen Richtungen hin ausstrahlend, kaufend und verkaufend, geduldig, redebegabt und geschäftstüchtig, dabei trotzdem fest in ihrem Volkstum wurzelnd, auch in weiter Entfernung von ihrer Heimat freundlich und entgegenkommend in ihrem Wesen, dem Heidentum durch ihre mohammedanische Kultur überlegen, den Fanatikern des Glaubens wenigstens nicht unebenbürtig, gründen sie allüberall ihre Niederlassungen, die gar bald zu einem nicht nur geduldeten, sondern anerkannten Zentrum des wirtschaftlichen Lebens werden" (LUKAS 1942, 21).

2 A. H. M. KIRK-GREENE notes: "Indeed, it is often said that you will find Hausa-speakers from Dakar to Port Sudan, from Leopoldville to Fez" (KIRK-GREENE 1963, 25).

restricted to the *Hausa* communities themselves, who in their contacts with the rest of the population had to use the leading language in each case. Only in Northern Nigeria and in the bordering countries HAUSA was able to achieve a greater importance as lingua franca as well.

*Development since 1800*

326 A new epoch in the history of HAUSA started at the beginning of the 19th Century. Amongst the *Hausa* population, members of the preponderantly nomadic *Ful* people had settled for some time, who, coming from the extreme West African territories, advanced further and further to the east in search of grazing grounds for their cattle. They were dependant on the *Hausa* princes, to whom they had to pay tribute. In 1804 a great leader, Osman dan Fodio, rose up amongst them. At the age of 60 this Moslem priest became one of the outstanding generals in African history. In few years he conquered the *Hausa* states and adjoining territories such as, for example, Adamawa. Osman established a great empire, which, still during his lifetime, he divided up between his son and his brother.

327 The importance of HAUSA was not encroached upon by this development, but was even considerably furthered. FUL, the language of the conquerors, could not gain a foothold[3], and thus it was the *Ful* people themselves who recognized the advantage of the already existing lingua franca and on the whole willingly aided in the spread of HAUSA within the domain of their rule. Thus the expansion of the *Ful* followed in the footsteps of the spread of HAUSA.

328 When towards the end of the 19th Century the British settled in Northern Nigeria, they found in HAUSA a medium of communication, which they had to take into account in their language policy. After HAUSA had for a long time only been written in Arabic letters, it now received an orthography based on the Latin alphabet, and a copious literature was founded in this new script. Institutions sprang up, devoting themselves to the standardization of HAUSA and publishing new works; this was done chiefly by the *Translation Bureau* in Zaria, the work of which was continued after World War II by the *Northern Region Literature Agency* (Norla) (LUKAS 1964, 275). The question of standardization is studied chiefly within the scope of the *Language Board* founded by the government in 1955 (loc. cit. 276). Fresh avenues of use were also opened up by the Press, such as by *"Gaskiya"*, a HAUSA periodical meaning "truth", and by radio broadcasts.

329 Since 1960 HAUSA enjoys equal rights with English as debating language in the parliament of Northern Nigeria, i.e. not only in the *House of Assembly* but also in the *House of Chiefs*. Beyond that, efforts were not

---

3 Only in Adamawa with its relatively high percentage of *Ful* people, FUL as a lingua franca achieved major importance (see par. 261–268).

lacking to turn HAUSA into the official language of the entire state of Nigeria. Remarkable in this connection is that amongst supporters of this language there were also prominent people from the south of the country, i.e. mostly members of the tribes *Yoruba* and *Ibo*, although especially amongst those tribes the resistance against HAUSA was particularly great.

Thus, Olu Akinfosile, the then *Federal Minister of Communications,* as well as Dennis Osadebay, President of the Nigerian Senate, took up a strong stand to make HAUSA the lingua franca of Nigeria, on account of its large spread in West Africa (KIRK-GREENE 1963, 25/6). Also Tai Solarin, the *Yoruba* journalist, through his weekly newspaper columns became an important protagonist of HAUSA as lingua franca of this most richly populated state in Africa (SCHWARZ 1965, 43).

330 These efforts, however, were condemned to failure. As preponderantly the language of the northern region of Nigeria, HAUSA meets with little sympathy on the part of the majority of the population in the southern part of this country. HAUSA became the subject of ethnic rivalries and the introduction of this language as a national language is deemed by many inhabitants a menace to the particularities of the smaller ethnic groups. In addition, the standard school education amongst the HAUSA-speaking population — compared with that of other groups of the population — is terrifyingly low, a fact which in a modern national state is not without importance.

*Present extent of spread*

331 HAUSA is spoken today by approximately 20 to 25 million people[4]. This estimate tallies with the data supplied by KIRK-GREENE in 1967. Accordingly, there exists "an approximate total number of at least twenty million speakers of Hausa in Northern Nigeria and most likely 25 million in Africa" (KIRK-GREENE 1967, 89). Pursuant to the Nigerian census of 1952, 5,488,446, i.e. 32.6% of the population of Northern Nigeria were members of the "Hausa tribe". Calculated on the basis of the census of 1963 the total number of *Hausa* population in the northern region of Nigeria would amount to about ten million. Thereby, however, the number of people using Hausa as first language is not fully defined. Although a not unimportant part of the population of Northern Nigeria speaks Hausa as first language, it confesses its adherance to other ethnic groups — in particular to the *Ful.* The following data recorded in the census of 1931 in the town of Kano are characteristic of this. Kano at that time amounted to 89,162 inhabitants (loc. cit. 100). This population can be broken down ethnically and linguistically as follows:

---

4 Large differences occur between the various authors in their estimates of the number of users, for example, MEYER, 261: 6 million; LUKAS 1964, 275: 13 million; KIRK-GREENE 1963, 25: 20 million.

|  | Tribe | Language |
|---|---|---|
| Hausa | 77.15% | 97.79% |
| Ful | 11.67% | 0.28% |
| Kanuri | 6.61% | 0.95% |
| Arab | 0.49% | 0.22% |
| Tuareg | 1.62% | 0.43% |
| Shuwa | 0.27% | — |
| Nupe | 1.43% | 0.06% |
| Yoruba | 0.76% | 0.27% |
| Total | 100.00% | 100.00% |

In this case, therefore an important, difference results between ethnic and linguistic memberships. Thus, for instance, only about every fortieth member of the *Ful* tribe spoke FUL as first language. The number of those who speak HAUSA as mother tongue, however, is more than 20% higher than those who belong ethnically to the *Hausa*. Apart from HAUSA no language is spoken by more than 1% of the population of Kano.

In regard to Northern Nigeria, KIRK-GREEN has compiled detailed data on the total number of users of HAUSA. In this connection he also took into consideration those people who speak the language as lingua franca. These data consist of estimates, which, however, were based on the results of the census of 1952 and that of 1963. Accordingly, the following numbers of users apply to the various districts of administration (loc. cit. 86/7):

a) Territories, in which HAUSA is understood by almost 100% of the population

| Districts of administration | Number of users of HAUSA |
|---|---|
| Kano province | 5,775,000 |
| Katsina province | 2,545,000 |
| Sokoto province | 4,335,000 |
| Zaria emirate | 1,180,000 |
| Bauchi emirate | 850,000 |
| Katagum emirate | 520,000 |
| Misau emirate | 175,000 |
| Jema'are emirate | 40,000 |

b) Territories, in which HAUSA is understood by about 50% of the population

| | |
|---|---|
| Jos | 230,000 |
| Gwari | 160,000 |
| Pankshin | 140,000 |

| Districts of administration | Number of users of HAUSA |
|---|---|
| Numan | 140,000 |
| Biu | 135,000 |
| Kontagora | 115,000 |
| Fika | 110,000 |
| Jema'a | 110,000 |
| Lowland | 105,000 |
| Zuru | 100,000 |
| Nasarawa | 80,000 |
| Kaduna | 75,000 |
| Abuja | 45,000 |
| Bedde | 45,000 |
| Wase | 35,000 |
| Yergam | 35,000 |
| Kamuku | 20,000 |
| Wushishi | 10,000 |

c) Territories, in which HAUSA is understood by about 25% of the population

| | |
|---|---|
| Adamawa | 175,000 |
| Gombe | 160,000 |
| Muri | 150,000 |
| Lafia | 60,000 |
| Akwanga | 45,000 |
| Borgu | 25,000 |
| Kanam | 25,000 |

d) Territories, in which HAUSA is understood by about 10% of the population

| | |
|---|---|
| Mubi | 50,000 |
| Bida | 40,000 |
| Dikwa | 30,000 |
| Wukari | 30,000 |
| Chamba | 20,000 |
| Gashaka | 10,000 |
| Gwoza | 7,000 |
| Lapai | 5,000 |
| Agaie | 5,000 |
| United Hills | 3,000 |

e) Territories, in which HAUSA is understood by about 5% of the population

| Districts of administration | Number of users of HAUSA |
|---|---|
| Idoma | 25,000 |
| Kwara | 4,000 |
| Lafiagi | 4,000 |
| Pategi | 2,000 |

f) Territories, in which HAUSA is understood by about 1% of the population

| Bornu | 20,000 |
|---|---|
| Tiv | 12,000 |
| Ilorin | 9,000 |
| Igala | 7,000 |
| Igbirra | 3,000 |
| Bunu-Ijumu-Kabba | 2,000 |

Accordingly, the total number of users of HAUSA in Northern Nigeria amounts to about 18.3 million. A large proportion is made up by the users of HAUSA also in the neighbouring state of Niger. Of its 3,128,000 inhabitants 1,497,000 are counted amongst the *Hausa,* but, as a total, two million people, i.e. 65% of the population of the country are alleged to have a command of HAUSA (loc cit. 88).

332 The compact area, in which HAUSA is spoken as mother tongue or as lingua franca, reaches from Agades in the north to the confluence of the Niger and Benue Rivers in the south, from Adamawa in the east until almost to Niamey in the west. Amongst the Song'ai, in whose area of settlement Niamey, the capital city of the state of Niger, is situated, HAUSA is said to be widespread (LUKAS n.d. 16). It is of less note as a lingua franca in some parts of the Republic of Cameroon. HUTTER remarked in 1905:
"The Hausa language has become the lingua franca in the whole of Adamawa, it is spreading still further, just like its users, and will become the future language from the boundary of the primeval forest to Lake Chad." *
From the study of other literature it appears, however, that HAUSA could not gain a preponderance in Adamawa and did not achieve the importance enjoyed there by FUL as lingua franca.

333 HAUSA has, furthermore, become widespread in the northern part of Dahomey, Togoland and Ghana (LUKAS 1942, 21; ZWERNEMANN 1962, 427).

---

\* "Die Haussasprache ist die Verkehrssprache in ganz Adamaua geworden, greift immer weiter um sich wie ihre Träger und wird die Zukunftssprache von der Urwaldgrenze bis zum Tsadsee werden" (HUTTER 1905, 235).

In these countries it is particularly widespread along the big traffic routes. In 1907, LIPPERT wrote:
"In the whole of North, Middle and South Togoland, the Hausa language already predominates as lingua franca, even though in a dialectally somewhat contaminated form." * As far as it concerns the southern part of Togoland, this statement is not justified. On the basis of observations of my own, which I was able to make in the town of Kpalimé and Hohoe (south-eastern Ghana), HAUSA, although being the preponderant lingua franca in the part of the town in which the Mohammedan immigrants from the north congregate, and which in both towns is known under the name of *Zongo* (cf. LIPPERT 1907, 197), it enjoys no importance and spread amongst the native population of southern Togo and of south-eastern Ghana.

334 Trade and labour migrations carried a large number of people from the central Sudan into the near-coastal territories in the south. Amongst them the *Hausa* represent a group of numerical importance. Already Julius LIPPERT noted: "In all trading centres of the Guinea coast, in L a g o s, L o m e, A c c r a and even in F r e e t o w n, ... they (i.e. the *Hausa*, author's note) can sometimes be found in colonies of 2,000 and more." ** In this way, HAUSA became lingua franca between Lagos and Accra amongst the immigrants from the north. Characteristic are the remarks of Rouch on the situation in southern Ghana:

"The immigrants between each other use Hausa as lingua franca, but only a few people speak Hausa on the coast." ***

335 HAUSA remained without noteworthy spread in Southern Nigeria (cf. par. 329). The reason for this must be looked for in the considerable cultural difference between the north and the south. In addition, two numerically very strong groups live in Southern Nigeria, the *Yoruba* and *Ibo*, which, as can be shown by other examples in Africa (cf. par. 176–79) frequently offered strong resistance to the spread of lingua francas. Also in the province of Bornu, in the sphere of influence of KANURI, HAUSA achieved but small importance. GREENBERG subsumes such reasons as follows:
"The Kanuri are a substantial population occupying a fairly large area, relatively undeveloped in the modern sense and hence with relatively restricted contacts with non-Kanuri speakers. A historical-psychological

---

* "Im ganzen Nord-, Mittel- und Südtogo herrscht bereits die Haussasprache, wenn auch in dialektisch etwas verdorbener Form, als Verkehrssprache" (LIPPERT 1907, 200).
** "An den sämtlichen Handelsplätzen der Guineaküste, in L a g o s, A n e c h o, L o m e, A k k r a und selbst in F r e e t o w n, ... sind sie (d. h. die *Hausa*, Anm. Verf.) manchmal in Kolonien von 2000 und mehr Köpfen zu finden" (LIPPERT 1907, 197).
*** "Les émigrants emploient entre eux le Hausa comme langue franche mais bien peu de gens parlent le Hausa sur la Côte" (ROUCH 1956, 162).

factor, however, also plays a definite role: Hausa was the language of the Fulani-dominated Muslim empire of Sokoto, which fought for supremacy with the Kanuri empire of Bornu in the pre-European period. This traditional attitude of hostility still finds expression in an unwillingness to recognize the dominant position of Hausa and to accomodate to it" (GREENBERG 1965, 53).

Charles ORR, however, notes that HAUSA is understood by the majority of educated people in Bornu (ORR 1965, 265).

## b) SONG'AI

336 SONG'AI (Songhai, Sonrhai) is the dominating language of the central Niger River. Its position amongst the languages of Africa has up till today not satisfactorily been clarified [5].

337 It may be alleged that the development of SONG'AI into a lingua franca can be connected with the history of the once powerful *Song'ai* empire. The political rise of the *Song'ai*, who were Islamized already in the 11th Century, took place in the 15th Century. Under their ruler Sonni Ali (1468–1493) the *Song'ai* advanced towards the west up the Niger River and conquered the important towns of Timbuktu and Djenne. If Sonni Ali was a great general, his successor Askia Mohammed I (Mohammed Ture, 1493–1528), a descendant of the *Soninke* tribe, proved his metal also as a great statesman. He introduced into his empire a well functioning administration, built up a permanent army and became an ardent supporter of religion, art and science. His military expeditions caused the Song'ai Empire to extend its domain immensely. It temporarily reached to the Lower Senegal River in the west and to the Air River in the east and therefore included the Hausa states. Under the successors of Askia Mohammed I the *Song'ai* empire went into a decline. At the end of the 16th Century, Moroccan armies marched into the Sudan and under their attack the empire collapsed.

338 Through the expansion of the *Song'ai* in the 15th and 16th Centuries, their language became temporarily one of the most widespread mediums of communication in Western Sudan. As soldiers or administrative officials, the *Song'ai* carried their language into far distant territories of their empire, where it spread as a lingua franca. Thus Askia Mohammed I after his victory

---

5 After Joseph H. GREENBERG could not at first ascertain any relationship between SONG'AI and other African languages (see GREENBERG 1955, 95), he placed it into the Nilo-Saharan family in 1963 (GREENBERG 1963, 130), the compilation of which, however, is based on insufficient linguistic material. Also the attempt by other authors to allocate SONG'AI to one or the other language groups (for example, MUKAROVSKY) did not lead to any satisfactory results. Pursuant to the *Handbook of African Languages* SONG'AI is not related to any other known language or language group (WESTERMANN/BRYAN 1952, 47).

over the Tuareg in Agades, had a number of *Song'ai* settlers there, and Diedrich WESTERMANN notes: "Still around the middle of the 19th Century Songhai was the leading language in Agades, and even today Songhai is spoken there next to Tuareg and Hausa." *

A special importance was acquired by SONG'AI as lingua franca along the Niger River from Djenne in the west via Timbuktu and Say towards the east. The century-long intensive use of this language has led towards various ethnic groups giving up their own language and adopting SONG'AI as mother tongue. Maurice DELAFOSSE reports that a number of *Soninke* in Djenne and Massina have relinquished their language in favour of SONG'AI (DELAFOSSE 1912, 366).

339 After the collapse of the *Song'ai* empire the spread of its language also gradually shrank, although it still continued to be of considerable note during the succeeding centuries. HACQUARD and DUPUIS ascertained in 1897:

"The Songay language is the most important language of the northern Sudan: in fact, it is spoken from the most western part of Lake Faguibine up to Agadès, in Air, and in the oasis of South Sahara, to the latitude of the Djenné and Say, i.e. throughout the whole ancient Askia empire." **

Still at the beginning of the 20th Century SONG'AI must have been used in trade and politics amongst the *Bozo, Soninke, Bambara, Ful*, and *Tuareg* settled in the central Niger River area, and the number of people employing it exceeded that of the *Song'ai* population by three times [6] (DELAFOSSE 1912, 366/7). In 1917 A. DUPUIS stated that SONG'AI was spoken in the west as far as Djenne on the Bani River, furthermore in Hambori, in the southeast as far as Central Dahomey, as well as in the town of Agades far away in the east (DUPUIS 1917, I).

340 Although SONG'AI has lost much of its former prominence, it is still spoken by various ethnic groups as second language. According to Jean ROUCH the entire population of the regions of Mopti and Djenne, as well as a part of the population of Masina, has a command of SONG'AI as lingua franca. In Djenne it has remained the predominant language up till today, although only a hundred SONG'AI people live there (ROUCH 1954, 12). Various

---

* "Noch um die Mitte des 19. Jahrhunderts war Songhai die herrschende Sprache in Agades, und auch heute wird dort neben Tuareg und Hausa Songhai gesprochen" (WESTERMANN 1952, 97).

** "La langue Songay est la langue la plus importante du Soudan septentrional: elle se parle, en effet, de l'extrémité occidentale du lac Faguibine jusqu'à Agadès, dans l'Air, et des oasis du sud du Sahara, jusqu'à la latitude de Djenné et de Say, c'est-à-dire dans toute l'étendue de l'ancien Empire des Askia" (HACQUARD/ DUPUIS 1897, I).

6 The census of 1909 gave the number of Song'ai in the then Haut-Senegal-Niger as 101,582, whereas according to DELAFOSSE more than 400,000 people had a command of SONG'AI (DELAFOSSE 1912, 367).

groups, for example, the *Arma, Zerma,* or *Kourtey,* have already adopted SONG'AI as their mother tongue, whereas others, *Tyanga, Ful, Koromba* and *Tuareg,* are also to an increasing extent being absorbed linguistically.

Apart from that, the DENDI dialect of SONG'AI in the northern part of Dahomey is employed as lingua franca. DENDI is the language of trade and for this reason is widespread particularly in the towns. BORGU (Bariba) is steadily being ousted by DENDI (HOUIS 1962, 108). DENDI, however, is above all language of the Islamic traders, be it *Mandingo, Song'ai, Hausa* or *Kanuri.* The extent to which its use is associated with this vocational group, is, inter alia, shown by the fact that the traders in some areas, such as in the town of Parakou, have become known under the designation of *Dendi* (LOMBARD 1961, 186). Finally it is asserted that amongst the immigrants from the states of Niger, Upper Volta, Dahomey and the north of Togoland, living in the Ashanti territory of Ghana, the ZERMA dialect of SONG'AI is the predominant lingua franca (SPENCER 1963, 139).

341 SONG'AI is today spoken as mother tongue by altogether 655,000 people (PROST 1956, 11). The total number of SONG'AI users is estimated by Jean ROUCH to amount to more than one million (ROUCH 1954, 12). The area of spread of the language extends from Djenne and Mopti along the Niger River via Timbuktu, Gao, the ancient capital city of the *Song'ai* empire as well as Niamey as far as Gaya. It further includes various language enclaves, such as around Hombori and Dori south of the Niger River. Accordingly it is spoken in the states of Mali, Niger, Upper Volta, Dahomey and to a smaller extent in Nigeria (see WESTERMANN/BRYAN 1952, 46).

Pursuant to the *Handbook of African Languages* SONG'AI is sub-divided into the dialects of SONG'AI, ZARMA and DENDI (op. cit. 46). R. P. A. PROST, on the other hand, notes: "From the point of view regarding dialects, a great contrast is to be noted between the groups situated in the west and south-west of Timbuktu (upstream) or, more exactly speaking in Arnasey, and those situated in the east." * The eastern group, in turn, is sub-divided by him into the following dialects: GAO, KADO, WOGO, ZERMA, and DENDI (op. cit. 15).

### c) MOSI

342 MOSI is counted amongst the *Gur* group of the *Niger-Congo* languages (GREENBERG 1963, 8). The name of MOSI *(mo-si)* signifies the members of the tribe of the same name and furthermore has largely established itself as

---

\* "Au point de vue dialectal, il y a à noter tout d'abord une opposition nette entre le groupe situé à l'ouest et au sud-ouest de Tombouctou (en amont) ou plus exactement d'Arnasey, et ceux situés à l'Est" (PROST 1956, 11).

designation of the language. The *Mosi* call their language *mo-re*, and this designation is frequently found in French literature.

343 The role of MOSI as lingua franca can in the main be traced back to the political importance of the *Mosi* empire at the bend of the Niger. Towards the end of the first post-Christian millenium, horsemen from the area around Lake Chad reached the Niger Bend and there, amongst the autochthonous population, founded states, from which, inter alia, the *Mosi* empires *Wagadugu* and *Yatenga* resulted. Both empires have survived the changing history of the Western Sudan and lost their independence only through the arrival of the French colonial power towards the end of the 19th Century.

344 MOSI spread wherever the empires made their influence felt. Various groups of the population relinquished their language and adopted MOSI as first language, thus, for instance, the *Yansi* and a large number of *Samo*[7]. According to Maurice DELAFOSSE it was learnt as a second language amongst others, by the major part of the *Dyula* population inhabiting the districts of Ouahigouya and Ouagadougou, furthermore by many *Ful* living in the territory of the *Mosi*[8], by the *Kurumba* (Nyonyose) as well as by the *Busa* (Busanse) settled in (the present Republic of) Upper Volta. Outside the sphere of influence of the *Mosi* rulers, MOSI is understood as lingua franca by various ethnic groups, whose languages are closely related to it, thus for instance the *Nankana* and *Dagari* in the south and the *Gurma* in the east (DELAFOSSE 1912, 369). Finally, MOSI is also widespread amongst the traders settled in the central Western Sudan, be they of *Soninke*, *Dyula* or *Hausa* origin.

345 It should not be forgotten either, that the spread of MOSI was furthered by the labour migrations, which already before the First World War had turned into an important factor in the economic and social life. The *Mosi* country is not very fertile and hardly suffices to feed the population. For this reason many *Mosi* emigrate in order to hire themselves out as wage-earning labourers in the southern states of the Ivory Coast and Ghana. Often their work is short-term and seasonal: after the harvest in November/December the *Mosi* leave their home country, work in the south and return in May in order to cultivate the fields. A large number of them, however, remains abroad for several years or does not return to the *Mosi* country at all. Thus it occurs every year in Ghana alone, that some 100,000 *Mosi* labourers come to work (SKINNER 1960, 375). Thereby, their language also has somewhat spread in Ghana. Henri LABOURET notes:

"Whoever travels in Ashanti or even in the coastal region of Accra as far

---

[7] Linguistically, the *Samo* belong to the *Mande* group (see WESTERMANN/BRYAN 1952, 41).

[8] One part of these *Ful* people has become known under the designation of *Silmi-Mosi* (WESTERMANN/BRYAN 1952, 64).

as Sekondi can see the whole extent of *more* (i.e. MOSI, author's note) which is spoken by almost all the foreigners."*

Amongst the indigenous population in the southern part of Ghana and the Ivory Coast, however, MOSI has never been able to gain importance. Also amongst the immigrants from the north it has spread only to a limited degree as a lingua franca. DYULA on the Ivory Coast and HAUSA in Ghana have in particular established themselves as a medium of communication amongst this group of population (ROUCH 1956, 162).

346   In 1912, Maurice DELAFOSSE stated the total number of MOSI speakers to be approximately 1,600,000, of which 1,387,000 used it as mother tongue (DELAFOSSE 1912, 369). According to more recent data this figure may well be a little higher. Pursuant to R. P. AEXANDRE, MOSI is spoken as mother tongue alone by 1,500,000 people; according to H. LABOURET and J. F. HALL[9] even by approximately 2 million (LABOURET 1931, 59). If the lingua franca speakers are added, this figure may well be more than two million. MOSI thereby forms the predominant language of the state of Upper Volta and is moreover, spoken and understood in Northern Ghana, to a lesser degree also further to the south.

## d) MANDINGO

347   MANDINGO comprises a group of dialects which are spoken in a wider sense in the entire western Sudan between the Atlantic Ocean in the west and the Black Volta in the East. MANDINGO is included in the *Mande* group, which, pursuant to Joseph H. GREENBERG belongs to the *Niger-Congo* family[10] (see GREENBERG 1963, 8).

*Development into a lingua franca*

348   The development of MANDINGO has to a considerable extent been determined by the history of the West African empire of *Mali*. *Mali* grew up east of the Futa Djalon mountains at the sources of the Niger River and succeeded to the *Gana* empire, the centre of which was situated further to the north. The beginnings of *Mali* may be traced back presumably to the 11th

---

* "Quiconque voyage dans l'Ashanti ou même dans la région littorale d'Accra à Sekondi peut se rendre compte de l'extension du *more* (= MOSI, note de l'auteur) qui est parlé par presque tous les étrangers" (LABOURET 1931, 60).
9  Cited from WESTERMANN/BRYAN 1952, 64.
10 The subsumation of the *Niger-Congo* languages into one family relies on an inadequate method and – as long as comprehensive comparative investigations have not taken place – must be looked upon as temporary. That Mande belongs to this family has recently been queried by Hans G. MUKAROVSKY (MUKAROVSKY 1966).

Century, but almost two centuries passed before its development into one of the largest state formations in Africa took place. Under the rule of *Mari Djata*, the 'Lion of Mali' (1230–1255), this empire rid itself of its most dangerous enemies, the *Susu-Soninke*. King Kankan Musa (Mansa Musa, 1312–1337) led Mali to the zenith of its power. It embraced the upper course of the Senegal River and extended towards the east beyond the Niger and Gao, the capital city of *Song'ai*. In the south it stretched as far as the rain forest boundary and in the north into the Sahara (WESTERMANN 1952, 79). Kankan Musa entertained friendly relations with Mecca, visited by him as a pilgrim, as well as with Egypt and Morocco, and he had Arab scientists come to his empire. Under his successors, the *Mali* empire went into a slow but steady decline.

349 MANDINGO has been known since the 11th Century (LABOURET/WARD 1933, 38). During the period between 1250 and the end of the 15th Century it was the official language of the *Mali* empire. As language of administration and trade it spread into all parts of the empire. "Often it spread amongst whole populations, — for instance the Khassonké, the Foulanké in the Wassulu, the Somono fishermen of the Niger River, the numerous groups of Sarakollé or Marka."* MANDINGO traders penetrated in the south into the rain forest, and their language could also gain a foothold there.

In the west, MANDINGO spread presumably as far as the coast. Thus P. E. H. HAIR presumes that, when the Venetian Ca da Mosto, who was in the service of the Portuguese, visited the Casamance territory in 1456, MANDINGO was the language of trade and possibly also of the administration, as well as being used as medium of communication between Africans and Europeans. The sphere of influence of MANDINGO embraced the entire coastal area between the Gambia and Rio Grande Rivers in the south. The Portuguese travellers in the second half of the 16th Century considered it purposeful to take, apart from WOLOF-speaking tribesmen, also interpreters of MANDINGO during their journeys along the West African coast (HAIR 1966, 14/5).

350 The final cause of the decline of the *Mali* empire was not least due to the rising power of the *Song'ai* people. Under the rule of Askia Mohammed I (1493–1528) who contributed towards Song'ai achieving its position of greatest importance, the *Mali* empire as a unit broke up. More and more groups of population abandoned the empire and developed into independent ethnic groups (DELAFOSSE 1901, 215). It presumably occurred during that time that MANDINGO became sub-divided into various dialects, the most important of which are MALINKE, BAMBARA and DYULA.

---

* "Il s'est souvent imposé à des populations entières – par exemple les Khassonké les Foulanké du Wassulu, les pêcheurs Somono du Niger, de nombreux groupements sarakollé ou marka" (LABOURET/WARD 1933, 38).

351 This splitting into dialects[11], however, has hardly impeded the further development of MANDINGO. Whereas the *mali* empire dwindled, its language, MANDINGO, continued to remain the predominant language of the western Sudan. When, in the 19th Century, the French conquered and colonised this territory, this did not have a detrimental effect on the prominence of MANDINGO — on the contrary, the spread of MANDINGO received fresh impulses and took a second upsurge. As the language of s o l d i e r s it accompanied the armies serving under the French on their campaign of conquest.

On the other hand, it was able to win new areas of spread as t r a d e language, on account of the expansion of trade and the improved traffic conditions, more particularly the introduction of the motor-car (LABOURET/ WARD 1933, 48).

### e) MALINKE

352 Pursuant to DELAFOSSE, MALINKE is the "oldest" and "purest" of MANDINGO dialects. The meaning of the name is 'the people of Mali' (DELAFOSSE 1901, 222). The area of its spread cradled the *Mali* empire. MALINKE is spoken in the wide spaces between the Atlantic Ocean in the west and the Black Volta in the east. It is sub-divided into the three following dialects:

West MALINKE. It is spoken in Gambia, in the Casamance, in Portuguese Guinea and in the near-coastal territories further south.

North MALINKE. Its area of spread lies particularly in eastern Senegal and in western Mali, i.e. in the valleys of the Falémé, Bafing and Bakoy Rivers.

South MALINKE, used on the upper course of the Niger River to south of Bamako and Ségou, and in the east as far as the Black Volta (DELAFOSSE 1901, 223). The territory in which it is distributed thus comprises the states of Guinea, Ivory Coast, Mali and Upper Volta.

353 MALINKE is spoken by more than one million people (WESTERMANN/BRYAN 1952, 33). Its spread, particularly in the west, has not yet come to a standstill. As well-to-do traders and ardent believers in Islam, the *Malinke* enjoy high repute amongst the tribes near the Atlantic coast (cf. BANTON 1957) and contribute towards the extent of its influence. Amongst the Moslem communities of many West African towns, such as Monrovia (see FRAENKEL 1964, 93), they form the leading class, and in the shadow of Islam MANDINGO also acquires more and more devotees.

---

11 According to Maurice HOUIS, it must be doubtful whether the traditional dialect division into MALINKE, BAMBARA and DYULA is justified from a linguistic point of view (verbal communication of 5. 7. 67).

## f) DYULA

354 The designation "Dyula", in the western Sudan, is almost synonymous with 'travelling traders'. DELAFOSSE already notes in 1901:

"One must not mix up the Dyula, Mandingo tribe, ... with the caravaning traders who, in Upper Senegal, are given the generic name of Dyula, but of whom a great part belongs to the Sarakollé." *

On the Ivory Coast, more particularly in the capital city of Abidjan (WALLERSTEIN 1965, 477), "Dyula" is frequently employed as a collective designation for the communities of immigrants coming from the north, because many traders of varying origins attempt to draw advantage from the high prestige of the *Dyula* by introducing themselves as members of the *Dyula* tribe, it is not always easy — neither from the ethnic nor from the linguistic standpoint — to separate the *Dyula* from the "non-*Dyula*".

355 The origin of the "Dyula tribe" has presumably occurred as follows: During their advance to the south a few centuries ago a number of *Mandingo* traders arrived in the area of Kong, in the north of the state of Ivory Coast. They settled there and amongst the autochthonous population spread their language and culture, more particularly their religion, i.e. Islam. On account of continual reinforcements by fresh *Mandingo* groups, these *Mandingo* in the diaspora retained their contacts with their homeland and simultaneously gained in numerical strength. They married women of the autochthonous tribes, more particularly from the *Senefu, Bobo* and *Anyi,* and from this mixture the new ethnic group of *Dyula* developed (DELAFOSSE 1901, 3). DELAFOSSE writes:

"... having an intelligence in general superior to that of autochthonous populations, showing a more open and more cultivated mind, also because of their conversion to the Islam, the Dyula acquired, all through peaceful means, a politically predominating position: their language spread amongst the indigenous people within the whole area and thus became the official language of the chiefs and persons of distinction, and at the same time it developed as diplomatic language and for commercial purposes amongst various tribes on whom the Dyula exercise a kind of moral protection. The chiefs of the indigenous population even borrowed their names from the Dyula, and they take it as an honour to be considered related to the Dyula chiefs. This is the reason why they have often been mixed up between each other, the Dyula and the Sénufo, who, however, speak quite different languages." **

* "Il ne faut pas confondre les Dyoula, tribu mandé, ... avec les marchands caravaniers auxquels on donne dans le haut Sénégal le nom générique de Dyoula, mais dont beaucoup aussi sont des Sarakolé" (DELAFOSSE 1901, 6).

** "... d'une intelligence bien supérieure en général à celle des peuplades autochtones, d'un esprit plus ouvert et plus cultivé aussi par suite de leur conversion

356 In comparison with the large area of spread of DYULA, the number of *Dyula* people is minute. The *Dyula,* however, do not live concentrated in one place, but dispersed over a wide area. Major groups of these people can be found most of all in the towns and trade centres, and thus it came about that their language is especially widespread there. Thus, for instance, a large number of *Dyula* is said to live in Djenne in Mali, their language being used as trade language there. The spread of DYULA, which owes its success in a large part to the prestige of the Moslem *Dyula* traders, was furthered especially in the south by the fact that it took place in an area which is linguistically cleft; numerous tribes inimical towards one another live here and often call on the *Dyula* as intermediaries and arbitrators during disputes (DELAFOSSE 1901, 6/7).

357 The figure of DYULA-speaking people is not known[12]. The territory where DYULA is spoken stretches in the north to beyond Sikasso and Bobo-Dioulasso and in the south to the far side of Séguéla and Bondoukou into the near-coastal districts of the Ivory Coast. In respect of the situation within the (present state of) Ivory Coast B. HOLAS notes that DYULA "is not only spoken in the area of the northern part of the country, but also along the main routes of trading roads linking the Islamic north with the southern markets. In fact, the Dyula language accompanies the travelling trader who, the Koran in hand, carries from the banks of the Bani and Niger Rivers the dried fish which he exchanges against nuts of the cola tree (bot. *Cola nitida* of the family of the Sterculiaces), precious forest trees of the south."\*

Pursuant to DELAFOSSE the eastern boundary is formed by the Black Volta and the frontier of Ghana. It is spoken as a lingua franca particularly by the

> à l'islam, les Dyoula ont acquis, par des moyens d'ailleurs tout pacifiques, la prépondérance politique: leur langue s'est répandue parmi les indigènes de toute la région et est devenue pour ainsi dire la langue officielle des chefs et des notables, en même temps qu'elle devenait la langue diplomatique et commerciale dont usent entre elles les diverses tribus sur lesquelles les Dyoula exercent une sorte de protectorat moral.
> Les chefs indigènes empruntèrent même aux Dyoula leurs noms de famille, et ils tiennent à honneur de passer pour les parents des chefs dyoula. C'est ce qui fait que l'on a souvent confondu les uns avec les autres les Dyoula et les Sénoufo, qui cependant parlent des langues bien différentes" (DELAFOSSE 1901, 4).

12 In accordance with H. LABOURET, the *Handbook of African Languages* states a figure of 140,000 (WESTERMANN/BRYAN 1952, 35). The total number of people speaking DYULA as first or second language is unequivocally larger.

\* DYULA "est parlé non seulement dans toute la partie septentrionale du pays, mais aussi le long des principales routes commerciales reliant le nord islamisé avec les marchés du littoral. En somme, le parler dioula accompagne le marchand ambulant qui, le Koran dans la main, transporte des bords de la Bani et du Niger le poisson sec qu'il échange contre les noix du kolatier (bot. *Cola nitida* de la famille des Sterculiacées), précieux arbre des forêts du sud" (HOLAS 1963, 8).

Senufo, Bobo, Lobi, Kulang'o, Baule, and Anyi (DELAFOSSE 1901, 5). Accordingly, its spread primarily comprises the states of Ivory Coast, Mali and Upper Volta.

## g) BAMBARA

358   The name "Bambara" derives from the *Ful* as well as *Soninke* (Sarakolé) and was adopted by the Europeans (DELAFOSSE 1901, 236). The *Bambara* call themselves the *bamana-nke* and their language *bamana ko-ma*[13]. Just as in the case of the name "Dyula" confusion exists over the name "Bambara". Thus, according to DELAFOSSE, the *Dyula* inhabiting the Niger Bend are often referred to as the *Bambara*, who themselves apply this name to the tribes not belonging to the *Mande* group, and more particularly to the *Senufo* (DELAFOSSE 1901, 236; WESTERMANN/BRYAN 1952, 55).

359   The *Bambara*, to be counted amongst the *Mandingo*, had to pay tribute to the Mali empire during the 13th Century and later on to the *Song'ai*. Upon the decline of the *Song'ai* empire as a consequence of the invasion by the Moroccans at the end of the 16th Century, the political rise of the *Bambara* started. At the beginning of the 17th Century the *Bambara*, with the help of immigrated *Ful* nomads, developed an independent state in the area between the *Niger* and the *Bani* rivers, the latter being one of the tributaries of the Niger. Around 1650 this state broke up into two rival empires, which have gone down in history under the designations of *Bambara-Ségou* and *Bambara-Masasi*[14]. Whereas *Bambara-Ségou* was concentrated around the town of Ségou on the right bank of the Niger River, *Bambara-Masasi* was situated further to the west in the area of Kaarta. The Ségou empire in particular achieved considerable importance and at times it included Djenne to the east as well as the trading metropolis of Timbuktu. At the beginning of the second half of the 19th Century both *Bambara* empires collapsed under the attacks of the *Ful* empire of *Tekrur*. El Hadj Omar, the ruler of *Tekrur*, attempted to proselytize the *Bambara*, who had remained predominantly 'heathen' up till then, to Islam. In 1890 the *Bambara* came under French rule.

360   As a result of the spread of the *Bambara* their dialect was carried beyond the borders of their territory. It "was used as lingua franca by traders and diplomats as far as the Atlantic coast in the west, the rain forest to the south and the region of Timbuktu to the east."* As a result of the later

---

13 Note on the etymology and history of the name *Bambara* (Banmana, Bamana) cf. BEUCHELT 1966, 143.

14 *Masasi* means 'King's Clan' (*masa* = 'king' or 'chief', *si* = 'clan'; WESTERMANN 1952, 105).

* wurde von Händlern und Diplomaten bis zur Atlantikküste im Westen, dem Regenwald im Süden und der Region von Timbuktu im Osten als lingua franca benutzt" (BEUCHELT 1966, 145).

development during colonial times BAMBARA out of all the MANDINGO dialects profited most. After the *Bambara* resisted at first the French administration they later on became obedient and diligent cooperators of the colonial power. The close contact with the Europeans achieved by them as labourers or domestic servants gained them important advantages in comparison with other ethnic groups of the inner Sudan. Their children were amongst the first to receive school education and thus already before the First World War there existed a considerable number of *Bambara* who were active as administration officials and teachers. The BAMBARA dialect was carried by them into other areas under French administration, inter alia, to Senegal, (the present state of) Niger and even as far as (the present state of) Mauritania (BEUCHELT 1966, 146).

361 Especial importance was achieved by BAMBARA as s o l d i e r ' s language. During their raids in the western Sudan, the French relied to a great extent on the aid of the *Bambara,* from whom they preferentially recruited their soldiers. BAMBARA became the predominant language of the troops and through them was spread to almost every territory under French rule. It became the lingua franca of the garrisons of French West Africa.

362 Today, BAMBARA is most likely to be the predominant lingua franca in Mali and in eastern Senegal. Altogether, it is used by approximately 3 million people, amongst whom ca. 1.2 million speak it as their mother tongue [15]. Its area of spread extends from Matam, Tambacounda and Kolda in the West via Kayes, Nioro, Nara, Bamako, Ségou and Mopti to the area east of the Upper Niger River. Outside the countries of Senegal and Mali, BAMBARA is spoken to some extent in other West African countries, such as (the present states of) Guinea and Upper Volta (see WESTERMANN/BRYAN 1952, 34). The nucleus of its spread is situated in Mali where every effort was made to elevate BAMBARA to the official language of the country next to French.

In Mali, BAMBARA is the language of the strongest ethnic group, making up a proportion of about 33% of the population of the country and is the vernacular language of the most important urban centres such as Ségou and Bamako. Thanks to an investigation carried out by Siegmund BRAUNER in Mali in 1967 amongst schoolchildren, more particularly in the town of Ségou and Markala, we are in possession of some detailed information on the spread of BAMBARA in this territory (BRAUNER 1967). Although the

---

15 "Pursuant to unpublished estimates by the Ministry of Education in Bamako there exist ca. 1,200,000 persons speaking Bambara as mother tongue and approximately 4 million people – 2 million according to other estimates – using it in inter-tribal communication." ("Nach unpublizierten Schätzungen des Erziehungsministeriums in Bamako gibt es heute ca. 1,200,000 Personen, die Bambara als Muttersprache sprechen, ca. 4 Millionen – nach anderen Vermutungen: 2 Millionen – die es im interstammlichen Verkehr gebrauchen können" [BEUCHELT 1966, 147].)

share of the *Bambara* amongst the persons questioned amounted only to 33%, 69.15% of the pupils stated that they spoke BAMBARA as their only language. Altogether, this language is mastered by even 99.75% of the 2,325 persons interviewed, and for 93.50% of them it is the language most used. Only six pupils — four of them of French nationality — confessed to having no knowledge of BAMBARA.

The extent of BAMBARA having gained a foothold as lingua franca in the family is demonstrated by the fact that it is spoken at home by more than 88% of the persons interrogated, of whom, however, 8.04% speak it together with one or several other languages. On the other hand, BAMBARA is used considerably less in the schools, where French has been prescribed as educational language since the time of the French colonial rule. Nevertheless, 17.76% of the pupils — preponderantly from the lower forms — declared using BAMBARA exclusively in contact with their mates at school, whereas 9.64% converse in French only.

### h) KANGBE

363   A further dialect of MANDIGO is KANGBE (phonet. $k\tilde{a}gb\varepsilon$), the 'white, clear language', also called "Common MANDINGO". As a result of the fact of MANDINGO being used as lingua franca by a number of tribes in the West Sudan, a pidgin dialect, namely KANGBE, developed. This was chiefly spread through trade. E. BEUCHELT presumes that this dialect originated already during the 14th Century, i.e. at a time when the Mali empire had reached its zenith (BEUCHELT 1966, 144).

Only little information exists on KANGBE. It is little known where or by whom it is spoken [16]. T. D. P. DALBY, in an account on the spread of languages in Sierra Leone notes, however:

"Speakers of various Mandinka and Bambara dialects, with their descendants, make up the existing Mandinka communities in Sierra Leone, and the language used by them is normally the Mandinka vehicular dialect or Kangbe..., lit. 'clear language'. Still used elsewhere in Mandinka-speaking areas as a trade language, Kangbe has become the common language of most Mandinka communities in Sierra Leone" (DALBY 1962, 63).

It may be presumed that the structure of KANGBE is not uniform, but shows differences according to the area of spread. Thus, there probably

---

16 Linguistic data are lacking also in respect of KANGBE. The present available data is restricted to such general remarks as, for example: "This dialect repudiates real dialectal forms and expressions and uses only phrases and expressions common to different dialects or at least used in a great number of dialects." ("Ce parler répudie les formes et locutions proprement dialectales et n'use que des expressions communes aux divers dialectes ou tout au moins usitées dans le plus grand nombre de dialectes" [LABOURET/WARD 1933, 48].)

exists one form of KANGBE intimately connected with MALINKE, and another form resembling DYULA or BAMBARA, respectively (BEUCHELT 1966, note 4).

*

364 These dialects of MANDINGO differ only slightly – speakers of different dialects can converse with one another without great difficulty. The changeover from one dialect to the other is continuous, and often it is hardly possible to determine the border between them. Within the range of these dialects quite a considerable number of different forms can be found (LABOURET/ WARD 1933, 39).

In summary it can be said that MANDINGO spread over an area which in extent is matched only by few other languages in Africa. It is spoken today by altogether five million people, of whom approximately three million speak it as mother tongue, whereas for the other two million it serves as lingua franca only [17].

---

[17] These figures coincide with the estimates arrived at by H. LABOURET and I. C. WARD (LABOURET/WARD 1933, 38). In 1934 LABOURET stated the total number of MANDINGO speakers to be 5.6 million, of which 2.8 million spoke it as their mother tongue. On the other hand, the estimates provided by DELAFOSSE are considerably lower (see DELAFOSSE 1912, 367/8).

# Bibliography *

AJAYI, J. F. A. 1960: How Yoruba was reduced to writing. Odù 8, 49–58.
ALEXANDRE, P. 1956: Manuel élémentaire de la langue bulu (Sud Cameroun). Paris 1956.
— 1961: Problèmes linguistiques des états négro-africaines à l'heure de l'indépendence. Cahiers d'Etudes Africaines 6, 177–195.
— 1961a: Sur les possibilités expressives des langues africaines en matière de terminologie politique. Afrique et Asie 56, 13–28.
— 1963: Aperçu sommaire sur le Pidgin A 70 du Cameroun. Cahiers d'Etudes Africaines 12, 577–582.
— 1966: Système verbal et prédicatif du bulu. Langues et Litteratures de l'Afrique Noire I. Paris.
— 1967: Langues et langage en Afrique Noire. Paris.
— 1967a: Note sur la réduction du système des classes dans les langues véhiculaires à fonds bantu. In: La classification nominale dans les langues négro-africaines. Paris.
ALEXANDRE, R. P. 1953: La langue mōré. Tome I. Dakar.
ALLEN, J. W. T. 1959: The rapid spread of Swahili. Swahili 30, 70–73.
— 1965: The case for developing Swahili. East African Journal 2, 2, 29–34.
AMONOO, R. F. 1963: Problems of Ghanaian *lingue franche*. In: Spencer, J. (Edit.): Language in Africa. Cambridge 1963. 78–85.
ANDRZEJEWSKI, B. W. 1962: Speech and writing dichotomy as the pattern of multilingualism in the Somali Republic. In: Colloque sur le multilinguisme. Brazzaville 1962. 177–181.
ANNICQ, Camille 1967: Le Swahili véhiculaire. Lubumbashi, Imbelco.
ARDENER, E. 1956: Coastal Bantu of the Cameroons. London.
ARMSTRONG, R. G. 1963: Vernacular Languages and Cultures in Modern Africa. In: Spencer, J. (Edit.): Language in Africa. Cambridge 1963. 64–72.
ASAMOA, E. A. 1955: The problem of language in education in the Gold Coast. Africa 25, 1, 60–78.
ASHTON, E. O. 1944: Inter-Territorial Language (Swahili) Committee. Africa 14, 346.
ATKINS, Guy 1950: The Nyanja-speaking population of Nyasaland and Northern Rhodesia (a statistical estimate). African Studies 9, 1, 35–39.
BAKER, R. H. 1947: Portuguese words in Chimanyika. Nada 24, 62–64.
BAMGBOSE, A. 1966: A grammar of Yoruba. Cambridge.
BARAKANA, G. 1952: L'unification des langues au Ruanda-Urundi. Civilisations (Bruxelles) 2, 67–78.
BARNEY, J. A. 1934: Notes on the Bangala language. Africa 7, 2, 220–223.
BARNOUW, A. J. 1934: Language and the race problem in South Africa. The Hague.
BAXTER, P. T. W. and BUTT, A. 1953: The Azande and related peoples of the Anglo-Egyptian Sudan and Belgian Congo. London.

---

* For further references see MOLNOS 1969.

BEAUDOIN, L. 1948: De l'influence des langues congolaises Bantu sur le Ki-Swahili. Bull. Jurid. indig. 16, 10, 293–301.
BERRY, J. 1959: The origins of Krio vocabulary. Sierra Leone Studies 12, 298–307.
— 1959a: Creole as a language. West Africa 2207, 745.
— 1961: English loanwords and adaptations in Sierra Leone Krio. In: Creole Language Studies 2, 1–16.
— Pidgins and creoles in Africa. In: Colloque sur le multilinguisme. Brazzaville 1962, 219–225.
— The Madina project, Ghana. Paper read at the Ninth International African Seminar, University College Dar es Salaam 1968.
BERRY, J. and GREENBERG, J. H. 1966: Sociolinguistic research in Africa. African Studies Bulletin (Stanford) 9, 2, 1–9.
BEUCHELT, E. 1966: Die kulturhistorische Entwicklung des Bambara zur Verkehrssprache. Afrika heute 10, 143–147.
BIEBUYCK, D. and DOUGLAS, M. 1961: Congo. Tribes and parties. London.
BOECK, L. B. de 1949: Taalkunde en de taalenkwestie in Belgisch-Kongo. Bruxelles.
— 1952: Het lingala op de weegschaal! Zaire 6, 2, 115–153.
— 1952a: Lingala. Bull. militaire (Léopoldville) 53, 275–299.
— 1953: Taaltoestand te Leopoldstad. Kongo-Overzee 19, 1, 1–9.
BOELAERT, E. 1936: Naar een nationale inlandsche taal in Kongo? Kongo-Overzee 2, 4, 240–248.
BOLAMBA, A. R. 1956: Le problème des langues dans nos écoles. Voix du Congolais 12, 119, 85–88.
BOLD, J. D. 1951: Dictionary and phrase-book of Fanagalo, Kitchen Kafir: the lingua franca of Southern Africa, the Rhodesias, Portuguese East Africa, Nyasaland, Belgian Congo & Capetown.
— 1964: Dictionary, phrase-book and grammar of Fanagalo. Sixth edition (revised), Johannesburg.
BOT BA NJOCK, H. M. 1966: Le problème linguistique au Cameroun. Afrique et Asie (Paris) 73, 3–13.
BRADSHAW, A. T. von S. 1965: Vestiges of Portuguese in the languages of Sierra Leone. Sierra Leone Language Review 4, 5–37.
BRAUNER, S. 1967: Structure ethnique et situation linguistique dans la région de Ségou. Paper read at the Second congrès international des africanistes, Dakar 11–20 décembre 1967.
BRAUNSHAUSEN, N. 1928: Le bilinguisme et la famille. In: Le bilinguisme et l'éducation. Travaux de la conférence internationale tenue à Luxembourg du 2 au 5 avril 1928. Genève–Luxembourg.
BRETON, F. H. Le 1936: Up-country Swahili exercises. London. 15th edition 1964.
BRIERLY, T. G. 1962: Hausa for all? West Africa 15 Dec.
BRIGHT, W. 1966: Proceedings of the UCLA Sociolinguistics Conference, 1964. The Hague.
BROOMFIELD, G. W. 1930: The development of the Swahili language. Africa 3, 516–522.
— 1931: The Re-Bantuization of the Swahili Language. Africa 4, 1, 77–85.
BROSNAHAN, L. F. 1961: Problems of linguistic inequivalence in communication (English-Nigerian). Ibadan 13, 26–30.
— 1963: Some historical cases of language imposition. In: Spencer, J. (Edit.): Language in Africa. Cambridge 1963. 7–24.
— 1963a: Some aspects of the linguistic situation in tropical Africa. Lingua 12, 1, 54–65.

Bryan, M. A. 1959: The Bantu languages of Africa. Handbook of African Languages. London.
Bulck, R. P. G. van 1948: Les recherches linguistiques au Congo belge. Bruxelles.
Bull, A. F. 1961: Looking back thirty years, and forward: the story of the East African Swahili Committee. Swahili n. s. 1, 20–23.
Bürgi, E. 1902: Welcher Dialekt der Evhesprache verdient zur Schrift- und Verkehrssprache im Evhelande (Süd-Togo) erhoben zu werden? Zeitschrift für afrikanische, ozeanische und ostasiatische Sprachen 6, 4, 223–233.
Burssens, A. 1939: Le Tshílúbà, langue à intonation. Africa 12, 3, 267–284.
— 1954: Introduction à l'étude des langues bantoues du Congo belge. Anvers.
Buschman, F. 1956: Kituba grammar. Kafumba (Congo).
Butler, G. 1964: The future of English in Africa. Optima 14, 2, 88–97.
Calloc'h, J. 1911: Vocabulaire français-sango et sango-français, langue commerciale de l'Oubangui-Chari, précédé d'un abrégé grammatical. Paris.
Calvet, M. 1964: Interférences du phonetisme wolof dans le français parlé au Sénégal dans la région du cap vert. BIFAN B 26, 3–4, 518–531.
Caeneghem, R. van 1944/5: Le luba, langue commune congolaise. Lovania 5, 118–123.
— 1950: Les langues indigènes dans l'enseignement. Zaire 4, 707–720.
Cassidy, F. G. 1962: Toward the recovery of early English-African pidgin. In: Colloque sur le multilinguisme. Brazzaville 1962. 267–277.
Cepollaro, A. 1962: I swahili e la loro lingua. Africa (Roma) 17, 2, 67–82.
Chabrelie, L. 1935: Notes sur la langue des sara. Journal de la Société des Africanistes 5, 2, 125–151.
Chataigner, A. 1963: Le créole portugais du Sénégal: observations et textes. Journal of African Languages 2, 1 (1963), 44–71.
Childs, G. M. 1949: Umbundu kinship & character. London.
Christaller, J. G. 1875: A grammar of the Asante and Fante language called Tschi (Chwee, Twi). Basel.
Christophersen, P. 1948: Bilingualism. London.
Clarke, P. H. C. 1962: A note on school slang (English and Swahili). Tanganyika Notes 58/59, 205–206.
Cleene, N. de 1935: Naar een nationale taal in Kongo. Elckerlyc.
Cohen, D. 1963: Le dialect arabe Ḥassânîya de Mauritanie. Paris 1963.
Cole, D. T. 1953: Fanagalo and the Bantu languages in South Africa. African Studies 12, 1, 1–9.
Coleman, J. S. 1958: Nigeria: background to nationalism. Berkeley and Los Angeles.
Comhaire-Sylvain see Sylvain.
The Congo's language problem. African World 11, 1943, 184.
Cook, C. L. 1955: Languages in the southern provinces of the Sudan. The Bible Translator 6, 3, 122–127.
Cotting, C. 1960: Le cibemba aux prises avec l'industrialisation. Tendences du temps 18, 2, 23–26.
Courboin, A. 1908: "Bangala". Langue commerciale du Haut-Congo. Anvers.
Crowder, M. 1962: Senegal. A study in French assimilation policy. London.
Cuvelier, J. 1944: Note sur la langue Kongo (Kikongo). Institut Royal Colonial Belge. Bulletin des Séances 15, 220–221.
— 1944a: La 'lingua franca' du Bas-Congo. Institut Royal Colonial Belge. Bulletin des Séances 15, 73–75.
Dalby, T. D. P. 1962: Language distribution in Sierra Leone: 1961–1962. Sierra Leone Language Review 1, 62–67.

— 1964: Problems of language-mapping in West Africa. Zeitschrift für Mundartforschung (Marburg) 31, 4, 356–361.
DAMMANN, E. 1961: Die sprachlichen Verhältnisse in Ghana. Babel (Berlin) 7, 4, 168–176.
DANNAUD, J.-P. 1965: Avenir de la langue française dans les pays d'Afrique noire. Revue politique et parlementaire May 1965, 54–64.
DEANS, W. A. 1947: Congo-Swahili Translator Committee Meeting. Congo Mission News 139, 22.
DECAMP, D. 1962: Creole language areas considered as multilingual communities. In: Colloque sur le multilinguisme. Brazzaville 1962. 227–231.
DELAFOSSE, M. 1901: Essai de manuel pratique de la langue mandé ou mandingue. Paris.
— 1912: Haut-Sénégal-Niger (Soudan Français). Tome 1. Le pays, les peuples, les langues. Paris.
— 1928: La langue mandingue et ses dialectes (Malinké, Bambara, Dioula). 1er vol. Paris.
— 1955: La langue mandingue et ses dialectes (Malinké, Bambara, Dioula). 2e vol. Dictionnaire mandingue-français. Paris.
DELANAYE, P. 1955: Position des missions catholiques en matière d'emploi des langues indigènes. Aequatoria 18, 91–95.
DEMOZ, A. 1963: European loanwords in an Amharic daily newspaper. In: Spencer, J. (Edit.): Language in Africa. Cambridge 1963. 116–122.
DIAGNE, P. 1967: Vernacular languages in a changing society. Unesco courier (Paris) 20, 6, 29–32.
DIANOUX, H. J. de 1961: Les mots d'emprunt d'origine arabe de la langue songhay. Bulletin IFAN B 23, 3–4, 596–606.
Dictionnaire français-lingala, lingala-français. Manuel No. 32. Léopoldville 1960.
DIEBOLD, A. R., Jr. 1961: Incipient bilingualism. Language 37, 97–112.
— A laboratory for language contact. Anthropological Linguistics 4, 1, 41–51.
DIOP, A. B. 1960: Enquête sur la migration Toucouleur à Dakar. Bulletin IFAN B 22, 3–4, 393–418.
— 1965: Société Toucouleur et migration (Enquête sur l'immigration Toucouleur à Dakar). Dakar.
DOKE, C. M. 1928: The linguistic situation in South Africa. Africa 1, 4, 478–485.
— 1931: Report on the unification of the Shona dialects. London.
— 1939: European and Bantu languages in South Africa. Africa 12, 3, 308–319.
— 1954: The southern Bantu languages. Handbook of African Languages. London.
DREWES, A. J. 1966: De verspreiding van het Amhaars. Kroniek van Afrika (Leiden) 6, 4, 333–338.
DUISBURG, A. von 1913: Grundriß der Kanuri-Sprache in Bornu. Archiv für das Studium deutscher Kolonialsprachen, Band 15, Berlin.
— 1930: Die Bevölkerung des Tschadsee-Gebietes und die Bedeutung der Kanuri für den mittleren und westlichen Sudan. Koloniale Rundschau 22, 4/6, 112–117.
— 1942: Im Lande des Cheghu von Bornu. Despoten und Völker südlich des Tschad. Berlin.
DUNCAN, P. 1954: Origin of Fanagalo. African Studies 13, 1, 45.
DUPUIS (Yakouba), A. 1917: Essai de méthode pratique pour l'étude de la langue Songoi ou Songai. Paris.
EAST, R. M. 1937: Modern tendencies in the languages of Northern Nigeria. Africa 10, 1, 97–106.
EDWARDS, A. C. 1962: The Ovimbundu under two sovereignities. London.

ELIET, E. et al. 1953: Les langues spontanées dites commerciales du Congo: le monokotuba comparé au lingala et au lari de la Région du Pool. Brazzaville.
ELLIS, J. 1965: Linguistic sociology and institutional linguistics. Linguistics 19, 5–20.
ENDEMANN, K. 1911: Über die Wiedergabe von Fremdwörtern und -namen in Bantusprachen. Zeitschrift für Kolonialsprachen 1, 4, 284–289.
EPSTEIN, A. L. 1959: Linguistic innovation and culture on the Copperbelt, Northern Rhodesia. Southwestern Journal of Anthropology 15, 235–53.
EVERBROECK, R. van: Grammaire et exercices lingala. Anvers/Léopoldville 1958.
FABULÉE, J. 1964: Langues nationales de jeunes états et orientalisme. Revue Ecole nat. langues orient. 1, 95–110.
FALLERS, M. C. 1960: The Eastern Lacustrine Bantu (Ganda, Soga). London.
FEHDERAU, H. W. 1962: The place of the Kituba language in Congo. Congo mission news (Léopoldville) 196, 9–10.
— 1963: Descriptive grammar of the Kituba language, a dialectal survey. Leopoldville (mimeographed).
— 1963a: Kituba-English-French dictionary. Leopoldville. (MS)
— 1966: The origin and development of Kituba (lingua franca Kikongo). University Microfilms, Inc., Ann Arbor, Michigan.
FERGUSON, C. A. 1959: The Arabic koiné. Language 35, 616–630.
— 1959a: Diglossia. Word 15, 325–340.
— 1962: Background to second language problems. In: Rice, F. A. (Edit.): Study of the Role of Second Languages in Asia, Africa and Latin America. Washington 1962, 1–7.
— 1962a: The language factor in national development. In: Rice, F. A. (Edit.): Study of the Role of Second Languages in Asia, Africa and Latin America. Washington 1962, 8–14.
— 1962b: The language problem in national development. Anthropological linguistics 4, 1, 23–28.
— 1965: Directions in sociolinguistics: report on an interdisciplinary seminar. Items 19, 1, 1–4.
— 1966: National sociolinguistic profile formulas. In: Bright, W. (Edit.): Proceedings of the UCLA Sociolinguistics Conference, 1964. The Hague, 309–324.
FEYER, Ursula 1947: Haussa als Verkehrssprache. Zeitschrift für Phonetik und vergl. Sprachwissenschaft 1, 3, 108–129.
FISHMAN, J. A. 1964: Language maintenance and language shift as a field of inquiry. Linguistics 9, 32–70.
— 1965: Who speaks what language to whom and when? La linguistique 2, 67–88.
— 1968: Sociolinguistic perspective on the study of bilingualism. Linguistics 39, 21–50.
FODOR, I. 1966: The problems in the classification of the African languages. Budapest.
— 1966a: Linguistic problems and "language planning" in Africa: suggestions with regard to the reports of a conference. Linguistics 25, 18–33.
FONLON, B. 1963: A case for early bilingualism (in Cameroon). Abbia 4, 56–94.
FORD, D. 1951: The Yoruba-speaking peoples of South-Western Nigeria. London.
FORTUNE, G. 1958: The future of African languages. Report of the Conference on Teaching of English in African Schools. Salisbury, March 1958, 14–17.
— 1963: Symposium on Multilingualism, Brazzaville, 16–21 July 1962. Journal of Modern African Studies 1, 102–103.
— 1968: The languages of Barotse Province. Paper read at the Eastern African Regional Conference on Language and Linguistics, Dar es Salaam, December 18–21, 1968.

FREEMAN, S. A. 1960: Africa in the world language picture. Modern Language Journal 44, 107–112.

FREEMAN-GRENVILLE, G. S. P. 1959: Medieval evidences for Swahili. Journal of the East African Swahili Committee 29, 1, 10–23.

FRISCH, A. 1963: Sprachennationalismus: Hindernisse für die afrikanische Einheit. Neues Afrika 5, 3, 109–110.

FUNKE, E. 1916: Die Stellung der Haussasprache unter den Sprachen Togos. Mitteilungen des Instituts für Orientalische Sprachen 19, 116–128.

GALLAIS, J. 1962: Signification du groupe ethnique au Mali. L'Homme 2, 2, 106–129.

GAMBLE, D. P. 1957: The Wolof of Senegambia. Together with notes on the Lebu and the Serer. London.

GELDERS, V. 1944: La langue commune au Congo. Inst. Roy. Col. Belge. Bulletin des Séances 15, 2, 77–104.

GIL, B., ARYEE, A. F. and GHANSAH, D. K.: 1960 Population Census of Ghana. Special Report 'E'. Tribes in Ghana. Accra 1964.

GLUCKMAN, M. 1942: Prefix concordance in Lozi, lingua franca of Barotseland. African Studies 1, 2, 105–114.

GOODMAN, M. F. 1964: A comparative study of creole French dialects. The Hague.

GORMAN, T. P. 1968: Bilingualism in the educational system of Kenya. Comparative Education 4, 3, 213–221.

GORMAN, W. A. R. 1950: Simple Silozi. London.

GOWER, R. H. 1952: Swahili borrowings from English. Africa 22, 2, 154–156.

GRAFFIN, R. & PICHON, F. 1930: Grammaire éwondo. Paris.

GREENBERG, J. H. 1955: Studies in African linguistic classification. New Haven.

— 1956: The measurement of linguistic diversity. Language 32, 109–115.

— 1957: Essays in linguistics. Chicago.

— 1960: Linguistic evidence for the influence of the Kanuri on the Hausa. Journal of African History 1, 205–212.

— 1962: The study of language contact in Africa. In: Colloque sur le multilinguisme, Brazzaville 1962. 167–175.

— 1963: The languages of Africa. The Hague.

— 1965: Urbanism, migration, and language. In: Urbanization and migration in West Africa. Edited by Hilda Kuper. Berkeley and Los Angeles 1965. 50–59.

GREENFIELD, R. 1965: Ethiopia. A new political history. London.

GUILBERT, D. 1954: Langues tribales et civilisation en Afrique centrale. Bull. Centre d'étude des problèmes sociaux indigènes (Elisabethville) 24, III–XIV.

GUMPERZ, J. J. 1962: Types of linguistic communities. Anthropological Linguistics 4, 1, 28–40.

GURREY, P. 1948: The relationship between a vernacular and a second language. Oversea Education 19, 3, 683–687.

GUTHRIE, M. 1939: Grammaire et dictionnaire de lingala. Cambridge.

— 1943: The lingua franca of the middle Congo. Africa 14, 3, 118–123.

— 1948: The classification of the Bantu languages. London.

— 1953: The Bantu languages of Western Equatorial Africa. London.

GUTHRIE M. and TUCKER, A. N. 1956: Linguistic survey of the northern Bantu borderland. Vol. I, Part I–III. London.

HACQUARD & DUPUIS, A. 1897: Manuel de la langue Songay parlée de Tombouctou à Say dans la boucle du Niger. Paris.

HAGEN, G. T. v. 1914: Lehrbuch der Bulu-Sprache. Berlin.

HAIR, P. E. H. 1962: Bibliography of the Mende language. Sierra Leone Language Review 1, 39–61.

— 1965: Susu studies and literature: 1799–1900. Sierra Leone Language Review 4, 38–53.
— 1966: The use of African languages in Afro-European contacts in Guinea, 1440–1560. Sierra Leone Language Review 5, 5–26.
— 1966a: A layman's guide to the languages of the Sudan Republic. Sudan Notes and Records 47, 65–78.
— 1967: Ethnolinguistic continuity on the Guinea Coast. Journal of African History 8, 2, 247–268.
HALL, R. A., Jr. 1952/3: Pidgin English and linguistic change. Lingua 3, 138–146.
— 1958: Creolized languages and "genetic relationships". Word 14, 367–373.
— 1962: The life cycle of pidgin languages. Lingua 11, 151–156.
HAMILTON, J. A. C. (Edit.) 1935: The Anglo-Egyptian Sudan from within. London.
HAMLYN, W. T. 1935: A short study of the western Mandinka language. London.
HARRIES, L. 1955: Swahili in the Belgian Congo. Tanganyika Notes and Records 39, 12–15.
— 1956: Congo Swahili. Tanganyika Notes and Records 44, 50–53.
— 1961: Some grammatical features of recent Swahili prose. African Language Studies 2, 37–41.
— 1966: Letter on 'sociolinguistic' research. African Studies Bulletin (Stanford) 9, 3, 124–127.
HARRIS, Z. S. and LUKOFF, F. 1940: The phonemes of Kingwana-Swahili. Journal of the American Oriental Society 60, 333–338.
HAUGEN, E. 1950: Problems of bilingualism. Lingua 2, 271–290.
— 1950a: The analysis of linguistic borrowing. Language 26, 210–231.
— 1958: Language contact. Proceedings of the VIII International Congress of Linguistics, Oslo 1958. 772–785.
— 1966: Linguistics and language planning. In: Bright, W. (Edit.): Sociolinguistics. The Hague 1966. 50–71.
— 1966a: Dialect, language, nation. American Anthropologist 68, 4, 922–935.
HAUSER, A. 1954: La frontière linguistique bantoue oubanguienne entre le Bas-Oubangui et ses affluents de droite. Zaire 8, 1, 21–26.
HEEPE, M. 1920: Die Komorendialekte Ngazidja, Nzwani und Mwali. Hamburg.
HEINE, B. 1963: Swahili, die wichtigste afrikanische Sprache. Neues Afrika 5, 9, 335–336.
— 1968: On the distribution of Swahili in Western Kenya. Paper read at the East African Regional Conference on Language and Linguistics, December 18–21, Dar es Salaam 1968 (to be published in Language in Eastern Africa).
— 1968a: Afrikanische Verkehrssprachen. Infratest, Schriftenreihe zur empirischen Sozialforschung, Band 4. Cologne.
— 1969: Zu einer Verbreitungskarte des Swahili im westlichen und zentralen Kenya. Die Erde (Berlin) 1969 (in print).
— 1969a: Urbanisierung und Sprachsoziologie afrikanischer linguae francae. Linguistics (in print).
— 1969b: Lingua franca und Familie in Afrika. Sociologus 1970 (in print).
— 1969c: Verbreitung und Ausbreitung afrikanischer linguae francae innerhalb der männlichen und weiblichen Bevölkerung. (mimeographed).
— 1969d: Tribalismus und Sprache. Internationales Afrika-Forum (Munich) 5, 11, 707–710.
HEINE, B. and WIESE, B. 1969: Geographische Grundlagen der Verbreitung des Swahili im westlichen Kenya. Paper read at the Tagung der Vereinigung von Afrikanisten in Deutschland, Marburg, 18–20 July, 1969.
HENRICI, E. 1891: Lehrbuch der Ephe-Sprache (Ewe). Stuttgart & Berlin.

Herzog, R. 1959: Die Ergebnisse der ersten sudanischen Volkszählung in ethnologischer Sicht. Zeitschrift für Ethnologie 84.
— 1961: Sudan. Bonn.
Hesbacher, P. and Fishman, J. A. 1965: Language loyalty: its functions and concomitants in two bilingual communities. Lingua 13, 145–165.
Hill, T. 1958: Institutional linguistics. Orbis 7, 441–455.
Hiskett, M. 1965: The historical background to the naturalization of Arabic loanwords in Hausa. African Language Studies 6, 18–26.
Hjemslev, L. 1938: Caractères grammaticaux des langues créoles. 2e Congrès International des Sciences Anthropologiques et Ethnologiques (2e session), Comtes-rendus. Kopenhagen 1938. 373.
Hodge, C. T. 1958: Non-native Hausa. Monograph Series on Languages and Linguistics 11, 57–69.
Höftmann, H. 1961: Möglichkeiten zur Wiedergabe europäischer Begriffe im Ewe. Beiträge zur Völkerforschung, Hans Damm zum 65. Geburtstag. Berlin. 276–284.
— 1963: Untersuchung zur Eingliederung moderner Begriffe in Bantusprachen, dargestellt am Suaheli, Zulu und Herero. Ethnographisch-Archäologische Zeitschrift 4, 60–65.
Hoijer, H. 1948: Linguistic and cultural change. Language 24, 335–345.
Holas, B. 1963: Côte d'Ivoire. Passé — présent — perspectives.
Hopgood, C. R. 1944: The future of Bantu languages in Northern Rhodesia. Human Problems in British Central Africa 2, 8–15.
— 1948: Language, literature, and culture. Africa 18, 112–119.
Hopkin-Jenkins, K. 1947: Basic Bantu. Pietermaritzburg.
Houis, M. 1950: Les minorités ethniques de la Guinée côtière: situation linguistique. Etudes guinéennes 4, 25–48.
— 1961: Mouvements historiques et communautés linguistiques dans l'Ouest Africain. L'Homme 1, 3, 72–90.
— 1962: Aperçu sociologique sur le bilinguisme en Afrique noire. Notes Africaines 96, 107–113.
— 1963: Etude déscriptive de la langue susu. Dakar.
Hughes, H. G. A. 1948: Language problems and policies in Africa. Linguistic Review 25, 115, 13–15.
Hulstaert, G. 1946: Les langues indigènes et les Européens au Congo Belge. African Studies 5, 2, 126–135.
— 1950: Carte linguistique du Congo Belge. Bruxelles.
— 1953: Lingala-invloed op Lomongo. Zaire 7, 3, 227–244.
— 1959: De bronnen van het lingala. Zaire 13, 5, 509–515.
Hunter, W. F. 1960 (?): A manual of Congo Swahili grammar. Mission Baptiste du Kivu.
Hunwick, J. O. 1964: The influence of Arabic in West Africa. Transactions of the Historical Society of Ghana 7, 24–41.
Hussey, E. R. J. 1932: The languages of literature in Africa. Africa 5, 2, 169–175.
Hutter 1905: Völkerbilder aus Kamerun. Globus 87, 234–238, 301–304, 365–371.
Hyder, Mohamed 1966: Swahili in the technical age. East African Journal 2, 11, 3–10.
Ikeleve sans peine. Banningville (Congo) 1958.
Inglehart, R. F. and Woodward, M. 1967: Language conflicts and political community. Comp. Stud. Soc. Hist. 10, 1, 27–45.
Jacquot, A. 1960: Esquisse phonologique du Sango urbain (Bangui). Journal de la Société des Africanistes 30, 2, 173–191.

— 1960a: Les langues Bantu du nord-ouest. Etat des connaissances. Perspectives de la recherche. Recherches et Etudes Camerounaises 2, 5–34.

— 1961: Notes sur la situation du Sango à Bangui: résultats d'un sondage. Africa 31, 2, 158–166.

— 1962: Notes à propos des éléments non africains du lexique sango (République Centrafricaine). Bulletin de l'Institut de Recherches Scientifiques au Congo 1, 55–61.

JACOTTET, E. 1896: Etudes sur les langues du Haut-Zambèze. Première partie. Paris.

JADOT, J. M. 1950: Notions pratiques de lingala. Tournai: Monobloc.

JAVABU, D. D. T. 1947: The influence of English on Bantu literature. Lovedale Press.

JEFFREYS, M. D. W. 1955: The impact of the Arab language on East Africa. Muslim Digest 5, 10, 209–212.

JENSEN, A. E. 1947: Die Rotse. In: Bernatzik, H. A. (Edit.): Afrika. Handbuch der angewandten Völkerkunde. Innsbruck 1947. 1126–1139.

JESPERSEN, O. 1922: Language, its nature, development and origin. London.

JOHNSON, F. 1930: Zamani mpaka siku hizi. London.

JOHNSON, W. 1946: People in quandaries. New York.

JONGHE, E. de 1933: Les langues communes au Congo Belge. Congo 2, 4, 509–523.

— 1935: Vers une langue nationale congolaise. Bulletijn der Zittingen van het Koninklijk Belgisch Koloniaal Instituut 6, 2, 340–351.

— 1944: L'unification des langues congolaises. Institut Royal Colonial Belge. Bulletin des Séances 15 (Bruxelles), 272–282.

JUNOD, H.-P. 1963: Langues vernaculaires et véhiculaires en Afrique. Genève-Afrique 2, 1, 21–45.

KEHOE, M. 1963: The language dilemma in Ethiopia. Overseas Education 34, 4, 162–165.

KELLER, B. B. 1963: Contact languages in Africa. Kroeber Anthropological and Sociological Papers 28, 49–71.

KERKEN, G. van der 1944: Le Swahili, langue de grande expansion. Institut Royal Colonial Belge. Bulletin des Séances 15 (Bruxelles), 234–267.

KILSON. M. 1962: Multilingualism among African students. Harvard. (MS)

KIRK-GREENE, A. H. M. 1963: Neologisms in Hausa: a sociological approach. Africa 33, 1, 25–44.

— 1963a: A preliminary survey of neologisms in Hausa (summary). In: Actes du second colloque international de linguistique négro-africaine, Dakar 12–16 avril 1962. Dakar 1963. 204–209.

— 1964: The Hausa Language Board. Afrika und Übersee 47, 3–4, 187–203.

— 1965: An excursion into Ghanaian Hausa. Nigerian Citizen (Kaduna), June 30.

— 1967: The linguistic statistics of Northern Nigeria: a tentative presentation. African Language Review 6, 75–101.

Kikwango grammar. Kafumba (Congo) 1945.

KISOB, J. A. 1963: A live language: Pidgin English. Abbia 1 Feb., 25–31.

KITUMBOY, L. W. H. 1960: Kiswahili usages, Congo Belge & Ruanda Urundi. Swahili 31 (New series 1, 2), 227–230.

— 1961: Swahili in Rwanda Urundi and Congo Republic. Swahili 32 (New series 1, 3), 65–66.

KIWANUKA, B. 1967: Bi-lingualism in education: the role of the vernacular languages. East African Journal 4, 7, 21–24.

KLEINICKE, D. 1959: An etymology for "pidgin". International Journal of American Linguistics 25, 271–272.

KLINGENHEBEN, A. 1943/4: Die Mande-Völker und ihre Sprachen. Zeitschrift für Eingeborenen-Sprachen 34, 1.

— 1966: Deutsch-Amharischer Sprachführer nebst einer grammatischen Einführung ins Amharische. Wiesbaden.
KLOSE, H. 1899: Togo unter deutscher Flagge. Reisebilder und Betrachtungen. Berlin.
KLOSS, H. 1927: Spracherhaltung. Archiv für Politik und Geschichte 8, 456–462.
— 1929: Sprachtabellen als Grundlage für Sprachstatistik, Sprachkarten und für eine allgemeine Soziologie der Sprachgemeinschaften. Vierteljahresschrift für Politik und Geschichte 1, 103–117.
KNAPPERT, J. 1958: De bronnen van het lingala. Kongo-Overzee 24, 4–5, 193–200.
— 1963: Languages and societies. EAISR (East African Institute of Social Research) Conference Paper.
— 1963a: New nations and national languages. EAISR Conference Paper.
— 1964: Le swahili, langue de culture. Présence africaine 50–52, 178–182.
— 1964a: Languages unite and divide. EAISR Conference Paper.
— 1965: Wijzigingen in Afrika's taalkaart. Kroniek van Afrika 5, 2, 143–156.
— 1968: The function of language in a political situation. Linguistics 39, 59–67.
KÖHLER, O. 1960: Sprachakkulturation im Herero. Ethnologica N.F. 2, 331–362.
KRUMM, B. 1932: Wörter und Wortformen orientalischen Ursprungs im Suaheli. Hamburg.
KUNENE, D. P. 1963: Southern Sotho words of English and Afrikaans origin. Word 19, 3, 347–375.
KURATH, H. 1962: Interrelation between regional and social dialects. In: Preprints of Papers for the Ninth International Congress of Linguistics. Cambridge (Mass.) 1962. 185–190.
KYATANGALWA, J.-R. 1957: Le kirega, une langue qui meurt. Voix du Congolais 138, 690.
LABOURET, H. 1931: La situation linguistique en Afrique Occidentale Française. Africa 4, 1, 56–62.
— 1934: Les Manding et leur langue. Paris.
— 1947: Introduction. In: Trenga, G.: Le Bura-Mabang du Ouadai. Paris. V–XI.
LABOURET, H. et WARD, I. C. 1933: Quelques observations sur la langue mandingue. Africa 6, 38–50.
LACROIX, P.-F. 1959: Observations sur la "koine" peule de Ngaoundéré. Travaux de l'Institut de Linguistique 4.
— 1962: Distribution géographique et sociale des parlers peul du Nord-Cameroun. L'Homme (Paris) 2, 3, 75–101.
LAMAN, K. E. 1928: Languages used in the Congo basin. Africa 1, 3, 372–380.
LANG, K. 1923/4: Arabische Lehnwörter in der Kanuri-Sprache. Anthropos 18/19, 1063–1074.
The language of Ethiopia. Ethiopia Observer 2, 3 (1958), 98–128.
LAROCHETTE, J. 1950: Problèmes culturels et problèmes linguistiques au Congo Belge. Zaire 4, 123–165.
— 1952: Le problème des langues dans l'enseignement aux indigènes du Congo Belge. Prob. Afr. Centrale (Bruxelles) 5, 16, 72–78.
LEBLANC, M. 1955: Evolution linguistique et relations humaines. Zaire 9, 8, 787–800.
LECOSTE, B. 1954: Le Ngwana. Variété congolaise du Swahili. Kongo-Overzee 20, 4–5, 391–408.
— 1955: Vocabulaire Ngwana. Kongo-Overzee 21, 3/4, 289–297.
— 1960: A grammatical study of two recordings of Belgian-Congo Swahili. Swahili 31 (New series 1, 2), 219–226.
LEKENS, B. 1952: Dictionnaire Ngbandi (Ubangi-Congo Belge). Annales du Musée du Congo-Belge, Tervuren, série in-8°, sciences de l'Homme, Linguistique, I.

LEMARCHAND, R. 1961: The bases of nationalism among the Bakongo. Africa 31, 4, 344–354.
LESLAU, W. 1956: Arabic loanwords in Tigré. Word 12, 125–141.
LESLIE, J. 1959: Swahili slang. Swahili 29, 1, 81–87.
LESTRADE, G. P. 1946: Some problems of Bantu language development. South African Journal of Science 42, 70–83.
LETHEM, G. J. 1920: Colloquial Arabic. Shuwa dialect of Bornu, Nigeria, and of the region of Lake Chad. London.
LEWIS, E. G. 1962: Conditions affecting the "reception" of an official (second/foreign) language. In: Colloque sur le multilinguisme, Brazzaville 1962. 83–102.
LIEBERSON, S. 1964: An extension of Greenberg's linguistic diversity measures. Language 40, 4, 526–531.
LIESENBORGHS, O. 1938: Wat is Kingwana? Kongo-Overzee 4, 5, 233–249.
— 1941/2: Beschouwingen over wezen, nut en toekomst der zoogenaamde 'linguae francae' van Belgisch Kongo. Kongo-Overzee 7/8, 1/3, 87–99.
LINDBLOM, G. 1925: Notes on the Kamba language. Upsala.
Lingala, Collection des Frères Maristes. Buta (Congo) 1951.
Linguistic survey of the northern Bantu borderland. Volume I. London 1956.
LINTON, R. (Edit.) 1940: Acculturation in seven American Indian tribes. New York.
LIPPERT, J. 1907: Über die Bedeutung der Haussanation für unsere Togo- und Kamerunkolonie. Mitteilungen des Seminars für Orient. Sprachen zu Berlin 10, 193–226.
LLOYD, G. O. 1955: A study of some Xhosa words of Afrikaans origin. South African Outlook 85, 1010, 90–93.
LOEWEN, J. A. 1968: Why minority languages persist or die. Practical Anthropology 15, 1, 8–15.
LOMBARD, J. 1961: Les bases traditionelles de l'économie rurale bariba et ses fondements nouveaux. Bulletin IFAN B 23, 1–2, 179–242.
LOUW, J. A. 1963: The development of the Bantu languages in South Africa. Afr. Inst. Bull. 3, 5, 133–141.
LUKAS, J. n. d.: Das westafrikanische Verkehrssprachenproblem von Togo bis nach Wadai. (MS)
— 1936: The linguistic situation in the Lake Chad area in central Africa. Africa 9, 3, 332–349.
— 1937: A study of the Kanuri language. Grammar and vocabulary. London.
— 1939: Linguistic research between Nile and Lake Chad. Africa 12, 3, 335–349.
— 1942: Das afrikanische Verkehrssprachenproblem. Beiträge zur Kolonialforschung 2, 15–24.
— 1943: Zur Entwicklung der afrikanischen Verkehrssprachen. Beiträge zur Kolonialforschung. Tagungsband 1, 118–127.
— 1964: Hausa, eine umfassende Verkehrssprache für Westafrika. Neues Afrika 6, 8, 275–277.
MCCULLOCH, M. 1952: The Ovimbundu of Angola. London.
MCDAVID, R. I., Jr. 1966: Dialect differences and social differences in an urban society. In: Bright, W. (Edit.): Sociolinguistics. The Hague 1966. 72–83.
MACDOUGALD, D. 1944: Languages and press of Africa. University of Pennsylvania.
MACKENZIE, N. 1960: The outlook for English in central Africa: an inaugural lecture, University College of Rhodesia und Nyasaland. London.
MCLOUGHLIN, P. F. M. 1964: Language-switching as an index of socialization in the Republic of the Sudan. Berkeley and Los Angeles.
MAKWARD, E. C. 1963: The language problem. West African Journal of Education 7, 2, 87–93.

MALAMI, S. 1961: The claims of Hausa. West Africa 2292, 483.
MALHERBE, E. G. 1946: The bilingual school: a study of bilingualism in South Africa. London.
MANESSY, G. 1964: Les langues négro-africaines de grande extension et l'unification linguistique de l'Afrique noire. L'Homme 4, 3, 71–86.
Manifeste d'un groupe de Bakongo. Vers l'unification de la langue Kikongo. Kongo-Overzee 19, 2–3, 1953, 178–181.
MAROUZEAU, J. 1951: Lexique de la terminologie linguistique (français, allemand, anglais, italien). Paris.
MAZRUI, A. A. 1967: The national language question in East Africa. East African Journal 4, 3, 12–19.
MEEK, C. K. 1931: Tribal studies in Northern Nigeria. 2 vols. London.
MEEUS, D. F. de 1953: Le problème des langues en Afrique. Rythmes du Monde (Paris, Bruges) N.S. 1, 2, 154–164.
MEINHOF, C. 1910: Die moderne Sprachforschung in Afrika. Berlin.
— 1928: Die Sprachenfrage in Südafrika. Koloniale Rundschau 12.
— 1939: Verkehrs-Sprachen, Pidgin-Sprachen, Sonder-Sprachen. Zeitschrift für Eingeborenen-Sprachen 29, 4, 312–313.
MERCIER, P. 1949: Création de mots nouveaux. Notes africaines IFAN 41, 10.
MEYER, E. 1944: Das Problem der Verkehrssprachen von Tropisch-Afrika, insb. von Kamerun. Mitt. geogr. Ges. Hamburg 48, 253–288.
MIGEOD, F. W. H. 1908: The Mende language. London.
MOLNOS, A. 1969: Language problems in Africa. A bibliography (1946–1967) and summary of the present situation, with special reference to Kenya, Tanzania and Uganda. Nairobi.
MONTEIL, V. 1963: Sur l'Arabisation des langues négro-africaines. Genève-Afrique 2, 1, 12–20.
MORENO, M. M. 1952: La modernisation et l'unification des langues en Somalie. Civilisations 2, 61–66.
MORRISON, W. M. 1906: Grammar of the Buluba-Lulua language as spoken in the upper Kasai and Congo basin. Luebo.
MORTIER, R. 1946: Ubangi onder linguistisch opzicht. Aequatoria 9, 3, 104–112.
MUKAROVSKY, H. G. 1966: Zur Stellung der Mandesprachen. Anthropos 61, 679–688.
MUKUNA, P. C. 1957: Ne déprécions pas notre langue maternelle. Voix du Congolais 136, 508.
MULIRA, E. M. K. 1951: The vernacular in African education. London.
MURRAY, W. A. 1963: English in the Sudan: trends and policies: relations with Arabic. In: Spencer, J. (Edit.): Language in Africa. Cambridge 1963. 86–95.
NATALIS, E. 1965: La langue swahilie. Première partie. Cours méthodique. 2e édition. Liège.
NAUMANN 1915: Die Bajasprache. Einführung in die Grammatik und systematisches Wörterverzeichnis. Mitteilungen des Seminars für Orient. Sprachen 18, 42–51.
NEKES, P. H. 1911: Lehrbuch der Jaunde-Sprache. Lehrbücher des Seminars für Orient. Sprachen 26. Berlin.
— 1912: Jaunde und seine Bewohner (Süd-Kamerun). Koloniale Rundschau 1912, 8, 468–484.
— 1927: Zur Entwicklung der Jaunde-Sprache unter dem Einfluß der europäischen Kultur. Festschrift Meinhof, Wien 1927. 301–314.
NEWELL, H. W. 1930: Notes on Ki-Swahili as spoken by the King's African Rifles (MS).
NGIJOL, P. 1964: Nécessité d'une langue nationale. Abbia 7, 83–99.

NIDA, E. A. 1949: Some language problems in the Congo. Congo Mission News 145, 14–16.
— 1955: Tribal and trade languages. African Studies 14, 4, 155–158.
— 1956: The role of language in contemporary Africa. Practical Anthropology 3, 3, 122–137.
NNUNDUMBA, B. E. 1959: Written Swahili in the Belgian Congo. Swahili 29, 1, 24–33.
NSIMBI, M. B. 1952: African languages in Uganda Primary Schools. Oversea Education 23, 240–242.
NUTTALL, C. E. 1962: Problems of English teaching in Northern Nigeria. In: Colloque sur le multilinguisme. Brazzaville 1962, 109–120.
OBOTE, M. 1967: Language and national identification. East African Journal 4, 1, 3–6.
O'HARA, A. 1965: Swahili: la lingua dell' "uhuru". Nigrizia 83, 3, 14–18.
ORNSTEIN, Jacob 1964: Africa seeks a common language. Revue politique et parlementaire (Paris) avril 1964, 205–214.
ORR, C. 1965: The making of Northern Nigeria. Second edition. London.
OWIREDU, P. A. 1957: Towards a common language for Ghana. African Affairs (London) 56, 225, 232–241.
— 1964: Proposal for a national language for Ghana. African Affairs 63, 142–145.
LE PAGE, R. B. (Edit.) 1961: Proceedings of the conference on creole language studies. Creole Language Studies, No. 2. London.
— 1964: The national language question. Linguistic problems of newly independent states. London.
PANKHURST, S. 1955: Ethiopia. A cultural history. London.
PARKIN, D. J. 1968: Language choice in two Kampala housing estates. Paper read at the Ninth International African Seminar, December 1968, Dar es Salaam.
PATEL, R. B. 1965: The borrowing of Swahili words in spoken Gujarati. Swahili 35, 2, 14–16.
PERREN, G. E. 1958: Bilingualism or replacement. English in East Africa. English Language Teaching 8, 1.
PHILIPPS, J. E. T. 1926/27: The Azande. Journal of the African Society 26, 21–26.
PIA, J. J. 1966: Language in Somalia. Linguistic Reporter 8, 3, 1–2.
POLOMÉ, E. 1963: Cultural languages and contact vernaculars in the Republic of the Congo. Studies in Literature and Language (Texas) 4, 4, 499–511.
— 1967: The position of Swahili and other Bantu languages in Katanga. Paper read at the Second congrès international des africanistes, Dakar 11–20 décembre 1967.
— 1967a: Swahili language handbook. Center for applied linguistics, Washington D.C.
— 1968: Multilingualism in an African urban centre: the Lubumbashi case. Paper read at the Ninth International African Seminar, December 1968, Dar es Salaam.
— n.d.: Lubumbashi Swahili (MS).
PORTER, P. W. 1956: Population distribution and land use in Liberia. Phil. Diss. London.
PRAETORIUS, F. 1886: Äthiopische Grammatik mit Paradigmen, Litteratur, Chrestomathie und Glossar. Karlsruhe und Leipzig.
PRICE, T. 1940: Nyanja linguistic problems. Africa 13, 2, 125–137.
PRINS, A. H. J. 1961: The Swahili-speaking peoples of Zanzibar and the East African coast (Arabs, Shirazi and Swahili). London.
Het probleem van de inlandse onderwijstaal in Leopoldstad. Kongo-Overzee 19, 1, 1953, 7–9.

Prost, R.P. A. 1956: La langue soṅay et ses dialectes. Mémoires IFAN. Dakar.
— 1966: Mots mossi empruntés au Songay. Bulletin IFAN B 28, 1–2, 470–475.
Rapp, E. L. 1955: Zur Ausbreitung einer westafrikanischen Stammessprache (Das Twi). In: Lukas, J. (Edit.): Afrikanistische Studien. Berlin 1955. 220–230.
Raum, O. F. 1937: Language perversions in East Africa. Africa 10, 2, 221–225.
Ray, P. S. 1962: Language standardization. In: Rice, F. A. (Edit.): Study of the role of second languages. Washington 1962. 91–104.
Redden, J. E., Bongo, F. and Associates 1963: Lingala basic course. Washington.
—, Owusu, N. and Associates 1963: Twi basic course. Washington.
Reinecke, J. E. 1938: Trade jargons and creole dialects as marginal languages. Social Forces 17, 107–118. Reprinted in: Hymes, D. (Edit.): Language in Culture and Society. A reader in linguistics and anthropology. New York, Evanston, and London 1964. 534–542.
Rendinger, Général de 1949: Contribution à l'étude des langues nègres du Centre-Africain. Journal de la Société des Africanistes 19, 2, 143–194.
Report of the Rejaf Language Conference, 1928. London.
Reusch, R. 1953: How the Swahili people and language came into existence. Tanganyika Notes and Records 34, 20–27.
Reyburn, W. D. 1963: The penetration of world languages into Africa. Practical Anthropology 10, 6, 259–270.
Richards, A. I. 1955: Economic development and tribal change. Cambridge.
Richardson, I. 1961: Some observations on the status of Town Bemba in Northern Rhodesia. African Language Studies 2, 25–36.
— 1962: Linguistic change in Africa with special reference to the Bemba-speaking area of Northern Rhodesia. In: Colloque sur le multilinguisme. Brazzaville 1962. 189–196.
— 1963: Examples of deviation and innovation in Bemba. African Language Studies 4, 128–145.
— 1967: Linguistic evolution and Bantu noun class systems. In: La classification nominale dans les langues négro-africaines. Aix-en-Provence 1967.
Roberts, J. 1962: Sociocultural change and communication problems. In: Rice, F. A. (Edit.): Study of the role of second languages. Washington 1962. 105–123.
Rommes, M. 1951: La situation linguistique dans les vicariats de Stanleyville et de Wamba. Kongo-Overzee 17, 240–249.
Rop, A. de 1953: De Bakongo en het Lingala. Kongo-Overzee 19, 2–3, 170–174.
— 1960: Les langues du Congo. Aequatoria 23, 1, 1–24.
Ross, A. S. C. 1962: On the historical study of pidgins. In: Colloque sur le multilinguisme. Brazzaville 1962. 243–249.
Rouch, J. 1954: Les Songhay. Paris.
— 1956: Migrations au Ghana (Gold Coast). Journal de la Société des Africanistes 26, 1–2, 33–196.
Roulet, E. M. 1957: The linguistic situation in French West Africa. Bible Translator 8, 1, 37–40.
Roux, M. 1930: La question des langues en Ouganda. Le Bulletin des Missions 11, 12, 533–536.
Rowlands, E. C. 1963: Yoruba and English: a problem of coexistance. African Language Studies 4, 208–214.
Sabbadini, E. 1951: Il Swahili, lingua franca dell'Africa orientale. Lingue del Mondo 16, 11.
Sacleux, C. 1909: Grammaire des dialectes swahilis. Paris.
Sakiliba, D.-F. 1957: Présent et futur des langues africaines. Présence africaine, N.S. 12, 127–141, and 13, 65–73.

Samarin, W. J. 1953: Learning Sango. A pedagogical grammar. Mission Evangélique de l'Oubangui-Chari, Bozoum.
— 1955: Sango, an African lingua franca. Word 11, 2, 254–267.
— 1958: The phonology of Pidgin Sango. Word 14, 62–70.
— 1961: The vocabulary of Sango. Word 17, 1, 16–22.
— 1962: Lingua francas, with special reference to Africa. In: Rice, F. A. (Edit.): Study of the role of second languages. Washington 1962. 54–64.
— 1962a: Une *lingua franca* centrafricaine. In: Colloque sur le multilinguisme. Brazzaville 1962. 257–265.
— 1966: Self-annulling prestige factors among speakers of a creole language. In: Bright, W. (Edit.): Sociolinguistics. The Hague 1966. 188–213.
Sauvageot, A. 1953: Le problème des langues vernaculaires. Education nationale (Paris) 11, 3–4, 7.
Sauvageot, S. 1965: Description synchronique d'un dialecte wolof: le parler du Dyolof. Dakar.
Sauvant, Mgr. 1925: Manuel Bambara. 3ᵉ Edition. Alger.
Schmidt, P. W. 1902/3: Welcher Dialekt der Evhesprache verdient zur Schrift- und Verkehrssprache in Evheland (Togo) erhoben zu werden? Beiträge zur Kolonialpolitik und Kolonialwirtschaft 4, 65–70.
Schmidt-Rohr, G. 1932: Die Sprache als Bildnerin der Völker. Jena.
— 1936: Ein Fragebogen zum Problem der Zweisprachigkeit. Deutsche Arbeit 36, 9, 443–444.
Schneider, G. D. 1960: Cameroons creole dictionary. First draft. Bamenda Settlement, Southern Cameroons (mimeographed).
Schramm, J. 1965: Gambia. Bonn.
Schultze, E. 1933: Sklaven- und Dienersprachen (sogenannte Handelssprachen). Sociologus 9, 4, 377–418.
Schwarz, F. A. O., Jr. 1965: Nigeria. The tribes, the nation, or the race – the politics of independence. Cambridge (Mass.).
Scott, D. C. and Hetherwick, A. 1951: Dictionary of the Nyanja language. Being the Encyclopaedic Dictionary of the Mang'anja Language. Reprint, London.
Scotton, C. M. M. 1965: Some Swahili political words. Journal of Modern African Studies 3, 4, 527–541.
Shelton, A. J. 1964: Some problems of inter-communication. Journal of Modern African Studies 2, 3, 395–403.
Shepherd, A. 1926: Dictionnaire Kingala: Kikongo commercial. Brussels.
Sierra Leone Creo. West Africa 31, 1564, 1947, 62–63.
Silvey, J. 1963: Formal and informal learning through the medium of a second language: applications of a theory of sociolinguistics to East Africa. EAISR Conference paper.
Skalnikova, O. 1964: Ethnological research into the present changes in the mode of life of urban population in Africa. In: Proceedings of the First International Congress of Africanists. Accra 1964. 286–297.
Snoxall, R. A. 1938: Word importation into Bantu language with particular reference to Ganda. Uganda Journal 5, 4, 267–283.
— 1951: How Swahili is changing. East Afr. Inter-Territ. Language (Swahili) Committee Bulletin 21, 8–11.
Southall, A. W. 1955: Alur migrants. In: Richards, A. I. (Edit.): Economic development and tribal change. Cambridge 1955. 141–160.
Spencer, J. (Edit.) 1963: Language in Africa. Papers of the Leverhulme Conference

on universities and the language problems of tropical Africa, held at University College, Ibadan. Cambridge.
SPITZER, L. 1966: Creole attitudes towards Krio: an historical survey. Sierra Leone Language Review 5, 39–49.
STAPLETON, W. H. 1910: Propositions pour une grammaire du "Bangala" et un vocabulaire Français–Bangala–Swahili. Nouvelle Edition.
STAPPERS, L. 1952: Het Tshiluba als omgangstaal of unifiatie van de Luba-dialekten? Kongo-Overzee 18, 50–65.
STEINDORFF, G. 1951: Lehrbuch der Koptischen Grammatik. Chicago.
STEWART, J. M. 1967: A note on Akan-centered linguistic acculturation. Research Review (Accra) 3, 2, 66–73.
STEWART, W. A. 1962: An outline of linguistic typology for describing multilingualism. In: RICE, F. A. (Edit.): Study of the role of second languages. Washington 1962. 15–25.
STIGAND, C. H. 1915: A grammar of dialectic changes in the Kiswahili language. Cambridge.
STIRKE, D. W. 1922: Barotseland: eight years among the Barotse. With an introductory chapter by Sir Harry Johnston, G.C.M.G., K.C.B. London.
STRUCK, B. 1912: Die Sprachverhältnisse im "Moyen Congo". Koloniale Rundschau 1912.
— 1921: Die Einheitssprache Deutsch-Ostafrikas. Koloniale Rundschau 1921, 164–196.
SUTHERLIN, R. E. 1962: Language situation in East Africa. In: RICE, F. A. (Edit.): Study of the role of second languages. Washington 1962. 65–78.
SWARTENBROECKX, P. 1953: Dictionnaire kikongo simplifié – français, français – kikongo simplifié. Banningville (Congo).
COMHAIRE-SYLVAIN, S. 1949: Le lingala des enfants noirs de Léopoldville. Kongo-Overzee 15, 5, 239–250.
Symposium on the linguae francae in the Belgian Congo. Institut Royal Colonial Belge, Bulletin des Séances 15, 2, 1944.
TABER, C. R. 1964: French loan words in Sango: a statistical analysis of incidence. Hartford Studies in Linguistics. Hartford.
TAESCHNER, F. 1964: Geschichte der arabischen Welt. Stuttgart.
TANGHE, J. 1930: Le Lingala, la langue du fleuve. Congo 11, 341–358.
— 1944: Le Swahili, langue de grande expansion. Institut Royal Colonial Belge, Bulletin des Séances 15, 2, 174–197.
TASTEVIN, R. P. 1956: L'appelation 'Mandé'. Notes africaines IFAN 72, 124–126.
TESSMANN, G. 1932: Die Völker und Sprachen Kameruns. Petermanns Mitteilungen 78, 5/6, 113–120 and 78, 7/8, 184–190.
THIRIET, A. n.d.: L'enseignement du français en Afrique I. Le Sénégal: population, langues, programmes scolaires. Dakar.
THOMAS, H. B. and SCOTT, R. 1935: Uganda. London.
THOMAS, N. W. 1914: Slang in Southern Nigeria. Man 14, 3, 3–4.
THOMSON, T. D. 1955: A practical approach to Chinyanja. Zomba.
THORBECKE, F. 1914: Auf der Savanne. Berlin.
TRAPP, O. 1908: Die Isikula-Sprache in Natal, Südafrika. Anthropos 3, 508–511.
TRENGA, G. 1947: Le Bura-Mabang du Ouadai. Notes pour servir à l'étude de la langue Maba. Paris.
DE TRESSAN, de Lavergne 1953: Inventaire linguistique de l'Afrique Occidentale Française et du Togo. Dakar.
TUCKER, A. N. 1934: The linguistic situation in the southern Sudan. Africa 7, 1, 28–36.

- 1940: The eastern Sudanic languages. Volume I. Oxford.
- 1947: My recent linguistic tour in East Africa. Makerere 2, 4, 22–25.
- 1952: Taaleenmaking in Oost-Afrika. Kongo-Overzee 18, 312–317.
- 1958: The present status of Swahili in Africa. Indian Linguistics – Turner Jubilee. Vol. 1, 363–375.
TUCKER, A. N. and BRYAN, M. A. 1956: The non-Bantu languages of north-eastern Africa, with a supplement on the non-Bantu languages of southern Africa, by E. O. J. Westphal. London.
TURNER, V. W. 1952: The Lozi peoples of north-western Rhodesia. London.
ULLENDORFF, E. 1949: A Tigrinya language council. Africa 19, 1, 63–64.
- 1955: The languages of Ethiopia. A comparative phonology. London.
- 1960: The Ethiopians. An introduction to country and people. London.
- 1965: An Amharic chrestomathy. London.
- 1965a: The challenge of Amharic (Inaugural Lecture). School of Oriental and African Studies. London.
UNESCO 1953: The use of vernacular languages in education. Paris.
URVOY, Y. 1942: Petit atlas ethno-démographique du Soudan entre Sénégal et Tchad. Paris.
VALKHOFF, M. F. 1966: Studies in Portuguese and creole. With special reference to South Africa. Johannesburg.
VERBREKEN, A. 1928: Abrégé de grammaire Tshiluba. Bruxelles.
Vocabulary: English–Kituba, Kituba–English. Kafumba (Congo) 1958.
VOEGELIN, C. F. 1965: Sociolinguistics, ethnolinguistics, and anthropological linguistics. American Anthropologist 67, 2, 484–485.
VOEGELIN, C. F. and F. M. 1964: Languages of the world: African fascicle one. Anthropological Linguistics 6, 5.
- 1964a: Languages of the world: Ibero-Caucasian and pidgin-creole fascicle one. Anthropological Linguistics 6, 8.
- 1961: Languages now spoken by over a million speakers. Anthropological Linguistics, Archives of languages of the world 3, 8, 13–22.
VOEGELIN, C. F. and HARRIS, Z. S. 1951: Methods for determining intelligibility among dialects of national languages. Proc. Amer. Philos. Soc. 95, 322–329.
VOORHOEVE, J. 1962: Creole languages and communication. In: Colloque sur le multilinguisme. Brazzaville 1962. 233–242.
VORBICHLER, A. 1964: Das Sprachenproblem im Kongo (Léo). Neues Afrika 6, 5, 167–169.
VORST, G. VAN DER 1958: Le Kiswahili, langue classique. Kongo-Overzee 24, 203–213.
WALKER, A. 1933: Les néologismes dans les idiomes gabonais. Journal de la Société des Africanistes 3, 2, 305–314.
WARD, I. C. 1935: A linguistic tour in Southern Nigeria. Africa 8, 90–97.
WARMELO, N. J. VAN 1957: Neuere Entwicklungen und Bestrebungen in den Bantusprachen Südafrikas. Zeitschrift für Phonetik und Allgemeine Sprachwissenschaft 10, 2, 167–176.
WEIL, P. M. 1968: Language distribution in the Gambia: 1966–67. African Language Review 7, 101–106.
WEINREICH, U. 1958: Research frontiers in bilingualism studies. Proceedings of the Eighth International Congress of Linguistics. Oslo 1958. 786–797.
- 1963: Languages in contact. 2nd edition. The Hague.
WELMERS, W. E. 1953: African languages and Christian missions. Civilisations 3, 545–564.

— 1959: A survey of the major languages of Africa. The Linguistic Reporter, suppl. 1, 1–2.
WESTERMANN, D. 1905: Wörterbuch der Ewe-Sprache. I. Teil. Ewe-Deutsches Wörterbuch. Berlin.
— 1929: The linguistic situation and vernacular literature in British West Africa. Africa 2, 4, 337–351.
— 1933: Swahili as the lingua franca of East Africa. The Church Overseas 6, 21, 20–31.
— 1940: Sprache und Erziehung. In: Baumann, H., Thurnwald, R. and Westermann, D.: Völkerkunde von Afrika. Essen 1940. 375–452.
— 1949: Sprachbeziehungen und Sprachverwandtschaft in Afrika. Berlin.
— and BRYAN, M. A. 1952: The languages of West Africa. London.
WESTON, A. B. 1965: Law in Swahili: problems in developing the national language. Swahili 35, 2, 2–13.
WESTPHAL, E. O. J. 1946: The unification of Bantu languages. African Studies 5, 1, 54–56.
— 1962: An example of complex language contacts in Ngamiland, B.P. In: Colloque sur le multilinguisme. Brazzaville 1962. 205–210.
WHINNOM, K. 1965: Origin of the European-based creoles and pidgins. Orbis 14, 2.
WHITE, C. M. N. 1944: A Lwena-English vocabulary. Balovale.
— 1949: A short Lwena grammar. London.
— 1949a: The Balovale peoples and their historical background. The Rhodes-Livingstone Journal 8, 26–41.
— 1951: Modern influences upon an African language group. The Rhodes-Livingstone Journal 11, 66–71.
WHITELEY, W. H. 1955: Kimvita: an enquiry into dialectal status and characteristics. Journal of the East African Swahili Committee 25, 10–43.
— 1956: The changing position of Swahili in East Africa. Africa 26, 4, 343–353.
— 1956a: Present-day position of Swahili in East Africa. Conference paper, East African Institute of Social Research, 6.
— 1957: The work of the East African Swahili Committee 1930–1957. Congo-Overzee 23, 242–255.
— 1962: Swahili as a *lingua franca* in East Africa. In: Colloque sur le multilinguisme. Brazzaville 1962. 183–187.
— 1964: Problems of a lingua franca: Swahili and the trade-unions. Journal of African Languages 3, 3, 215–225.
— 1967: Linguistics and Africa: 1962–1967. Paper read at the Second congrès international des africanistes, Dakar 11–20 décembre, 1967.
— 1969: Swahili. The rise of a national language. London.
— and HOUIS, M. 1962: Les problèmes linguistiques dans les situations multilingues. Introduction. In: Colloque sur le multilinguisme. Brazzaville 1962. 153–164.
WILLIAMSON, J. 1951: Congo Swahili. East African Inter-Territorial Language (Swahili) Committee Bulletin 21, 15–17.
WILSON, W. A. A. 1962: The Crioulo of Guiné. Johannesburg.
WING, J. VAN 1953: Het Kikongo en het Lingala te Leopoldstad. Kongo-Overzee 19, 2/3, 175–178.
WINTERBOTTOM, J. M. 1949: Some problems of the use of African vernaculars. Human Problems in British Central Africa 7, 67–74.
WIOLAND, F. et CALVET, M. 1967: L'expansion du wolof au Sénégal. Bulletin IFAN B 29, 3/4, 604–618.

WOLFF, H. 1967: Language, ethnic identity and social change in Southern Nigeria Anthropological Linguistics 9, 1, 18–25.
WONDERLY, W. L. 1966: At home in a second language. Practical Anthropology 13, 3, 97–102.
WRIGHT, M. 1965: Swahili language policy, 1890–1940. Swahili 35, 1, 40–48.
ZWERNEMANN, J. 1961: Kulturen und Sprachen in Tanganyika. Neues Afrika 3, 11, 432–435.
— 1962: Die Verkehrssprachen Afrikas. Neues Afrika 4, 11, 426–430.

## Index of Authors

References are to paragraphs. I = Introduction

Alexandre, P. 245, 250, 251, 281, 317
Alexandre, R. P. 37, 346
Andrzejewski, B. W. 46, 49, 236
Atkins, G. 98–9

Banton, M. 324
Barney, J. A. 119
Berry, J. I, 6
Beuchelt, E. 358, 363
Boeck, L. B. de 5, 34, 114, 132, 134–6, 141
Brauner, S. 362
Broomfield, G. W. 150
Brosnahan, L. F. 29
Bryan, M. A. 57, 119, 198, 200, 203
Bulck, R. P. G. van 122
Burssens, A. 19, 105, 128

Callaway, C. 52, 60
Calvet, M. 318
Chabrelie, L. 215
Childs, G. M. 72–3
Christaller, J. G. 305
Cole, D. T. 51–2, 59–60
Comhaire-Sylvain, S. 119, 134

Dalby, T. D. P. 363
Delafosse, M. 262, 338–9, 344, 346, 352, 354–5, 357–8, 364
Diop, A. 316
Duisburg, A. von 219–20, 222
Duncan, P. 52
Dupuis, A. 339

Edwards, A. C. 73
Epstein, A. L. 61, 75
Everbroeck, R. van 140

Fallers, M. C. 201
Fehderau, H. W. 109, 112–4, 116–7
Ferguson, C. A. 38, 47–8, 229

Greenberg, J. H. 26, 31, 36, 206, 212, 215, 217, 220, 224, 270, 272, 307, 322, 335–6, 347
Guthrie, M. 119, 122–3, 140, 238, 247, 251

Hacquard 339
Hagen, G. T. v. 239, 246
Hair, P. E. H. 311, 316, 349
Hall, J. F. 346
Harries, L. 163, 189
Henrici, E. 294
Hill, T. I, 48
Holas, B. 357
Houis, M. 28–9, 312, 314, 351
Hulstaert, G. 101, 121–2, 163
Hutter 332

Jacquot, A. 5–6, 19, 22, 281, 284, 286–8, 290–1
Johnson, F. 149, 152

Kähler-Meyer see Meyer, E.
Kerken, G. van der 101, 103, 105
Kirk-Greene, A. H. M. 324, 332
Kitumboy, H. 191
Klingenheben, A. 211
Knappert, J. 122
Köhler, O. 322
Krumm, B. 152

Labouret, H. 345–6, 357, 364
Lacroix, P. F. 268
Lavergne, de Tressan de 314, 317
Leblanc, M. 5, 164
Lecoste, B. 163
Lekens, B. 276
Lethem, G. J. 233
Lewis, E. G. 39
Liesenborghs, O. 105
Lindblom, G. 205

Lippert, J. 334
Ludolf, H. 208
Lukas, J. 29, 210, 217, 219–20, 222, 226, 233, 293, 322, 324, 331

Manessy, G. 27
Meinhof, C. 51
Meyer, E. 29, 35, 119, 157, 258–9, 331

Natalis, E. 189
Naumann 271
Nekes, H. 249
Nida, E. A. 20, 24, 26, 115

Pankhurst, S. 210
Polomé, E. 166
Prins, A. H. J. 198
Prost, R. P. A. 341
Ptolemy 155

Rapp, E. L. 9, 303, 306
Reinecke, J. E. 2
Rendinger, General de 232
Reusch, R. 152, 189, 198
Richards, A. I. 202
Richardson, I. 4, 22, 24, 56, 75, 87, 92
Roberts, J. 129, 203, 308
Roehl, K. 183
Rop, A. de 133, 137
Rouch, J. 334, 340–1
Rowlands, E. C. 293

Samarin, W. J. 6, 22, 33, 275, 277, 279, 281, 283, 286–7, 289–90
Schoen, J. F. 307
Schuchardt, H. I

Schultze, E. I, 2, 305
Schweinfurth, G. 215
Southall, A. W. 202
Stapleton, W. H. 119
Stappers, L. 102, 106–7
Steindorff, G. 228
Struck, B. 153, 161, 169, 171, 189, 191, 204
Sutherlin, R. E. 187–9
Swift, L. B. 109, 115

Tanghe, M. J. 119, 121, 189
Thorbecke, F. 270
Trapp, O. 51–2, 58, 60
Trenga, G. 225–6, 231
Tucker, A. N. 198, 214, 234, 322
Tucker, Th. 73

Ullendorff, E. 211

Valkoff, M. F. I
Verbreken, A. 101

Ward, I. C. 364
Weinreich, U. I
Westermann, D. 30, 230, 294, 338
Westphal, E. O. J. 4, 62
White, C. M. N. 74
Whitehead, J. 130
Whiteley, W. H. I, 188
Wing, J. van 133, 141
Wioland, F. 318
Wolff, H. 25

Zola, E. W. A. 109, 115

## General Index

References are to paragraphs. I = Introduction

Abd el Kerim 225
Abua 25
Adama 263–4
Adamawa Ful 30, 35, 261–8, 270
Adang'me 296, 303, 306
Adele I, 303
Afrikaans I, 51, 56, 59
Afroasiatic 206, 322
Akan see Twi
Akinfosile, O. 329
Akpafu-Lolobi 297
Akuapem 46, 305
Alur 202
Amadi 213
American Presbyterian Mission 11, 240
Amharic 206–11
Ang'lo 49, 295, 297–8
Anyi 355, 357
Animere I
Arabic 9, 17, 30, 37, 46, 149, 151, 183, 221, 225–37
'Arabiyyah 229
Arma 340
Asante 305
Ashanti 9, 300–1, 303, 305
Askia Mohammed Ture I 337–8, 350
assimilating language 27
Avatime 18, 297
Avongara 9, 213

Bade 222
Bafia 250
Baga 312–3
Bajue 240
Bakongo 34, 114, 117, 133–5, 138, 140, 142–3
Bakwa Mbalayi 105
Bakwa Mbiye 105
Bakwa Mputu 105
Balante 317

Balemi 297, 303
Bali 259–60
Bambara 3, 37, 318, 350, 358–63
Bambara-Masasi 359
Bambara-Ségou 359
Bamvele 250
Banda 272, 288
Bangala 119, 123, 140
Banta 318
Banyun 317
Basic Bantu 50
Basic Nguni 50
Basic Zulu 50
Basilides 209
basis form 14–20, 295
Baule 357
Bell 254
Bemba 18, 37, 76, 81–2, 86, 89
Bena Kanyoka 105
Bena Mpang'u 105
Bene 250
Benguela railway 72
Berber 227–8
Berti 217
Biombo 105
Bobangi 119, 121–2
Bobo 355, 357
Bolewa 222
Boloki 122
Bongo-Bagirmi languages 215
Borgu 340
Bowili 303
Bozo 339
Buduma 222
Buganda 10, 34, 161, 177–9, 201–2
Bula-Matari 108
Bulala 218
Bulom 308–9
Bulu 11, 23–4, 26, 238–46, 251
bulu bediliva 23, 251

193

Bum 271, 308
Buraka 273–4
Busa 344

Ca da Mosto 349
Cewa 97, 100
Cenge 71
Chad-Arabic 216, 282
Chaga 176, 180
Chaka 53, 64
Chamba 259
church language 256
Cikabanga 50
Cikopabeeluti 75
Cilapalapa 50
Coillard 67
Cokwe 74, 105
"command" language 80
Conversational Zulu 50
Coptic 228
Creole I, 14, 20, 111, 113, 286
Creolization 14, 166
Crioulo I

Dagari 344
Dagomba 22
Daudi Chwa 34, 177
Daza 217
Dendi 340–1
diachrony 24–30
dialect-continuum 48–9
Digo 190
domestic servants 23, 90, 360
Duala 32, 250, 254–8, 260
Duruma 147
Dyalonke 310, 314
Dyola 320
Dyolof see Wolof
Dyula 3, 9, 344–5, 350, 354–7, 358, 363

El Hadj Omar 359
elite 33, 95
Embu 193
Enoa 250
Esperanto I
Eton 238, 250–1
evolués 33, 279
Ewe 18, 40, 49, 295–8, 303
Ewondo see Yaunde

Fanagalo 4, 13, 22, 24, 33, 42, 47, 50–61, 78–80, 83–4, 88, 96

Fang 37, 238, 245, 251
Fante 46, 299, 301, 305–6
Fanti see Fante
Fiote 108
Fong 246, 250
Ful 9–10, 27, 29, 221, 230, 259, 261–8, 270, 314, 316, 318, 326–7, 332, 339–40, 344, 358–9

Ga 298, 303, 305
Galla I
Gana 348
Ganda 10, 34, 37, 176–8, 191, 196, 201–3
Gbanu 288
Gbanziri 273–4
Gbaya 271–2, 288
Ge'ez 207–10
Giriama 147
Gola 308
Gowers, W. F. 177
Griqua-Hottentots 64
Guang 299, 301
Gurma 344
Gusii 193
Gwandu 9

Hanya 72
Hassani 231
Hausa 3, 9, 12–3, 22, 27, 30, 33–4, 36, 38, 45, 47, 221, 230, 262, 322–35, 340, 344–5
Hausa states 323, 326
Haya 176
Higi 222

Ibo I, 25, 34, 37, 329, 335
Idris Aloma 219
Ijo 25
Ikeleve 108
Ila 66
Indians 7, 52
industrial labourers 79
institutional linguistics I
Inter-Territorial Language (Swahili) Committee see Swahili Committee
interviews 288–9
Isikula 50, 52
Isilololo 50
Isipiki 50
Islam 9, 30, 155, 163, 172, 175, 179, 227–30, 234, 237, 265, 353, 355, 359
Isungu 290

Jesuits 209–10
Jukun 269

Kajanga 225
Kaka 240, 244
Kalabari 25–6
Kalenjin 193
Kamba 188, 193, 195, 205
Kanem-Bornu 9, 218–20
Kanembu 217, 223
Kangbe 363
Kankan Musa 348
Kanuri 9, 13, 30, 34, 36, 217–23, 230, 257, 332, 335, 340
Kare 279
Kashmere 225
Kasongi 71
Katanga-Swahili 166
Kaya 271
Kebu 297, 303
Kentu 269
Kete 105
Keyo 193
Khoisan 62
Kibangi 121
Kibulamatadi 108
ki-Hindi 7, 200
Kikongo 6, 24, 34, 101, 105, 108–11, 113, 116, 118, 133–4, 138, 143,
Kikongo commercial 6, 108
Kikongo keleve 108
Kikongo ya Léta 108
Kikuyu 34, 176, 188, 193, 195–6, 199
Kikwango 108
Kileta 6, 11, 108
Kimbundu 69
Kipsigis 176, 193, 195
ki-Setla 7, 42, 200
ki-Shamba 7, 200
Kisodi 6, 108
Kisii see Gusii
Kissi 308
Kisuaheli see Swahili
Kiswahili see Swahili
Kitchen-Kafir 6, 50
Kituba 6, 11, 20, 24, 27, 108–18, 129, 138
ki-Vita 7, 200
Koine 48–9, 229
Kololo 9, 63–6
Kono 308
Koromba 340

Kotoko 222
Kourtey 340
Kposo 297
Krapf 182
Krim 308
Krobo 306
Kuba 103–5
Kulang'o 358
Kurumba 344

labour migration 6, 10, 74, 142, 195, 202, 334, 345
Lake Nyanja 97, 100
Landuma 312
"language nationalism" 143
language of administration 4, 201, 225
language of religion 9, 302
language policy 36, 39, 43, 46, 97, 112, 185–6, 188
Lari 134
Leopold II 165
Lewanika 66
Likpe 18, 297
Limba 309, 314
Lingala 3, 5, 12, 20–2, 27, 34, 42–3, 113–4, 119–47, 166, 197, 282
lingua franca form 14–20, 233, 257, 295, 312
linguistics 1
Livingstone, D. 65, 94
Lobi 357
Logba 18, 297
Loko 309
Lozi 9, 63–8
Luala 105
Luba 101–7, 166
Luba lingua franca 101–7, 114
Luchazi 74
Luganda see Ganda
Luhya 193–6
Lunda 66, 74
Luo 34, 176, 188, 193–6, 199
Luyi 64–7

Maba 224–6
Mabaale 119
major language 38
Mali 9, 348–52, 359, 363
Malinke 37, 317, 350, 352–3, 363
Mandara 222
Mandingo 9, 12–3, 27, 30, 36, 230, 262, 310, 316, 340, 347–64

Mandjia 288
Mandyak 317
Mangala 119
Mang'anja 97, 100
Mani 312
Mankanya 317
Marakwet 193
Mararit 225
Margi 222
Mari Djata 348
market 22, 35, 266, 287, 298, 303
Masai 29, 36, 161, 176, 191, 193–4, 196, 204–5
Mbakamandjia 288
Mbala 134
Mbangani 104
Mbo 95
Mbum 267, 270
Mbunda 66
Meinhof, C. 181
Mende 307–10
Mengisa 250
Mina 49, 295, 297–8
Mine-Kafir 6, 50
mission 11, 25, 36, 49, 67, 97, 113, 140, 172–3, 175–6, 240–1, 256–7, 259, 278, 284, 291, 297
missionary 25, 41, 46, 86, 94, 97, 104, 108–9, 111, 117, 130, 172, 198, 278, 303, 305–6
"mixed language" 66, 151
Mongallese 234
Mosi 17, 37, 300, 342–6
Munukutuba 108, 112
Mvae 246
Mvele 250
Mvita 198

Nachtigal, G. 254
Nalu 312
Namba 71
Nandi 176, 193, 195–6
Nankana 344
national language 43, 280, 330
natural language 14, 18, 20
Nembe 25–6
Ngala group 119, 121
Ngamo 222
Nganda 72
Ngbandi 18, 272
Ngizim 222
Ngongo 134

Ngoni 95, 97, 159
Ngumba 240–1
Nguni 42, 51
Ngwana 57, 163–4, 173, 199
Njem 240, 244
Njemps 193
Nkunya 303
Ntum 245–6
Nubi 193, 234
Nupe 332
Nyamwezi 160, 176, 191
Nyangbo-Tafi 18
Nyanja 3, 17, 33, 37, 85, 88, 93–101
Nyika 147

Odual 25
official language 34, 39, 62, 95, 127, 137, 177, 186, 203, 210, 221, 321, 329, 349, 362
Ogbia 25
orthography 41, 44–6, 170, 184, 284
Osadebay, D. 329
Osai Osibe Kwamina 300
Osai Tutu 300
Osman dan Fodio 263, 326
Ovimbundu see Umbundu

Pende 105
Petit-Nègre see Français-Tirailleur I
Peul see Ful
pidgin I, 7, 14–5, 18, 20, 42, 107, 110–1, 113, 117, 130, 141, 188, 234, 252, 268, 286, 363
Pidgin A 70 22–3, 47, 251–3
Pidgin Bantu 50
Pidgin-English I, 32, 257, 260, 305
Pidgin Ewondo 251
Pidgin Sango 272, 278
pidginization 14, 16, 18, 42, 200, 232, 276
Pokot 193
Portuguese I, 257
Praetorius, F. 210
prestige 58, 114, 117, 131, 145, 356
prestige language 87, 131, 137, 279
primary language I, 5, 113, 117, 312
prostitute 23, 87, 90

Rabeh 218
radio 11, 110, 112, 114, 176, 328
Rebmann 182
Rhodes, C. 55

Richter, J. 175
rival lingua franca 31, 226, 257, 260, 303
river language 3, 6, 12
Rotse 62

Sabaot 193, 195
Sala Mpasu 105
Samo 344
Sanga 71
Sango 3, 5–6, 12, 17–9, 21, 27, 29, 33, 43, 128, 216, 272–91
Sango commercial 6, 272
Santrokofi 297
Sara 215–6, 282
school language 4, 11, 41, 67, 243, 256
Sebitwane 64–5
second language I, 14, 27, 34, 164, 196, 222, 235, 257, 274, 312, 340, 344
secondary language I
Senufo 355, 357–8
Serer 37, 317–8
Shona 317
Silunguboi 4, 50
Simple Kikongo 108
Sokoto 9
Solarin, T. 329
soldier language 3, 6–7, 14, 108, 125, 351, 361
Somali I, 29, 46, 236–7
Song'ai 230, 332, 336–41, 348, 350, 359
Song'e 103, 105
Soninke 337–9, 344, 348, 358
Sonni Ali 337
Sotho 66–7
South Sudan Arabic 234
stable bilingualism 27
standardization 38, 181–4
Stanley, H. M. 105, 163, 165
"substitute languages" 2
Sukuma 176, 199
Sumbwa 165
Susneos 209
Susu 309–14, 348
Swahili 2, 5, 7, 12–3, 22, 27, 29–30, 34, 36–7, 39, 42, 44, 47, 57, 121, 125, 146–200, 203–5, 230
Swahili Committee 182–3

Tawana see Tswana
Teda 217
Tekrur 359
Temne 303, 314
Terik 193
Teso 193, 195
Tetela 105
Theodore II 210
Tigre 235
Tonga 66
Town Bemba 13, 18, 21–4, 33, 47, 57, 68, 74–92, 96
trade language I, 1, 6, 14, 27, 225, 254, 256–7, 294, 351, 356
tribal language I, 86
Tshiluba 42, 101–3, 107, 138
Tshituba 42, 107
Tswana 4, 11, 62
Tuareg 222, 332, 338–40
Tubeya 105
Tubu 222
Tugen 193
Tukuleur 10, 316–7
Turku 216, 233, 282
Twi 9, 17, 22, 33, 40, 46, 297–305
Tyenga 340

Umbundu 69–73
Unguja 147, 164, 198
"Union-Nyanja" 97
Vai 308
vernacular language I, 26–7, 40, 58, 76, 82, 89, 111, 130, 136, 138, 164, 186, 188, 278–9
Volapük I
Vute see Wute

Wagadugu 343
wa-ngwana 163–4
Wasaw 301
wa-shomvi 153
Wolof 10, 17, 27, 37, 315–21
Wolseley 300
working language 4, 6–7, 33, 56
written language 18, 38, 45, 47, 49, 84, 141, 147, 207, 209, 237, 278, 291, 297, 305
Wurbo 269
Wute 35, 264

Xhosa 51

Yaka 134
Yangere 271

Yansi 344
Yanzi 134
Yatenga 343
Yaunde 3, 238, 242, 247–51
Yei 62
Yelinda 246
Yembama 246
Yengono 246

Yoruba 34, 37, 45, 49, 292–4, 329, 332, 335
Zaghawa 217
Zaman 246
Zande 9, 27, 212–4
Zenj Empire 155, 198
Zerma 340–1
Zulu 50–1, 53

## Studies within the African Research Programme of the Ifo-Institut für Wirtschaftsforschung, Munich

**Published:**

*a) in the series "Afrika-Studien"*

(No. 1–18 by Springer-Verlag, Berlin – Heidelberg – New York; No. 19 ff. by Weltforum-Verlag, Munich)

No. 1 **Development Banks and Companies in Tropical Africa**
By Naseem Ahmad and Ernst Becher, 1964, 86 pages, in German

No. 2 **Agricultural Development in Tanganyika**
By Hans Ruthenberg, 1964, 212 pages, in English

No. 3 **National Accounting Systems in Tropical Africa**
By Rolf Güsten and Helmut Helmschrott, 1965, 69 pages, in German

No. 4 **Contributions to Internal Migration and Population Development in Liberia**
By Hans W. Jürgens, 1965, 104 pages, in German

No. 5 **Annotated Bibliography of Social Research in East Africa 1954—1963**
By Angela von Molnos, 1965, 304 pages, in German

No. 6 **The Political and Economic Role of the Asian Minority in East Africa**
By Indira Rothermund, 1965, 75 pages, in German

No. 7 **Land Tenure Reform in Kenya**
By Hanfried Fliedner, 1965, 136 pages, in German

No. 8 **Taxation and Economic Development in East Africa**
By Lübbe Schnittger, 1966, 216 pages, in German

No. 9 **Problems of Economic Growth and Planning: The Sudan Example**
By Rolf Güsten, 1966, 74 pages, in English

No. 10 **African Agricultural Production Development Policy in Kenya 1952—1965**
By Hans Ruthenberg, 1966, 180 pages, in English

No. 11 Land Use and Animal Husbandry in Sukumaland/Tanzania
By Dietrich von Rotenhan, 1966, 131 pages, in German

No. 12 Land Legislation in the Cameroons 1884—1964
By Heinrich Krauss, 1966, 156 pages, in German

No. 13 Investigations into the Productivity and Profitability of Smallholder Sisal in East Africa
By Hermann Pössinger, 1967, 172 pages, in German

No. 14 The Attitude of Various Tribes of the Republic of Togo, Especially the Ewe on the Plateau de Dayes, towards the Problem of Commissioned Cattle Herding by the Fulbe (Peulh) of West Africa
By Julius O. Müller, 1967, 124 pages, in German

No. 15 The Role of Co-operatives in the Economic Development of East Africa, and Especially of Tanganyika and Uganda
By Margarete Paulus, 1967, 156 pages, in German

No. 16 Gabun: History, Structure and Problems of the Export Trade of a Developing Country
By Hans-Otto Neuhoff, 1967, 273 pages, in German

No. 17 Continuity and Change in the Division of Labour among the Baganda
By Jürgen Jensen, 1967, 297 pages, in German

No. 18 Trade in Tanzania
By Werner Kainzbauer, 1968, 239 pages, in German

No. 19 Problems of Agricultural Development in the Coastal Region of East Africa
By Sigmar Groeneveld, 1967, 124 pages, in German

No. 20 The Monetary and Banking Systems of the Countries of West Africa
By Heinz-Günter Geis, 1967, 428 pages, in German

No. 21 The Role of the Transport Sector in the Development Policy — with Special Reference to African Countries —
By G. Wolfgang Heinze, 1967, 324 pages, in German

No. 22 Ukara: A Special Case of Land Use in the Tropics
By Heinz Dieter Ludwig, 1967, 251 pages, in German

No. 23 Applied Economics of Education — The Example of Senegal —
By Werner Clement, 1967, 224 pages, in German

No. 24 Smallholder Farming and Smallholder Development in Tanzania — Ten Case Studies —
By Hans Ruthenberg (ed.), 1968, 360 pages, in English

No. 25 Smallholders in the Tropical Highlands of East Africa. The Usambara Mts. in the Transition Period from Subsistence to Market Production
By Manfred Attems, 1968, 168 pages, in German

No. 26 Attitudes towards Family Planning in East Africa
By Angela Molnos, 1968, 408 pages, in English

No. 27 Smallholder Production under Close Supervision:
Tobacco Growing in Tanzania. A Socio-Economic Study
By Walter Scheffler, 1968, 184 pages, in German

No. 28 The Kilombero Valley/Tanzania: Characteristic Features of the Economic Geography of a Semihumid East African Flood Plain and Its Margins
By Ralph Jätzold and E. Baum, 1968, 147 pages, in English

No. 29 Investigations into Internal Migration in Tanzania
By Hans W. Jürgens, 1968, 166 pages, in German

No. 30 Studies in the Staple Food Economy of Western Nigeria
By Rolf Güsten, 1968, 311 pages, in English

No. 31 Agricultural Development in Angola and Moçambique
By Hermann Pössinger, 1968, 284 pages, in German

No. 32 Rural Economic Development in Zambia, 1890—1964
By J. A. Hellen, 1968, 297 pages, in English

No. 33 Small Farm Credit and Development — Some Experiences in East Africa with Special Reference to Kenya —
By J. Vasthoff, 1969, 144 pages, in English

No. 34 Crafts, Small-Scale Industries, and Industrial Education in Tanzania
By Karl Schädler, 1969, 264 pages, in English

No. 35 Money and Banking in East Africa
By E.-J. Pauw, 1969, 278 pages, in German

No. 36 Reorganization of Land Use in Egypt (three case studies)
By E.-S. El Shagi, 1969, 175 pages, in German

No. 37 Energy Supply and Economic Development in East Africa
By H. Amann, 1969, 254 pages, in English

No. 38 The African Settlers and how They Organize Their Life in the Urambo-Scheme (Tanzania)
By Axel v. Gagern, 1969, 130 pages, in German

No. 39 Irrigation in Kenya's Agriculture with Special Reference to the Mwea-Tebere Project
By R. Golkowsky, 1969, 149 pages, in German

No. 40   Economic Statistics in Developing Countries: the Example of Uganda
By Hanns Hieber, 1969, 244 pages, in German

No. 41   Problems of Land-Locked Countries: Uganda
By W. Fischer, 1969, 274 pages, in German

No. 42   Investigations into Health and Nutrition in East Africa
By H. Kraut/H.-D. Cremer (eds.), 1969, 342 pages, in English

No. 43   The African as Industrial Worker in East Africa
By O. Neuloh a. o., 1969, 440 pages, in German

No. 44   Rice Cultivation in West Africa — A Presentation of the Economic and Geographical Differences of Cultivation Methods
By B. Mohr, 1969, 163 pages, in German

No. 45   Structure and Growth of the East African Textile and Garments Industry
By H. Helmschrott, 1969, 130 pages, in German

No. 46   Social Change in Kiteezi (Buganda), a Village within the Sphere of Influence of the Township of Kampala (Uganda)
By E. C. Klein, 1969, 160 pages, in German

No. 47   Balance of Payment Problems in a Developing Country: Tanzania
By M. Yaffey, 1970, 284 pages, in English

No. 48   Fodder Plants in the Sahel zone of Africa
By R. Bartha, 1970, 306 pages, in German, English und French

No. 49   Status and Use of African Lingua Francas
By B. Heine, 1970, 206 pages, in English

No. 50   Cultural Change and Anxiety Reaction among the Yoruba of Nigeria
By Staewen/Schönberg, 1970, ca. 430 pages, in German (with an English Summary)

No. 51   Studies in Production and Trade in East Africa
By P. Zajadacz and Contributors, 1970, 441 pages, in English

No. 52   Planning Processes: The East African Case
By R. E. Vente, 1970, 224 pages, in English

**To be published shortly in the series "Afrika-Studien":**

No. 53   Financial Aspects of Development in East Africa
By P. Marlin and Contributors (in English)

No. 54   Administration and Economic Exploitation of German East Africa before 1914
By D. Bald (in German)

*b) in the African Studies special series "Information and Documentation"*

No. 1  Africa-Vademecum (basic data on the economic structure and development of Africa)
Prepared by F. Betz, 1968, 163 pages, in German, with additional headings in English and French

No. 2  Development Banks and Institutions in Africa
By H. Harlander and D. Mezger, 1969, 211 pages, in German

*c) as mimeograph* (African Research Reports)

Economic Planning and Development Policy in Tropical Africa
By N. Ahmad, E. Becher and E. Harder, 1965, 283 pages, in German (out of print)

The Human Factor in the Development of the Kilombero Valley
By O. Raum, 1965, 56 pages, in English (out of print)

The EEC Market Regulations for Agricultural Products and their Implications for Developing Countries
By H. Klemm and P. v. Marlin, 1965, 95 pages, in German (out of print)

The Impact of External Economic Relations on the Economic Development of East Africa
By P. v. Marlin, 1966, 110 pages, in English (out of print)

Crop Cultivation on the Island of Madagascar with Special Reference to Rice Growing
By Alfred H. Rabe, 1965, 346 pages, in German (out of print)

Economic Research in Tropical Africa. Results of an Informatory Trip to Egypt, Ethiopia, Kenya, Uganda, Tanzania, Malawi, Zambia, Congo (Kinshasa), Nigeria, Ghana and Senegal in April and May 1966
By Hildegard Harlander, 1966, 193 pages, in German

Israeli Aid to Developing Countries with Special Reference to East Africa
By F. Goll, 1967, 189 pages, in German

The Economy of South West Africa (a Study in Economic Geography)
By Axel J. Halbach, 1967, 210 pages, in German (out of print)

Co-operative Farming in Kenya and Tanzania
By Nikolaus Newiger, 1967, 157 pages, in English (out of print)

Game Protection and Game Utilization in Rhodesia and in South Africa
By Wolfgang Erz, 1967, 97 pages, in German (out of print)

Zoological Studies in the Kivu Region (Congo-Kinshasa)
By Fritz Dieterlen and Peter Kunkel, 1967, 138 pages, in German

Recent English Economic Research in East Africa. A Selected Bibliography
By Dorothea Mezger and Eleonore Littich, 1967, 383 pages, in German (out of print)

The Attitude of Various Tribes of the Republic of Togo, Especially the Ewe on the Plateau de Dayes, towards the Problem of Commissioned Cattle Herding by the Fulbe (Peulh) of West Africa
By Julius O. Müller, 1967, 187 pages, in French

Examination of the Physical Development of Tanzanian Youth
By H. W. Jürgens, 1967, 152 pages, in English

The Chemical and Allied Industries in Kenya
By Hans Reichelt, 1967, 182 pages, in English

Traditional Farming and Land Development in the Kilombero Valley/Tanzania
By Eckhard Baum, 1967, 150 pages, in German

The Organization of Milk Markets in East Africa
By Helmut Klemm, 1967, 164 pages, in German

Botanical Investigations in the Masai Country/Tanzania (an Example from the Semi-Arid Areas of East Africa)
By H. Leippert, 1968, 184 pages, in German

Evaluation of Aerial Photography in East Africa (an Inventory)
By K. Gerresheim, 1968, 225 pages, in German

Manufacturing and Processing Industries in Tanzania
By K. Schädler, 1969, 55 pages, in English

Agricultural Development in Malawi
By H. Dequin, 1969, 248 pages, in English

Development Aid to Africa – with Special Reference to the Countries of East Africa
By K. Erdmann, 1969, 186 pages, in German

Vegetable Cultivation in Tropical Highlands: the Kigezi Example (Uganda)
By F. Scherer, 1969, 227 pages, in English

Science and Development Policy. The Problem of Application of Research Results
By M. Bohnet, 1969, 35 pages, in German

Importance, Volume, Forms and Development Possibilities of Private Saving in East Africa
By G. Hübner, 1970, 343 pages, in German

Operational Concepts of the Infrastructure in the Economic Development Process
By H. Amann, 1970, 203 pages, in German

**In preparation:**

The Present State of Legislation in East Africa
By G. Spreen

Development Possibilities of the Pig and Poultry Industry in East Africa
By H. Späth

Comparative Investigations into the Efficiency of Utilizable Ruminants in Kenya
By Walter/Dennig

Farm Management Systems in Kenya
By v. Haugwitz/Thorwart

Problems of the Transport Economy in Tanzania with Special Reference to Road Transport
By R. Hofmeier (in English)

The Influence of Urbanization upon the Development of Rural Areas — with Special Reference to Jinja (Uganda) and Its Surroundings
By Gerken/Schubert/Brandt

The Interrelationship between Man, Nature and Economy: the Example of Madagascar
By W. Marquardt

The Implications of Tanzania's Administrative System for Her Economic Development
By K. v. Sperber (in English)

Autonomous Institutions in East African Agricultural Production
By H. Blume (in English)

Applied Research in East Africa and Its Influence on Economic Development
By M. Bohnet and H. Reichelt (in English)

Co-operatives in the Sudan: Their Characteristics, Functions and Suitability in the Socio-Economic Development Process
By M. Bardeleben

Mining and Regional Development in East Africa
By T. Möller

The Economico-Geographical Pattern of East Africa
By K. Engelhard

Iraqw Highland/Tanzania: Resource Analysis of an East African Highland and its Margins
By J. Schultz (in English)

Methods and Problems of Farm Management Surveys in Africa South of the Sahara
By H. Thorwart

The Mau-Mau Movement: Its Socio-Economic and Political Causes and Implications upon British Colonial Policy in Kenya and Africa
By J. Muriuki (in English)

Beef Production in East Africa with Special Reference to Semi-Arid Areas
By K. Meyn (in English)

The Requirements for the Means of Transport in East Africa with a View to the Economic Expansion of these Countries
By H. Milbers

Population Trends and Migration in Malawi with Special Reference to the Central Region of Lake Malawi
By U. Weyl

Population Trends in Kenya and Their Implications for Social Services in Rural and Urban Areas
By M. Meck (in English)

Education's Contribution to Economic Development of a Tropical Agrarian Country — the Example of Tanzania
By H. Desselberger

Agrarian Patterns in Ethiopia and their Implications for Economic Growth
By V. Janssen

Development of Law in Malawi
By F. v. Benda-Beckmann (in German)